COOKING IN

OZ

Hi Tracy –

Jennifer and I saw this book at the Hotel del Coronado in California in January. We thought of you immediately, I hope you don't have it. I hope all is well.

Debby
April 2008

Much of MGM's original print advertising for The Wizard of Oz *featured early Al Hirschfeld art.*

COOKING IN
OZ

Kitchen Wizardry and a Century of Marvels
from America's Favorite Tale

ELAINE WILLINGHAM AND STEVE COX

Foreword by
MARGARET PELLEGRINI
(Munchkin in MGM's *The Wizard of Oz*)

Recipes Edited by
TINA CASSIMATIS AND BLANCHE COX

CUMBERLAND HOUSE
Nashville, Tennessee

Published by Cumberland House Publishing, Inc., 431 Harding Industrial Drive, Nashville, TN 37211-3160.

Cover design: Harriette Bateman
Interior design: Gore Studio, Inc.
Typesetting: Mary Sanford

Back cover images courtesy of: Frito-Lay, Inc.; Beyond the Rainbow Archive; Norman Rockwell; MGM/UA; and Turner Entertainment.

Library of Congress Cataloging-in-Publication Data
Willingham, Elaine, 1954–
    Cooking in Oz: kitchen wizardry and a century of marvels from America's favorite tale / Elaine Willingham and Steve Cox ; foreword by Margaret Pellegrini ; recipes edited by Tina Cassimatis and Blanche Cox.
        p. cm.
    Includes index.
    ISBN 1-58182-051-8 (pbk.)
        1. Cookery, American. 2. Wizard of Oz (Motion picture) I. Cox, Stephen, 1966–
II. Cassimatis, Tina. III. Cox, Blanche. IV. Title.

TX715 .W7325 1999
641.5973--dc21
                                                                99-048258

Printed in the United States of America
    3 4 5 6 7 8—04

For my mom, Tina Cassimatis, who has truly a generous heart. She's helped me find my courage. Wherever she is, that's home for me. And perhaps I'd deserve her, and be even worthy erv her, if I only had a brain.

E. W.

—ᴑᴗᴑ—

For Mom—our family chef and culinary wizard. For Dad, who had a crush on Frances Gumm when he was young. And for my niece, Megan Dalton, who is just beginning her journey down the Yellow Brick Road, off to see the world.

S. C.

For one hundred years this story has given faithful service to the Young in Heart; and Time has been powerless to put its kindly philosophy out of fashion.

To those of you who have made that faithful return to the icebox

. . . and to those Craving
. . . we dedicate this cookbook.

Contents

A very young Margaret Williams celebrates her birthday with famous fan dancer Sally Rand in 1936. (Courtesy of Margaret W. Pellegrini)

Foreword

by MARGARET WILLIAMS PELLEGRINI

I'm pleased Steve Cox and Elaine Willingham have asked me to write this Foreword for their *Oz* cookbook. They came to the right place, because anybody who knows me knows that I love to cook and I love to eat. The hotter the taste, the better. They've seen me remove the lid from the pepper shaker and pour it. Nothing is too spicy for me.

What most people don't know is that I became a Munchkin in *The Wizard of Oz* because of potato chips. That's right, potato chips. When I was a teenager in Alabama (they called me "Li'l Alabam"), I went to Memphis to visit my sister and her husband; they asked me if I'd help pass out potato chip samples at the State Fair, and so I did. We'd pass out these little bags of potato chips and one day, while I was doing this at the Fair, a group of little people came walking down the midway and approached me. They knew I was a little person and they asked me my name. I was so young (just barely in my teens), I really didn't consider myself a little person at that time, but somehow they knew. They asked me if I was interested in joining their traveling Midget Troupe, and I told them I wasn't. I gave them my name and address on a piece of paper before they left and really, I didn't think any more about it. One of the little ladies in the group seemed to be in charge, Dolly Kramer. She was a nice little person, and her husband, Henry, was a much taller man.

A year later, I received a letter from an agent in Hollywood named Thelma Weiss, who got my address from the Kramers. Miss Weiss was contacting me to see if I'd be interested in

traveling to California, all expenses paid, for this motion picture they were making at MGM/Loew's called *The Wizard of Oz.* I was pretty excited, but my dad had a few questions about the details. He worked at the Sheffield Hotel as a maintenance man, and he had one of the managers get back to Miss Weiss. We got it all ironed out and in a matter of weeks, I was

Dolly and Henry Kramer with little Margaret Williams in 1939. Occasionally, they called Margaret "Li'l Alabam" or "Popcorn."

on my way, by train, to Los Angeles in November 1938. I wasn't an actor or a singer, but I liked the sound of fifty dollars a week. That was a lot of money in those days, especially since my father only made five dollars a week.

Now, since this is a cookbook, I've thought about what we did for meals when all of us little people—more than a hundred of us—were brought together in Culver City, California, for this film. Originally, I stayed at the Culver Hotel, which is where the majority of us little ones stayed. For the most part, when we were working, we all ate at the commissary, which was like a cafeteria at MGM. I distinctly remember meeting Lew Ayres in the commissary and getting his autograph. Other times, food was brought in to us Munchkins, catering style, and the studio had set up rows of lowered tables for us because we were pretty tiny people back then. (Most of us grew some after the movie, you know.)

Across the street from MGM was a small café that served family-style cooking. It was called Marie's. It was nothing fancy. I guess today it might be like a greasy spoon, but it was good. Most of us Munchkins were able to eat any meals we wanted there and sign for them, so many of us gathered there, and lined up for breakfast in the morning. There's one morning at Marie's I'll never forget.

I was there with my roommate, Jessie Kelley, a pretty little lady who kind of took me under her wing. She and her husband, Charley Kelley (also a little person), were separated, maybe even divorced by that time. They were not on good terms and they fought. He was a drinker and caused problems for her and for us, and a ruckus at the studio. Eventually, he got kicked out of the movie for causing so much trouble. Charley Kelley was one of the rowdy ones who eventually gave us Munchkins a bad

reputation. Well, one morning, Jessie and I came to Marie's and got in line with our trays. Charley was looking for her and when he saw Jessie, he got up from where he was sitting at a table, he came over to Jessie and grabbed her by the back of her long blonde hair and pulled her down to the floor and began wrestling her. A few of the little guys immediately got up and stopped him. The whole thing caused a commotion, and because of that incident and a couple of other violent acts, which I witnessed, Jessie and I moved to another hotel in Hollywood, the Vine Manor.

Marie's is where Jessie and I and Dolly and Henry Kramer and Meinhardt Raabe had Thanksgiving dinner in 1938. There might have been a few more people with us. You remember those holidays when you're away from home like I was, and I wasn't used to being so far away from home. I remember Thanksgiving because after our dinner (in the afternoon), we went for a ride around Hollywood sightseeing in Dolly and Henry's car, with Meinhardt, and later that evening Meinhardt asked me to go to a show with him. He brought me a one-pound box of Whitman's chocolates, which I'll never forget. I guess it was one of my first dates. He was a gentleman, and the chocolates really impressed me.

Speaking of sweets, Judy Garland was a sweet thing herself. I mean that. People always ask what she was like back then. She was a curious teenager, well-mannered, and respectful to all of us and we were respectful toward her. One day Judy presented all of us Munchkins a gigantic box of chocolates on the set of Munchkinland. I remember it was on the day the studio presented her with her own dressing room on wheels, with a ribbon-cutting ceremony. It was around Christmastime, and she announced to all of us that she'd love to give us all individual gifts, but that would be impossi-

"On another soundstage at MGM, they had special low tables set up for us because the normal-size tables in the commissary were big for us. That's me, in the flowerpot hat, walking to my seat with a tray of food. I was hungry!"

ble. She had this thirty-pound, huge box of chocolates brought on the set and she opened it and told us all to come around and have some. Then, she invited us to stream in and take a look at her new dressing room; inside she signed an autographed picture for each of us. I still have mine; it says, "To Margaret, from your pal, Judy."

While we were in Hollywood for almost two months making *The Wizard of Oz,* Jessie and I also went to a favorite German hofbrau in Hollywood to eat, and there was also a drug-store we liked, near Hollywood and Vine. We'd eat meals there on weekends but since Jessie drove a car, we were able to go anywhere. That was nice. And at Christmas, she and I had a lit-tle tree that we decorated in our room. My dad sent me a locket with the initials MVW, for Margaret Virginia Williams, engraved on it. I still have that. I don't remember where we had Christmas dinner or if we celebrated with a lot

of other little people, but I'm sure wherever I was, I was homesick. I couldn't call home to my dad because we didn't have a phone back at home, so we sent post cards and letters.

My mom died when I was two, so I more or less learned cooking from watching my step-mom, Annie Lee. She was a good cook. And I learned some kitchen skills from watching oth-ers. Years later, when I married my husband, Willie Pellegrini, I watched his mother and his family prepare Italian dishes. We lived in Chicago at the time. Willie liked the traditional dishes, like spaghetti with homemade meat-balls, and lasagna. I learned to make my own Italian sausage, pressed out of pork shoulder roast (the butcher grinds it coarse) and I add fennel seed, red peppers, salt, and the rest. My husband, who was also a good cook (he made a great stew), loved my food. My two children—and now grandchildren, and great-grandchil-dren—still tell me I'm a wizard in the kitchen.

Even though I'm just four feet tall, all of my kitchens have been big. Well, normal-size kitchens, I should say. (Some little people I know have had kitchen counters and other household facilities scaled down for convenience.) I've always just used a footstool or a small two-step ladder to reach things, cook, and do the dishes. And that's the only adjustment I've ever needed. No one looks twice in our house. I had an arrangement with my two kids when they were small. If we got separated in the grocery store (you know how little ones get panicky in the store when they can't find Mom) it was usually because I was already in line to check out while they were still in the cereal aisle looking for prizes. If they called out for me but couldn't see me, I'd hold up a box of cereal above my head, and when they spotted the floating box of Corn Flakes near a checkout line, they'd found me.

Another option for my kids was to find me in the aisle with the spices. I've loved spicy foods since I was a kid. I'd shake that black pepper on eggs and potatoes, and most of my foods. Lots of black pepper. Down south, that's the way we prepared collard greens—with pepper sauce. When I was a kid, if I had a headache, I could cure it with hot tamales and a Coke. It worked. I love hot and spicy barbecue, sliced barbecued pork sandwiches. Nothing like it. One of my favorite dishes is chicken-fried steak, tenderized round steak, breaded and fixed right. Not that pressed and quick-serve meat. In fact, to this day, I carry around a small bottle of Tabasco with me in my purse. They have this tiny sample size now— Munchkinized—that works great. If I come across something in a restaurant that I don't like, I put Tabasco on it or hot peppers in oil, and it gives it a whole new flavor. Sometimes it makes it palatable. I'm not picky. My family

knows there's just two things I won't eat: mushrooms and lamb. I don't know why. I just don't like either.

When my husband and I moved to Arizona years ago, I got a taste for Mexican food, hot and spicy corn bread, spicy chili. I love it all. In our house, it's been a tradition for me to put out a big spread of food on the holidays. Lots of guests, and lots of hungry friends would come by our house. Family galore at the holidays, or any day. There's nothing like settling down in the evening to talk with friends or family, or watch TV, with a nice cup of coffee and a slice of pie before bedtime; the coffee doesn't affect me. I guess that might be due to my hectic schedule.

Here I am, in my late seventies, and I'm traveling around the country more than I ever did in my entire life. Ever since the fiftieth anniversary of *The Wizard of Oz* ten years ago, I've been off and running, and loving every minute of it. I've been invited to just about every corner of the country, met some of the nicest folks around the U.S., and I've had the chance to taste some of the most diverse foods and eat in the most interesting restaurants along the way, I think I've become a connoisseur. It's a great opportunity for me, to meet so many fans, wave in parades, attend cocktail parties and special dinner events, and celebrate the popularity of *The Wizard of Oz* with all the enthusiastic fans. God's been good to me. I never imagined my life would take such a turn, all because I was a Munchkin. And because of potato chips . . . God bless 'em, every fried one of 'em.

Munchkin Love
Margaret Pellegrini
"Lil' Alabam"

Acknowledgments

The authors would like to extend a smile and a thank you to all of the individuals who graciously took time to rummage through their personal family cookbooks and scrapbooks and contribute something special. We only hope this book will serve up some wonderful memories, and tasty dishes. To the Baum family, in particular, we wish to thank you for your enthusiasm toward our little *Oz* endeavor—and the greater picture, the legacy that is *Oz*.

With special thanks for their assistance, encouragement, support, and love we would like to thank the following people and organizations:

Chris Aber, Robert Allison Baum Jr., Bill Beem, Steve Bertani, Ron Borst, Willard Carroll, The Cassimatises (Amy, Pete, Reyna, and Rileigh), Tina and Andy Cassimatis, Helen Cassimatis, Blanche and Jerry Cox, Froso Condoleos, Eric Daily, Dulcino Eisen, Scott Essman, Brad Farrell, Katie Fleming, John Fricke, Frito-Lay, Inc., Ron Gibbs, Katie Grové, Renee Hambley, Michael Hamilton, Hanna-Barbera, Inc., Billie Hayes (Pet Hope, Inc., P.O. Box 1847, Hollywood, CA 90078), Robyn Knutson, Jack Lane, Tod Machin, Lynn Markley, Scott Michaels, Scott Maiko, Gita Dorothy Morena, Ph.D., Francine and Kelly Murphy, Tim Neeley, Julie Pitkin, Ron Pitkin, Margaret Pellegrini, Phil Potempa, Mary Jane Probst, Jeff Rizzo, Jan Rooney, Mary Sanford, Bob Satterfield, Ray Savage, Jay Scarfone, Paula Shatley, Stephen Sisters, Kurt Steinruck, Brad Steppig, Bill Stillman, The Harburg Estate, Peter Theodore (TMBTC), Turner Entertainment, Betty Von Hoffmann, Warner Bros., Inc., Rose Washington, Jimmi Willingham, and Jasen Woehrle. We thank you very sweetly!

For assistance with research and preparation of the Baum Family Tree, we gratefully thank: Gita Dorothy Morena, Ph.D., Robert Allison Baum Jr., Ozma Baum Mantele, Tina Cassimatis, and Kurt Steinruck.

For information about The International Wizard of Oz Club, write: P.O. Box 266, Kalamazoo, MI 49004.

For information about *The Wizard of Oz* on line, you can access Beyond the Rainbow's Web site: www.beyondtherainbow2oz.com or write to P.O. Box 31672, St. Louis, MO 63131-0672, or call 314-799-1724.

The authors wish to praise the talented fraternity of artists whose unique visions of Oz grace this book: Thomas Blackshear, W. W. Denslow, Al Hirschfeld, Chuck Jones, Bil Keane, Tod Machin, John R. Neill, Mike Peters, Norman Rockwell, Kurt Steinruck, and Dave Woodman.

For information about Dave Woodman Illustrations *(page vi)*: 750 Kings Road, Suite 224, Los Angeles, California 90069.

A portion of the royalties from this book will go to The Make-A-Wish Foundation, and in memory of Toto and all his friends a donation is also being made to Pet Hope, Inc., on behalf of Billie Hayes and Kay Hobday.

INTRODUCTION

―⌖―

To the Kitchen as Fast as Lightning!

Pay no attention to that cook behind the apron . . . the proof is in the pudding.

For *Oz* creator Lyman Frank Baum, the proof was in the public's immediate embrace of his tale about a farmgirl's quest for a Wizard. "In the curtain speech Baum delivered on the opening night of his musical back in 1902," writes *Oz* historian Michael Patrick Hearn, "he likened the creation of this early stage production to the making of a plum pudding: He, as the author, may have provided the flour, but the composer brought the spice, the actors the plums, everyone else something flavorful of his own, the whole of which was beaten into shape by the master chef, the director. This metaphor is equally apt in describing the 1939 movie."

Today, the tale is commonplace. Of course, everyone knows the story of Dorothy and her whirlwind adventures through the magical Land of Oz, either by book or by film. Can you believe it? We've hit the sixtieth anniversary of a motion picture that has taken on a life of its own, rightfully earning the title "classic," if ever a film there wuz. The millenium marks the one-hundredth anniversary of Baum's original *Oz* story-book. Clearly demonstrated by an unprecedented and faithful following during the past century, *The Wizard of Oz* has become a twentieth-century cultural milestone.

Over the years, Metro-Goldwyn-Mayer's Technicolor jewel, *The Wizard of Oz,* has become a motion picture icon, a masterpiece experienced by more human beings than any other celluloid story, bar none. Remember, however, this is now a tale for the ages, a purely American tale that belongs to the people. The stargazing fable has proved ageless, retold countless times to dreamers everywhere. Rare is the person alive who does not know *Oz,* never having fallen under its spell. The magic all took hold in 1900 when storyteller L. Frank Baum published *The Wonderful Wizard of Oz* as a children's book. Today, the world has experienced but a tender century of *Oz,* with no end in sight. It is difficult to put into perspective just how consummately the world of *Oz* has saturated our culture, but we hope this book might provide at least a sweet taste of the century's phenomenon.

Remember, in the movie, when sentimental Auntie Em suggested Dorothy "find a place where you won't get into any trouble . . ."? Well, she meant the kitchen. So, don't be frightened if you're a little rusty. Have a little courage, that's all. Force yourself into that cataclysmic decision and head into the kitchen as fast as lightning. Why, anyone can cook, that's a very mediocre commodity. Keep in mind, some people without brains do an awful lot of cooking, so we've compiled a friendly collection of recipes that speak in the vernacular of the peasantry. There's something for everybody. This isn't just a clinking, clanking, clattering collection of caliginous junk food, you know.

We hope this cookbook will be a "keeper" for you. Keep it in the kitchen. Keep it on the coffee table. Everyone loves to reminisce. This is also a scrapbook that, we hope, will satisfy your appetite for *Oz* by way of a unique blend of edible pleasures mixed with classic images carefully culled from an incredibly vast array of *Oz* incarnations. We're confident that never before, not nowhere, not no how, have you seen such a menu of Oz à la Carte; we're also excited about serving up these nostalgic nuggets—a painstaking harvest of several eminent *Oz* collections.

You may be surprised when you dig in. Maybe a long-forgotten memory of *Oz* will reappear, or you might notice a new delicious detail, just like what happens when you sit down to watch *The Wizard of Oz* for the umpteenth time. The movie's magic allows you to extract a new morsel you didn't get the time before. Have you ever focused purely on one character? It's a wonderful way to experience the movie. Follow Toto continuously throughout the flick and you'll know why the pettable pooch was more than just decoration. Keep your eye on Ray Bolger and his graceful, nimble movement will amaze you.

For every admirer of *Oz*—including ourselves—we've been able to unearth fresh trivia, oddly appropriate recollections from *Oz* "celebrities," and astounding, never-before-published photographs. All of this is presented in the most delicious of ways, with recipes from the personal files of dozens of prominent *Oz* personalities—even a recipe from Judy Garland's own kitchen. These favorites are complemented by recipes and recollections contributed from fans around the country as well as members of the spirited International Wizard of Oz Club, established way back in 1957.

Along the way, you'll run into some well-known personalities who might appear to have no connection to *Oz*. Ahhhh . . . but look a little closer into the crystal ball and you'll see why entertainers Bill Cosby, Phyllis Diller, and Art Carney love *The Wizard of Oz*, too. Have lunch with a Munchkin or join Mr. Rogers for a snack and reminisce about his visit with the Witch. Share a salad with Sid Caesar, or a malt with The Mick. You never know who you're gonna stumble upon on this winding culinary journey down the Yellow Brick Road.

To Oz?

Steve Cox
Elaine Willingham

COOKING IN
OZ

WE WELCOME YOU TO MUNCHKINLAND FOR STARTERS

APPETIZERS

ARTICHOKE-CHILI DIP

1   14-ounce can artichoke hearts, drained and chopped
1   4-ounce can green chilies
1   cup mayonnaise or salad dressing
1   cup grated Parmesan cheese
     Tortilla chips or melba toast

In a small casserole dish mix together the artichoke hearts, chilies, mayonnaise, and Parmesan. Bake at 350° for 25 minutes until the top is golden.

Serve with tortilla chips or melba toast.

—MICKEY CARROLL, Munchkin in *Oz,* MGM

EMERALD CITY AVOCADO DIP

"Dip dip here, dip dip there . . ."

1   ripe avocado
1   tablespoon lemon juice
1   teaspoon Worcestershire sauce
½   teaspoon salt
     Few drops garlic juice
1   teaspoon finely grated onion
2   strips bacon, fried crisp

Peel and seed the avocado. Sprinkle immediately with lemon juice to prevent darkening. In a bowl mash with a fork and add the Worcestershire sauce, salt, and garlic juice. Put through a coarse sieve or process in the blender, and blend in the onion.

Just before serving stir in the crumbled bacon, reserving a few pieces to garnish the top.

Serve with corn chips or tostados.

Makes 1 cup.

Romance Over the Rainbow

Did romance bloom between any of the Munchkins? Certainly. Several marriages of little people resulted from the summit of midgets in Culver City for *The Wizard of Oz*. Munchkin villager Ruth Robinson met her husband, Fred Duccini (also a little person), while working on the film in 1938. Originally from Minnesota, Ruth had traveled west with a midget troupe of entertainers, all of whom worked in the film as Munchkins. Fred had employment elsewhere at an elite Beverly Hills hotel and did not work in *Oz*, but during the film's production he visited many of his little buddies at a restaurant across the street from MGM.

"We called it 'Ptomaine Marie's,'" laughs Ruth Duccini, "but it wasn't all that bad. That's where I met Fred for the first time, at Marie's." Fred and Ruth married a few years later in 1943, in El Paso, Texas. Why El Paso? Fred's car was stolen and located in El Paso. "We decided to go pick up the car and get married," says Ruth. The couple had two children, Fred and Margaret, and celebrated their golden wedding anniversary in 1993.

Today, Ruth Duccini, a widow, is in her eighties; she is a very proud great-grandmother and an active Munchkin at *Oz* Fests and events around the country—where she invariably finds more *Oz* trinkets and keepsakes for her grandchildren.

FESTIVE ROASTED RED PEPPER DIP

1   cup (8-ounce carton) sour cream
1   cup mayonnaise
1   5-ounce jar roasted red peppers, drained, finely chopped
1   4-ounce can chopped green chilies, drained
½   teaspoon garlic powder
       Vegetables for dipping or chips

In a medium bowl mix the sour cream, mayonnaise, red peppers, chilies, and garlic powder until well blended. Refrigerate.
    Serve with vegetable dippers or chips.

MAKES ABOUT 3 CUPS.

—RUTH DUCCINI, Munchkin in *Oz*, MGM

HIRSCHFELD'S CAVIAR APPETIZER

1   hard-boiled egg, chopped
1   small onion, finely chopped
1   tablespoon light mayonnaise
1   tablespoon black caviar
       Japanese rice crackers

In a small bowl mix the egg, onion, mayonnaise, and caviar gently with a fork.
    Serve on Japanese rice crackers.

SERVES 6.

—AL HIRSCHFELD

Legendary artist Al Hirschfeld created promotional artwork for MGM's original release of The Wizard of Oz *in 1939. Now in his nineties, Hirschfeld continues to draw every day. His Oz assignment was pre-NINA, so don't attempt to locate his trademark imprint— his daughter's name surreptitiously incorporated into the images.*

Harry Monty, ninety-two, holds a framed vest portion of his original Munchkin wardrobe. A veteran midget-stuntman in films, Monty was also a Winged Monkey in the film. (Photo by Steve Cox)

LAYERED RANCHERO DIP

1	10-ounce can jalapeño-flavored bean dip
½	cup sour cream
⅓	cup mayonnaise
½	package taco seasoning mix
1	4-ounce can chopped green chilies
1	package frozen avocado dip, defrosted
1	cup shredded sharp Cheddar cheese
1	cup sliced green onions
1	cup chopped tomatoes
1	6-ounce can sliced black olives
	Tortilla chips

On a large platter thinly spread the bean dip. In a small bowl combine the sour cream, mayonnaise, and taco seasoning mix. Spread over the bean dip. Sprinkle with the chilies. Spread avocado dip over the chilies. Sprinkle with cheese, onions, tomatoes, and olives.

Serve with tortilla chips.

MAKES 6 SERVINGS.

—JEAN NELSON, founder, Chesterton, Indiana, Annual Oz Fest; owner, Yellow Brick Road Shop

MONKEY WINGS

1	5-pound bag frozen chicken wings
½	cup butter
1	small bottle Louisiana hot sauce
¼	cup lemon juice
2	packages dry Italian salad dressing mix
1	teaspoon leaf basil

Bake the frozen chicken wings on a cookie sheet at 450° for 35 minutes.

In a saucepan melt the butter and add the remaining ingredients. Place the baked wings in a baking pan. Pour the sauce over the wings and bake another 10 minutes.

MAKES 8 SERVINGS.

—HARRY MONTY, Munchkin and Winged Monkey in *Oz*, MGM

Munchkin Coroner's Spinach Dip

It's really most sincerely good!"

1	10-ounce package frozen chopped spinach, thawed and well drained
1	pint sour cream
1	cup mayonnaise
1	package dry leek soup mix
½	cup chopped parsley
½	cup chopped green onions
1	teaspoon dry Italian salad dressing mix
	Assorted raw vegetable dippers

In a blender combine all of the ingredients except the raw vegetables until blended. Refrigerate until ready to serve. Serve the dip with assorted raw vegetables.

Makes 3 ½ cups.

—MEINHARDT RAABE, Munchkin in *Oz*, MGM

Little Oscar . . . Cooking in Oz

Before pronouncing the Wicked Witch "really most sincerely dead," in *The Wizard of Oz*, German midget Meinhardt Raabe (pronounced "mine-heart robby") was employed with the Oscar Mayer meat company as a most unique spokesman, "Little Oscar," the world's smallest chef. Raabe put the Weinermobile in park so he could travel to Hollywood for work in *Oz*, and his natural culinary interests were peaked along the way. In a Watertown, Wisconsin, newspaper interview (August 1939), the forty-eight-inch-tall Northwestern University alum–turned–actor described his adventures in Tinseltown:

Hollywood has intrigued Raabe, especially its restaurants. He passed many hours with Louis Albers, chef at the studio commissary, listing favorite recipes of many of the stars. He visited the odd eating places, Chinese, Russian, Viennese, and English, in the screen colony. "Hollywood," he says, "is the home of cosmopolitan cookery. I found restaurants of every nationality, from Hindu to Hawaiian. I don't believe there is a dish on earth that can't be found there somewhere. I suppose it is because people of all nationalities are in pictures and so there is a market for their international menus. . . ."

Raabe became a close friend of Edgar Allan Woolf . . . a scenario writer famous for the dinner parties he gives at which he personally cooks unusual dishes for his guests. Woolf is rated one of the finest cooks in the world and makes a hobby of it. During production of The Wizard of Oz, on which he was one of the scene-artists, Woolf and Raabe made a tour of some of the lesser known and unusual restaurants of the screen capital, investigating Indian curies, Turkish pilaf, and such foreign viands. Raabe took copious notes and gathered special recipes.

PROFESSOR MARVEL'S STUFFED ANAHEIM PEPPERS

12　Anaheim peppers (or jalapeño for more heat)
1　8-ounce package cream cheese, cut into 12 slices
1　8-ounce package shredded Cheddar cheese, divided
1　small tomato, diced, divided
2　tablespoons finely chopped onion, divided
12　strips smoked bacon

Wash, split, and seed the peppers. Stuff with cream cheese, then Cheddar, tomato, and onion. Wrap each with 1 slice of bacon and secure with toothpicks. Cook on the grill over indirect heat for 20 to 30 minutes. (For indirect heat, build the fire on one side of grill. Place the peppers on the other side of the grate and cover the grill.) Grill until the bacon is cooked to your liking.

MAKES 12 STUFFED PEPPERS.

—NANCIE AND ART GUARIGLIA

ROASTED NUT TREATS

Blanched whole almonds
Butter
Salt

Buy as many packages of almonds as you care to. Spread them on a cookie sheet and brush with melted butter. Place the cookie sheet in a 350° oven. Keep brushing and turning them as they bake until they are a medium dark brown. Be careful not to burn them. Remove from the oven, spread between paper towels to remove the excess butter, and sprinkle with salt. Cool.

—ALAN OPPENHEIMER, voice of the Wizard from the DIC Animated Series

In 1990, Oz became an ABC-TV weekly cartoon show with some astute vocal impressions based on the movie's characters. Produced by DIC Animation and Turner Entertainment, the short-lived Saturday morning series was later released on home video.

Tornado Logs

2	8-ounce packages cream cheese, softened
2	green onions, minced
1	1-ounce package Hidden Valley Ranch salad dressing mix
4	12-inch flour tortillas
1	4-ounce jar diced pimiento
1	4-ounce can diced green chilies
1	2.25-ounce can sliced black olives

In a medium bowl mix the cream cheese, onions, and salad dressing mix. Spread on the tortillas. Drain the vegetables and blot dry with a paper towel. Sprinkle equal amounts of the vegetables on top of the cream cheese. Roll the tortillas tightly into a log. Chill at least 2 hours.

Cut into 1-inch pieces. Discard the ends. Serve with spirals facing up.

MAKES 3 DOZEN.

—JEAN NELSON, founder, Chesterton, Indiana, Annual Oz Fest; owner, Yellow Brick Road Shop

Very Resourceful Pepper Jelly Snack

Cream cheese
Pepper jelly (red, green, or jalāpeno)
Crackers

Pepper jelly can be a great thing. For a quick fix when unexpected company shows up at your door, all you have to do is spread cream cheese about ½ inch thick on a serving dish. Gently spread red, green, or jalāpeno pepper jelly over it to glaze. Serve with any type of crackers—it's great! If there's time to chill it a bit first, that's even better.

You can also add some crabmeat to the cream cheese, and toss in some chopped chives, green onions, or pimiento.

—ELAINE WILLINGHAM

Western Salsa

1	4-ounce can chopped black olives
1	4-ounce can diced green chilies
2	green onions, chopped
1	large tomato, diced
1	tablespoon vinegar
1	tablespoon salad oil

Drain the excess liquid from the olives and chilies. In a medium bowl combine all and chill.

Serve as a dip with corn chips.

Note: If you like it hot, add some Louisiana hot sauce to your taste.

—PETE CASSIMATIS

A rare candid of Judy Garland rehearsing her bit as a carhop in a scene from the motion picture A Star Is Born, *circa October 1953. (Beyond the Rainbow Archive)*

The Oz Man

In 1910, Lyman Frank Baum explained in a Chicago newspaper story the state of children's fairy tales as he saw it. "The imagination of the writers of other days fell short of the achievements of the creators of the present . . . children no longer desire the old-time fairy tales, for what is Aladdin's lamp compared to wireless telegraphy? The modern age with all its wonderful inventions is itself a fairyland. Modern discoveries have outstripped the imagination of the old writers of fairy tales."

It's been exactly a century since Baum forced himself to sit at his unique harpsichord/desk, with pen in left hand, and finally scribble out *The Wonderful Wizard of Oz*; indeed he was a confident man, but still, it would be amusing to know if he honestly assumed his stories would endure, or capture the ages. Could he have forecast that one hundred years later his *Oz* creation would be such a prolific cultural phenomenon in America—much less a global classic?

Let it be known, Baum was visionary, fascinated by technological advances: the advent of automobiles, motion pictures, airplanes, and electrical gadgetry of all sorts. His place in time allowed him to witness wonders, and Baum realized society was pushing through an exciting era at warp speed. Amazingly, in his book *Tik-Tok of Oz* (1914), Baum made an insightful reference to a "wireless telephone." Of course, today cordless and cell phones are commonplace.

Baum, the Oz Man, in Del Mar, California, circa 1916. (Robert A. Baum Collection)

Born in Chittenango, New York (near Syracuse), on May 15, 1856, L. Frank Baum (usually called Frank), was the son of a wealthy oil exporter. Young Frank had access to some of the best literature available, and he was fascinated by books of fantasy and lore. He dabbled in a variety of careers in adulthood: store proprietor, playwright, business entrepreneur, and journalist, and he was a reporter at newspapers in New York, Chicago, and Aberdeen, South Dakota. In November 1882, Frank married Maud Gage of Fayetteville, New York, and eventually the couple had four sons.

"After we were married," said Maud Baum in a 1939 *Syracuse Herald* interview, "he told me he had resolved as a boy that if he ever had the chance and ability, he would write at least one fantasy which did not have horror and bloodshed."

Frank Baum was a master storyteller, full of enthusiastic tales that spontaneously burst from his mind. Usually he tested his tales out on his own children and then to groups of children who routinely gathered "round in curious amazement." Traditionally, Baum settled down in his favorite upholstered chair and created the stories as he went. "Frank would throw his legs over one of the arm rests and rattle on with no effort. I told him he ought to write some of his fairy tales out and try to get them published. Usually he would jot down his notes on backs of envelopes or scraps of paper." Legend has it that the Baums frequently had to replace the wallpaper in their bedroom because Frank would scribble ideas on the wall as they popped up in

L. Frank Baum (far right) wins a turkey carving contest at an Uplifter's Banquet at the L.A. Athletic Club, circa 1914. The newspaper item was clipped and saved by his wife, Maud, for the family scrapbook. (Robert A. Baum Collection)

L. Frank Baum enjoying a cigar in Southern California, around 1912. By observing the shadows, you could presume the photographer is probably Maud, wearing a hat, taking the picture about waist-level with a box camera of the day. (Robert A. Baum Collection)

the middle of the night. Although he created many stories, plays, songs, and books in his life, Oz became the favorite theme with his own kids as well as children around the world. Oz kept coming back to him, and so he became "the *Oz* man" to many a youngster who approached him or wrote to him.

The publishing road was a difficult one at first because Frank was not financially secure, and during his most trying times, no publisher was interested in taking a chance on his whimsical ideas. In 1899, Baum published *Father Goose: His Book,* illustrated by William W. Denslow. It was a book of poetry with lavish color illustrations, and as delectable as it was to the eye, every publisher rejected it due to the risk and expense of printing color, especially for a children's storybook. So Baum and Denslow purchased the plates themselves and published the book. A year later, *The Wonderful Wizard of Oz* was published under similar circumstances. Distributed by George M. Hill Company, *Oz* became a gargantuan success and sold more than a million copies in its first year.

Still considered a bit radical, Baum nonetheless received literally bales of mail begging for further *Oz* adventures. He did not intend to write more books about the Emerald City and Dorothy, but the characters and the fame—as well as his own talents—haunted him, prodded him. It was not until 1904 that a second installment, *The Marvelous Land of Oz,* was published. Eventually, some sixty diverse books followed (some under the pen names Edith van Dyne, Floyd Akers, and Schuyler Stanton), but none so popular as his *Oz* tales.

The Baums spent their golden years in a gray two-story Hollywood home on Cherokee Avenue that Frank christened "Ozcot." The corner-lot home with a towering palm tree in front was Frank's castle, his pride and joy, where he indulged in his hobby of cultivating flowers, and where he penned some of his fourteen *Oz* books. His final book, *The Tin Woodman of Oz,* was published in 1918, a year before his death. Following a lengthy heart ailment that weakened him throughout

his adult years, L. Frank Baum suffered a stroke and died at his home on May 6, 1919, just days before his sixty-third birthday. Today, the site where Ozcot once stood in Hollywood is now a parking lot.

Maud Baum—his loving wife and companion to whom he dedicated his original *Oz* book—survived to attend the premiere of MGM's *The Wizard of Oz* in 1939 and experience the world's love affair with *Oz.* By that time, forty years after *Oz* was created, reportedly millions of copies of *The Wonderful Wizard of Oz* were in print, and it became Maud's responsibility to oversee her husband's legacy. (Two of Frank's *Oz* stories were published posthumously, tales he had written and stored in a safe-deposit box in case he was too ill to write.) Maud eventually allowed the *Oz* stories to continue through the eyes of several writers including Ruth Plumly Thompson, who wrote eighteen additional *Oz* books. Maud was hired to work in a mild advisory capacity during the filming of MGM's extravagant musical version, and she participated in appearances and radio interviews to

L. Frank Baum in a caricature by A. B. Titus, circa 1915. (Robert A. Baum Collection)

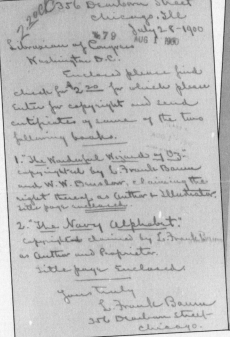

L. Frank Baum's original, handwritten copyright application for The Wonderful Wizard of Oz, addressed to the Library of Congress, and dated July 28, 1900. Registration was officially approved August 1, 1900. (Ron Borst Collection)

Founded in 1957, the International Wizard of Oz Club regularly publishes a magazine, The Baum Bugle, which strives to appeal to serious students of Oz, aficionados, and casual readers. This Winter 1982 edition featured a handsome portrait of L. Frank Baum, circa 1915, on the cover. (Courtesy of International Wizard of Oz Club. Reprinted by permission.)

promote the motion picture during its initial release in August 1939. Maud died in 1953.

Regarding *The Wizard of Oz,* the film that most significantly perpetuated the popular *Oz* story, Maud once revealed to a Kansas newspaper reporter she thought her husband would've been satisfied with the glorious Technicolor adaptation—but she wished there had been more music and no witch. "You see, Frank wouldn't have liked the witch part," she said. "He never wrote anything that might frighten children."

Maud Baum, widow of L. Frank Baum, was the guest of MGM and Judy Garland when the film was being made. Mrs. Baum had lunch with Garland, toured the studio, visited sets, and posed for publicity pictures such as this one, which she treasured in her personal scrapbook. (Robert A. Baum Collection)

THE *OZ* SERIES BY L. FRANK BAUM

The Wonderful Wizard of Oz (1900)
The Marvelous Land of Oz (1904)
Ozma of Oz (1907)
Dorothy and the Wizard in Oz (1908)
The Road to Oz (1909)
The Emerald City of Oz (1910)
The Patchwork Girl of Oz (1913)
Tik-Tok of Oz (1914)
The Scarecrow of Oz (1915)
Rinkitink in Oz (1916)
The Lost Princess of Oz (1917)
The Tin Woodman of Oz (1918)
The Magic of Oz (1919)
Glinda of Oz (1920)

The original *Oz* tale, *The Wonderful Wizard of Oz,* was illustrated by W. W. Denslow; all subsequent Baum *Oz* books were illustrated by John R. Neill.

L. Frank Baum
"The Wizard of Oz Man"

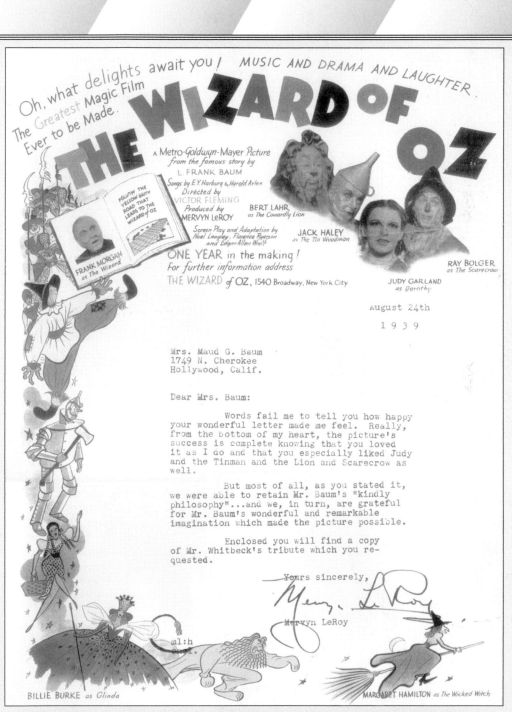

Oh, what delights await you! MUSIC AND DRAMA AND LAUGHTER.
The Greatest Magic Film Ever to be Made.

THE WIZARD OF OZ

A Metro-Goldwyn-Mayer Picture
from the famous story by
L. FRANK BAUM
Songs by E.Y. Harburg & Harold Arlen
Directed by
VICTOR FLEMING
Produced by
MERVYN LeROY

Screen Play and Adaptation by
Noel Langley, Florence Ryerson
and Edgar Allan Woolf

FOLLOW THE YELLOW BRICK ROAD THAT LEADS TO THE WIZARD OF OZ

FRANK MORGAN
as The Wizard

BERT LAHR
as The Cowardly Lion

JACK HALEY
as The Tin Woodman

JUDY GARLAND
as Dorothy

RAY BOLGER
as The Scarecrow

ONE YEAR in the making!
For further information address
THE WIZARD of OZ, 1540 Broadway, New York City.

August 24th
1939

Mrs. Maud G. Baum
1749 N. Cherokee
Hollywood, Calif.

Dear Mrs. Baum:

      Words fail me to tell you how happy
your wonderful letter made me feel. Really,
from the bottom of my heart, the picture's
success is complete knowing that you loved
it as I do and that you especially liked Judy
and the Tinman and the Lion and Scarecrow as
well.

      But most of all, as you stated it,
we were able to retain Mr. Baum's "kindly
philosophy"...and we, in turn, are grateful
for Mr. Baum's wonderful and remarkable
imagination which made the picture possible.

      Enclosed you will find a copy
of Mr. Whitbeck's tribute which you re-
quested.

      Yours sincerely,

      Mervyn LeRoy

ml:h

BILLIE BURKE as Glinda

MARGARET HAMILTON as The Wicked Witch

L. Frank Baum's widow, Maud, tucked away this kind letter in her scrapbook. Amused by the designed letterhead and Ozzy art, she eventually incorporated the concept into personalized stationery of her own. (The caricatures adorning the edges were created by Al Hirschfeld.)

St. Patrick's Dinner and Dance

Los Angeles Athletic Club

FRIDAY EVENING, MARCH 15TH

CEAD MILE FALTH!

AN EVENING OF BUOYANT JOY, EFFERVESCENT AS THE SPIRIT OF THE EMERALD ISLE, SPARKLING AS THE SAPPHIRE SEA KISSING ITS CASTELLATED SHORES, AND TRUE TO THE HAPPY TRADITIONS OF THE PATRON SAINT'S DAY

ALL THE IRISH TRIMMIN'S

DINNER AT 7. TWO AND A HALF DOLLARS PER PLATE. THE TIME TO MAKE SURE OF YOUR RESERVATION IS TODAY

FORMAL DRESS
A TOUCH OF GREEN O. K.

ENTERTAINMENT COMMISSIONERS

L. FRANK BAUM
MARCH CHAIRMAN
RALPH HAMLIN
DR. ALBERT BOILAND
SIM W. CRABILL
WILLIAM MAY GARLAND
LEO V. STARR
GEORGE T. CLINE
CHARLES SUMNER KENT
WM E. BUSH
L. E. BEHTYMER
JOHN F POWERS
SHIRLEY E. MESERVE

ST. PATRICK'S DINNER AND DANCE

SATURDAY, MARCH 17
LOS ANGELES ATHLETIC CLUB

A ROLLICKING GOOD TIME
IRISH BALLADS BY CLUB MEMBERS

IRISH MUSIC
AND BEGORRA! FAVORS OF OLD ERIN
DINNER AT 7 P.M.
$2.50 PER PLATE

DANCING FROM 9 P.M.
MAKE YOUR TABLE RESERVATION
TODAY
FORMAL DRESS

LOS ANGELES ATHLETIC CLUB
ENTERTAINMENT
BOARD

WILLIAM A. BUSH
WILLIAM W. WOODS
DR. GEO. KRESS
RALPH C. HAMLIN
GEORGE T. CLINE
L. FRANK BAUM,
MARCH CHAIRMAN

CHARLES SUMNER KENT
DR. ALBERT SOILAND
HARRY G. HOLABIRD
ANDREW MULLEN
JOHN F. POWERS
ROBT. B. ARMSTRONG

Patronesses

Mrs. John Maurer
Mrs. George L. Crenshaw
Mrs. Fred Hooker Jones
Mrs. J. T. Fitzgerald
Mrs. W. I. Hollingsworth
Mrs. Cecil Frankel
Mrs. Irving Hayes Rice

Entertainment Commissioners

John F. Powers
Ralph C. Hamlin
Wm. W. Woods
Geo. T. Cline
Harry G. Holabird
C. Sumner Kent
Andrew J. Mullen
Dr. Albert Soiland
Dr. George H. Kress
William E. Bush
Robert B. Armstrong
L. Frank Baum,
March Chairman

Menu

TOKE POINT OYSTERS
MIGNONETTE

HEARTS OF CELERY   OLIVES

CREAM OF GARDEN PEAS

BOILED CHINOOK SALMON, SAUCE VERTE
POTATO PERSILLADE

STUFFED BELL PEPPERS, VERTE PRE

CREME DE MENTHE PUNCH

BROILED SQUAB CHICKEN
POTATOES O'BRIEN AU GRATIN   CREAMED SPINACH

CRESSON SALAD

EMERALD ISLE ICE CREAM

DEMI TASSE

L. Frank Baum served as chairman for a variety of social events in Southern California, including annual St. Patrick's Day festivities. Obviously, Baum possessed a little spirit o' the Emerald Isle. These menus, circa 1915 and 1917, were preserved in Baum's family scrapbooks. (Robert A. Baum Collection)

BREAKFAST 'N' BRUNCH

ADDALIZA'S "GRAVY EGGS"

Great-great-grandma Addaliza cooked these on a wood stove and made good ol' buttermilk biscuits to go with them, too.

6   to 8 slices bacon
       All-purpose flour
       Salt and pepper
6   eggs
       Milk

In a large skillet fry 6 to 8 slices of bacon. Set aside on paper towels to drain. Pour off half of the bacon drippings. Sprinkle about ¼ cup of flour over the remaining drippings in the skillet—do not stir. Then sprinkle with salt and pepper.

Break the eggs over the flour in the skillet; then lightly sprinkle more flour over the eggs, plus more salt and pepper. Pour enough milk over the eggs to cover. Cover the skillet with a lid and cook over medium-low heat until the eggs are cooked to your liking, and the gravy thickened.

Try it with sausage, too.

MAKES 3 SERVINGS.

—JERRY COX

BREAKFAST WITH FRANK MORGAN

My father would often have the following big breakfast:

2   tablespoons butter
½   large onion, finely chopped
1   green onion, finely chopped
3   cloves garlic, finely chopped
1   16-ounce can tomatoes
1   teaspoon oregano
1   teaspoon basil
       Tabasco sauce
1   large Mexican pepper, finely chopped
3   eggs

In a large skillet melt the butter and sauté the onions and garlilc until tender. Add the tomatoes, oregano, basil, a good shake or two of Tabasco sauce, and the Mexican pepper. Set aside.

In a separate skillet scramble the eggs and transfer to a plate. Cover with the tomato mixture.

MAKES 1 SERVING.

—GEORGE MORGAN, son of Frank Morgan

Rancher Frank Morgan looks as if he's about to lead this bull to a "billowing bale of bovine fodder." The fifty-five-year-old actor owned a 550-acre ranch in Hemet Valley of Riverside County, California. On the ranch he had twenty Aberdeen-Angus heifers and the herd sire was named Hercules. He developed a genuine affection for the cows, and he had a pet name for each. (Photo circa 1944)

Edible Oz

Oz for a midnight snack . . . or anytime! L. Frank Baum was never at a loss for creatively jelling his characters with all sorts of edibles. In most of his books, he inventively conjured his characters into attending some nutritious event, consuming an unusual delicacy or stumbling upon some bizarre and tasty viand who happens to speak. For instance, during one adventure our Ozzy friends stumble upon Popcorn Mountain; in the land of Oogaboo, candy trees abound. In the Land of Oz, however, there was one specific thread throughout the adventures: no eating of animals.

Here is a selection of edible references and characters from the menu of Baum's books:

- JACK PUMPKINHEAD emerged in *The Land of Oz,* made by a boy named Tip who constructed Jack to scare away Mombi, the witch. She sprinkled Jack with magic powder to come alive. His head, which was of course made from a pumpkin, occasionally became detached from his wooden body and needed to be put back on again. Because his pumpkin head tended to spoil, he maintained a fresh pumpkin patch so he could always select a new one when necessary.

- Some have said THE WOGGLE BUG (shown at right), first described in *The Land of Oz,* was inspired by soft-shell crabs common to the beaches at the Hotel del Coronado in Southern California where Baum penned several *Oz* books. The Woggle Bug, grotesque and spidery in form, is a highly educated bug who actually invented square-meal tablets to conserve eating— but the concept was not well received.

- While trekking to Australia, Dorothy befriends a yellow hen named Bill, renamed BILLINA, in *Ozma of Oz.* The talkative fowl accompanies Dorothy through the underground world of the Nomes—who are terribly afraid of eggs. While in the king's domain, Dorothy is served coffee made of ground clay, which she finds surprisingly delicious. In the country of Ev, where Dorothy first lands with Billina, she realizes her hunger and discovers THE LUNCHPAIL TREE—that's right, a tree with lunchpails growing on it.

- In *Dorothy and the Wizard in Oz,* they go to the vegetable kingdom where all the dwellers are either live vegetable people or live flower people. The king (GWIG, a nasty sorcerer) is a cross between a potato and a turnip man. The vegetables do not like Dorothy. The Wizard ends up in a duel with Gwig and slashes the sorcerer in half, exposing his potato innards.

- The Wizard has learned to become an actual wizard in *The Emerald City of Oz,* and he takes Dorothy, Aunt Em, and Uncle Henry on a tour. While journeying through Oz, the Wizard magically makes a complete picnic appear for them to satisfy every meal. Dorothy gets separated from the group and lands in the town of BUNBURY where all who live there are made of buns or bread. Some of the more prominent citizens are neatly frosted, others have raisins for eyes and legs of cinnamon sticks. They roam on breadcrust sidewalks and live in elaborately constructed homes made of crackers, complete with porches with bread-stick posts and roofs shingled with wafer-crackers. (Toto takes a bite out of one citizen.) In this book, Baum also introduces the living kitchen utensils who live in the kingdom of Utensia, in the Quadling Country. Most unusual is the absence of a cook or a single thing to eat in the whole kingdom.

- CAYKE THE COOKIE COOK, a female Yip, is introduced in *The Lost Princess of Oz.* After her magic diamond-encrusted dishpan is stolen, she and the wise Frogman leave their mountaintop in search of it.

In "Thanksgiving in the Land of Oz," Dorothy makes another visit to the magical kingdom and greets some old friends, including the Lion, the Tin Man, and the Scarecrow, and meets some new ones, including Jack Pumpkinhead, Tik-Tok, the Hungry Tiger, Ozma, and U. N. Krust—a living, talking mince pie that used a different dialect every time he minced his words (voiced by Sid Caesar). The musical animated holiday special aired Tuesday, November 25, 1980, on CBS. (It later aired as "Dorothy in the Land of Oz" on Showtime and HBO.)

Caesar's Omelet

 Olive oil
2 green bell peppers, chopped
1 red bell pepper, chopped
 Chopped onions
 Basil
 Mushrooms, sliced
 Oregano
 Cayenne pepper
10 egg whites, 1 yolk
 Grated cheese (spicy)

In a skillet heat a little olive oil and lightly fry the peppers, onion, basil, and mushrooms until almost brown. Season with oregano and cayenne pepper. Set aside. In a bowl beat the egg whites until fluffy, then add the egg yolk and vegetable mixture. Mix together and return to the skillet to cook. Add the grated cheese. Serve.

—SID CAESAR

Flying Monkey Pancakes

1¾ cups all-purpose flour
½ teaspoon salt
1 tablespoon baking powder
1 tablespoon sugar
1 egg, beaten
1 cup milk
2 tablespoons melted shortening
2 bananas, cut in small pieces

In a large bowl sift the flour, salt, baking powder, and sugar together. In a medium bowl combine the egg, milk, and shortening. Add the liquid mixture to the dry ingredients, stirring just until moist. The batter will be lumpy. Add the bananas. Bake on an ungreased griddle.

Syrup: In a small saucepan mix 1 cup of white corn syrup and 2 teaspoons of banana extract. Pour the warm syrup over the pancakes.

May also be served sprinkled with confectioners' sugar or with whipped cream or Cool Whip and sliced bananas and nuts.

MAKES 6 TO 8 PANCAKES.

—VIOLA WHITE BANKS, child
Munchkin in *Oz,* MGM

HICKORY'S NUT WAFFLES

Well, don't start preparing for it now!

½   cup butter
1   cup confectioners' sugar
    Pinch salt
½   cup milk
1½ cups all-purpose flour (sifted before and
    after measuring)
1   cup chopped hickory nuts

In a large bowl cream the butter, sugar, and salt together. Add the milk and flour slowly. Pour the batter into a greased jelly roll pan or cookie sheet. Spread very thin and sprinkle with finely chopped hickory nuts. Bake in a 325° oven until lightly browned. Cut in squares and roll while still warm.

MAKES 4 SERVINGS.

SADIE'S "BUBBLE AND SQUEAK"

A good breakfast side dish for two.

When I was 9, I went on holiday to Salisbury. Every morning for breakfast, we either got fried potatoes or "bubble and squeak." I watched them cook it, and I've been making it ever since. We used to use leftover potatoes and meat drippings, but that has been altered for cholesterol purposes.

    Vegetable oil
1   clove garlic, finely chopped
1   small onion, finely chopped
4   medium potatoes, boiled, cooled
1   teaspoon butter
1   teaspoon milk
2   cups finely chopped boiled Brussels
    sprouts or cabbage, drained
½   teaspoon salt
¼   teaspoon pepper

Spread a little oil in a nonstick frying pan and place over low heat. Add the garlic and onion and sauté for a few minutes.

In a bowl mash the potatoes with the butter and milk until completely smooth. Add the rest of the ingredients to the potato mixture, including the garlic and onion. Mash it up very well. Turn the frying pan on high heat. Place the mixture into the pan and pat it down flat like a pancake. As it hits the pan, you should hear it sizzle, thus the name "Bubble and Squeak." Fry about 2 minutes until golden brown. Flip it over and brown the other side for another 2 minutes.

MAKES 2 SERVINGS.

—SADIE CORRÉ, Munchkin
in Disney's *Return to Oz*

Petite British actress Sadie Corré portrayed a Munchkin in Disney's Return to Oz, *filmed in England. "We shot it at Elstree Studios," Corré says, "and there were about eighty of us Munchkins. Some were children, dwarfs, and little people. We just walked behind Dorothy when she was going to see the witch. We just stood there like bloody fools.*

"Elstree Studios was used in the Star Wars *trilogy—I was an Ewok—and we also shot some of* The Rocky Horror Picture Show *there, which I was in as well. I remember Lord Snowden—or Tony, I call him—visited the set of* Return to Oz. *He used to be married to Princess Margaret. Tony is a photographer and we were friends from years earlier. When he saw me he threw his hands in the air and shouted, 'Hello, Sadie!' and we hugged."*

SAUTERNE EGGS

½	cup Sauterne wine
4	eggs
	Salt, pepper, grated nutmeg
2	tablespoons Parmesan cheese

Generously grease 4 custard cups. Pour 2 tablespoons of wine into each cup, then carefully slide in the eggs. Season with salt, pepper, and nutmeg. Sprinkle with cheese. Bake at 350° for 12 to 15 minutes or until the eggs are set as desired.

MAKES 4 SERVINGS.

—OZMA BAUM MANTELE, Granddaughter
of L. Frank Baum

Sunday Breakfast at Grandfather Baum's

Grandfather Baum liked to cook, as did my father. Breakfast was a favorite meal in their house. On Sunday mornings, we always had meat for breakfast, such as pork chops, lamb chops, or sautéed lamb kidneys (a particular favorite), plus popovers, which my father made with a great deal of success. Grandmother was a good cook as I remember, and it was always fun to eat at her house. She made a lot of jams, jellies, and relishes, which she shared with the family members.

—Ozma Baum Mantele

Working on the Yellow Brick Road

George Lillie, age eighty-one, worked at MGM during the production of *The Wizard of Oz* and recalls here some of his experiences on the film:

I started working at MGM in July 1937 as a painter. As you know, the motion picture studios employ many professional craftspeople and artisans, including carpenters, electricians, painters, etc. Most of us worked on the sets weeks prior to shooting. The famous Yellow Brick Road was in several scenes and it was constructed on three different soundstages. The Road began in a circular shape in Munchkinland and its route was about two hundred feet long in some places and it was about ten to twelve feet wide in some places. It ended at Emerald City, which was a different stage than Munchkinland.

In this new phase of moviemaking called Technicolor, we had to paint several samples on the road and these patches were photographed with the proposed lighting, and the Technicolor people chose the color that photographed best. From then on we painted the road in the various areas designated by the Art Department. In the 1930s, there were no rollers, nor any pressure spray guns so we used large paintbrushes called Dutch Brushes, which we used to hand-paint the entire Yellow Brick Road. The paint we used had to be quick drying; the paint was called shellac, which we tinted with various dry powder colors to create the selected shade. We made over a hundred gallons of the selected color to make sure all of the roads were painted consistently. Most of the stage floors were covered with a half-inch-thick product called Masonite, in one-foot by one-foot tiles. We had to fill the gaps where the Masonite came together with plaster so the road would look like one overall texture, showing no cracks. After the second coat, we were given yardsticks, and small paint brushes, called "liners," to paint the mortar lines. When you watch the movie, you cannot see all the detail we did on the grout lines because the bright lights wash it out on film. I think the scene with the Lion's appearance showed our grout work the best.

We also worked on the interior of Emerald City, lots and lots of green, and the interior of the Wicked Witch's castle was painted by our group. We also painted the horses "of a different color" in Emerald City. I had read later that "gelatin" coloring was used, but as I recall, we used powdered food coloring and water to paint these palominos. Along with the horses' trainers, we painted these white palominos with big brushes and sponges. We were careful with the animals and we had to get the color deep enough so not to see their natural white hair. When we finished shooting, we took the horses to the Pacific Ocean a few miles away and washed out the food coloring. One humorous thing happened, I remember. The purple horse did not wash as clean as we expected, so we had to do what we could and allow the horse's white hair to just grow back naturally. It was quite a sight to see a purple horse grazing with the other horses at the studio's equine area. The joke around the studio was that many a drinker quit altogether when they saw our purple horse.

—George Lillie

Scott's Healthy Breakfasts

"These things must be done delicately."
Cooking in Oz *wouldn't be complete without breakfast—how our heroes got through that entire land without one, I'll never know. I love breakfast, and make sure to compensate for my missed weekday meals by having a full breakfast at least one weekend morning. I gear my breakfasts around a moderately low-fat diet. Egg Beaters have always worked well for me. They tend to mix with other ingredients well and set up nicely in a frying pan. Another great breakfast ingredient is the shredded Healthy Choice light Cheddar cheese. Philadelphia Brand light and fat-free styles of cream cheese are quite suitable. Other ingredients you will need for my breakfasts include raw onion, Smuckers' Light Preserves (can anyone resist the 10 calorie strawberry?) and the muffin of your choice.*

The Omelet

After spraying Pam (an adequate fat-free butter substitute) into your nonstick frying pan, empty the entire 4-egg container of Egg Beaters into the pan, adjusting it slightly to be certain that the mixture spreads evenly throughout the pan. Allow the mixture to settle on medium heat, leaving it be for about 2 minutes. At this point, cut your muffin and ready it for toasting. Thomas' English Muffins are still and always my preferred brand. Check the edges of your omelet with your spatula, not disturbing the mixture until the edges have hardened first. At this

point, shake a generous but not excessive portion of your shredded cheese into the mixture, in a circular manner so as to distribute it throughout your omelet. By now, you may start gently pushing the sides of the omelet toward the center of the pan. Just before the bottom starts to harden, chop small shards of your onion in roughly the same portions as your cheese. You will sense the mixture's uni-

Producer Scott Essman with a cast of re-creations for a video tribute to the makeup wizardry of Oz in 1998.

formity, and the time is nearing when everything should be flipped. When you do so, the new up side will not yet be browned, but should be solid. Leave the remaining down side alone another 90 seconds or so and flip again. At this point, your muffin should begin toasting. Your breakfast is nearing completion.

When your omelet is slightly browning, you are getting very warm. Egg Beater omelets can take a few flips, but try to avoid flipping more than 2 or 3 times. Your onion and cheese will mix happily into the omelet without too much coercion, so leave well enough alone unless the emergency occurs—pieces breaking off! It's great to have a nice circle, but sometimes detachment does take place. Usually, Egg Beaters will let stray pieces of omelet back into the proverbial family if it's still early in the game. Once browning has initiated, the orphans are destined to forever remain separated! I usually time the pop of the toaster with the turning-down of heat on my stove. By the time I have moderately spread the cream cheese and light strawberry preserves atop my muffin halves, I am ready to take the sizzling delight off of the pan with spatula (or dumped onto my plate should detachment have occurred), and pour my glass of accompanying orange juice. Breakfast is served!

MAKES 1 SERVING.

—SCOTT ESSMAN

EGG BEATER FRENCH TOAST

Place three slices of whole wheat bread in the pan or skillet and pour a 4-egg container of Egg Beaters over the slices. Flip immediately. Leave alone for 90 seconds, flip once, and the mixture will conform to both sides of the bread. After each side has browned, serve with banana on top, and light maple or fruit syrup.

MAKES 1 SERVING.

—SCOTT ESSMAN

WE WELCOME YOU WAFFLES

My husband's grandmother (Gammy) used to make these waffles on Sunday morning and serve them with heaps of bacon, sausages, and eggs on the side. But, if you're watching fats, skip the side dishes, substitute vegetable oil for the butter, and eliminate the yolk from one of the eggs. These waffles are very different from the standard waffle: crispy golden outside, fluffy and tender inside.

½   cup warm water
1   package dry yeast
2   cups warm milk
½   cup melted butter
1   teaspoon salt
1   teaspoon sugar
2   cups all-purpose flour
2   eggs
¼   teaspoon baking soda

Pour the warm water in a large mixing bowl and sprinkle in the yeast. Let stand for 5 minutes. Add the milk, butter, salt, sugar, and flour to the yeast mixture and beat until smooth. Cover the bowl and let stand overnight at room temperature.

When you're ready to cook the waffles, while your waffle iron is warming up, beat in the eggs, then add the soda and stir until well mixed. The batter will be very thin.

Bake on a hot waffle iron until the waffles are golden and crisp to the touch.

Tip from Gammy: When the waffles stop sending up little puffs of steam, they're done. Don't open the waffle iron before the steam stops; you could interrupt the leavening process and the waffles will fall.

MAKES 8 AVERAGE-SIZE WAFFLES.

—BETTY ANN BRUNO, child Munchkin
in *Oz*, MGM

BEWITCHING BREWS

ANDY'S DANDY LION WINE

1 gallon boiling water
2 quarts dandelion blossoms
2 lemons, sliced
2 oranges, sliced
3½ pounds sugar
1 cake fresh yeast

In a large noncorrosive pot combine the water, dandelion blossoms, lemons, oranges, and sugar, and let come to a boil. Remove from the heat. When cold, add the yeast cake. Let stand, covered, five days. Transfer to a jug. Let stand 2 months.

MAKES 1 GALLON.

—ANDY CASSIMATIS

AUGUST TOMATO DRINK

4 very ripe tomatoes, peeled, seeded, and chopped
1 small onion, chopped
¼ cup chopped celery
¼ cup chopped carrot
½ cup chopped green bell pepper
2 tablespoons fresh parsley
1 bay leaf
  Salt to taste
½ teaspoon Worcestershire sauce
  Dash Tabasco sauce

In a heavy-bottomed pan cook the tomatoes, onion, celery, carrot, green pepper, parsley, and bay leaf over low heat until the vegetables are soft. Remove and discard the bay leaf. In a blender or food processor purée the mixture. Add the salt and sauces to taste. Chill. Serve over ice.

Note: No water in this recipe—vegetables form their own juice.

MAKES 2 SERVINGS.

Collectible Oz Sealtest tumblers, circa 1939, were made by Corning Glass Works and originally contained cottage cheese. In June 1999, an eBay Internet auction fetched $760 for one glass from the set of seven. (Photo courtesy of Willard Carroll)

CHAMPAGNE PUNCH

2   large bottles champagne
2   2-liter bottles ginger ale
2   12-ounce cans frozen lemonade
     Water
2   10-ounce packages frozen strawberries

In a punch bowl mix all of the ingredients together. Fill both empty lemonade cans with water and add to the mixture. Add ice cubes and serve.

MAKES ABOUT 18 SERVINGS.

—LINDA SHEETS

ALE TO DOROTHY! From the lush ever-green landscapes of Seattle (sometimes referred to as Emerald City) came a beer produced by the microbrewery Emerald City Brewing Company, a subsidiary of Ranier Brewing, in 1994. (Photo by Andy Cassimatis)

Flying Monkey Beer, a thirst-quencher from FMI microbrewery in Kansas City, Missouri, was first produced in 1996; available in pale and amber ale, the beer was a regional product sold by the keg and in bottles. (Beyond the Rainbow Archive)

EMERALD CITY COOLER

2   cups water
2   tablespoons instant tea or 3 tea bags
¼   cup mint jelly
2   cups unsweetened grapefruit juice
      Green food coloring (optional)
      Chilled ginger ale
      Fresh mint (garnish)

In a large saucepan boil the water. Remove from the heat and immediately add the tea. Allow to brew 3 to 5 minutes. Stir. Strain the hot tea over the mint jelly and stir until dissolved. Add the grapefruit juice and coloring if desired. Cool to room temperature. Divide among 8 tall glasses. Add ice cubes and cold ginger ale. Stir. Garnish with fresh mint.

MAKES 8 SERVINGS.

—LOIS JANUARY, Emerald City citizen in *Oz*, MGM

EMERALD CITY LIME FROST

1   3-ounce package lime-flavored gelatin
1   pint vanilla ice cream, softened
1   tablespoon fresh lime juice
½   cup heavy cream, whipped
⅔   cup flaked coconut

In a bowl prepare the gelatin according to the package directions. Chill to the consistency of egg whites. With a hand beater, beat in the slightly softened ice cream. Add the lime juice. When the mixture begins to hold a shape, pour into sherbet glasses or brandy snifters and refrigerate. Top with whipped cream and coconut. This also makes a delicious filling for a pre-baked pie crust.

MAKES 4 SERVINGS.

Lois January points to herself in Oz. In Emerald City she angelically sang to Dorothy, "We can make a dimpled smile out of a frown"

LEMON DROP PUNCH

It'll melt your troubles away . . . above the chimney tops.

9   whole cloves
6   cinnamon sticks
1   quart cranberry juice
6   cups water
⅔   cup sugar
1   12-ounce can lemonade concentrate, thawed

Tie the cloves and cinnamon in a cheesecloth bag. In a Crock Pot combine the cranberry juice, water, sugar, and spice bag, and heat on the high heat setting for 1 hour and 30 minutes.

Remove the spice bag, add the lemonade, and stir. Reduce the heat setting to low. Keep warm for serving.

MAKES 24 4-OUNCE SERVINGS.

—MICKEY CARROLL, Munchkin in *Oz*, MGM

LEMONCELLO

This makes a great gift. Keep it in the freezer and serve ice cold. My favorite is to mix with soda water, really refreshing in the summer.

24   lemons
2   bottles vodka (over 100 proof)
       Sugar
       Water

Peel the zest (the yellow part) of the rind from the lemons (be careful not to get any of the white part) and place in a jar. Cover with 1 bottle of vodka. Let stand for 15 days. Strain the liquid and discard the peels. Make a simple syrup of 2 parts sugar to 1 part of water, boiled together until slightly thickened, and add to the mixture along with another bottle of vodka. Let stand for another 15 days. If the liquid is cloudy, you may need to strain again.

—AUGIE AMATO

MICKEY AND JUDY'S MALT SHOPPE SPECIAL

1   egg
5   to 6 heaping scoops vanilla ice cream
⅛   teaspoon vanilla extract
¾   cup coconut flakes
4   cups milk
3   teaspoons malt powder (or chocolate syrup if you like)

In a blender mix all ingredients. For a thick, rich chocolate malted it is recommended to use vanilla ice cream but add the flavoring via malt and syrup. (For a delightful twist, instead of the coconut use one small package of M&M's plain candies. Additionally, a few tablespoons of Bailey's Irish Cream can give the malt a fresh flavor—for adults only.)

Serve in a tall iced-tea or malted-milk glass with a long spoon. Forget the straw, it won't work. The perfect treat on a hot summer day.

MAKES 3 TO 4 SERVINGS.

—MICKEY ROONEY

Studio head Louis B. Mayer drops in on some of his youngest—and brightest—stars, Mickey Rooney and Judy Garland, at the MGM commissary.

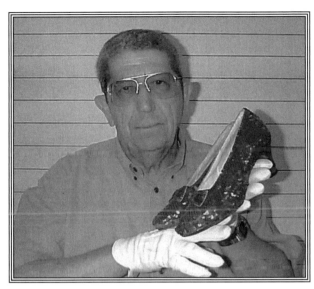

In June 1988, Anthony Landini purchased this pair of Dorothy's ruby slippers, size 6B, at auction from Christie's East, with a winning bid of $150,000. The official report from Christie's (with fees) was $165,000—the highest amount paid for a single item of Hollywood memorabilia. This particular pair of Garland's pumps—one of several used in the film—was owned by Roberta Bauman, a Memphis housewife who won them in a contest in 1940. After Landini acquired the sparkling slippers, he loaned them for display to the Disney/MGM Studio theme park in Florida. Another pair of ruby slippers are on permanent display at the Smithsonian Institution; it remains one of their most popular exhibits.

MUNCHKINLAND MAGICAL DRINK

1½	gallons frozen vanilla yogurt
5	cups white grape juice, chilled
5	cups red fruit drink, chilled

Divide the frozen yogurt evenly between two large pitchers. Pour the grape juice over the yogurt in the first pitcher. Pour the fruit drink over the yogurt in the second pitcher. Let stand for 10 minutes or until the yogurt is partially melted. Beat the contents of each pitcher with a wire whisk until smooth. Divide the grape juice mixture among 20 glasses. Carefully pour the fruit drink mixture along the inside edge of each glass to create a marbled look. Serve immediately.

MAKES 20 SERVINGS.

—KAREN ARMSTRONG

RUBY SLIPPER POWER PUNCH

". . . its magic must be very powerful."

2	large strawberries
1	14-ounce can pineapple cubes
64	ounces cranberry juice
12	ounces cherry soda
12	ounces pink champagne (or ginger ale)
2	tablespoons lemon juice
	Cherry or strawberry sherbet

Half fill a round mold with water. Partially freeze.

Place 2 large strawberries in the center; and surround with pineapple cubes (to represent ruby slippers and the yellow brick road). Freeze to anchor the fruit.

Fill with ice water and freeze until firm.

In a punch bowl combine the cranberry juice, cherry soda, champagne, and lemon juice just before serving. Top with the ice mold, and float 5 to 10 scoops of sherbet around the mold.

MAKES 16 SERVINGS.

—ANTHONY LANDINI

SHERBET PUNCH

1½   quarts sherbet (rainbow flavor)
1   6-ounce can frozen lemonade, diluted
1   6-ounce can frozen orange juice, diluted
1   14-ounce can crushed pineapple
2   large bottles ginger ale

Place the sherbet in a punch bowl. Add the remaining ingredients. Serve.

MAKES 16 SERVINGS.

RING AROUND THE ROSIE, A POCKETFUL OF JEERS Comedienne Roseanne stomped and screeched as the Wicked Witch in a hugely successful 1997 Madison Square Garden summer stage production of The Wizard of Oz *in New York. Theatre critics were not kind to Roseanne; however, fans were delighted by the show, which was chock full of special effects and splashy sets.*

SUMMER RUMPOT

This is a great liqueur for sipping and of course for serving over ice cream, pound cake, on top of whipped cream in a small wineglass, anything that needs a lift. Makes a great Christmas gift, along with homemade Pound Cake.

Start with a large crock or jar for this recipe.

Wash and dry strawberries and remove the stems. Weigh the fruit and place in the jar with an equal weight of sugar. Cover this with rum, just until the fruit-sugar mixture is covered. Cover the jar to prevent evaporation.

Wait until the sugar dissolves before adding more fruit. You can stir, but be careful not to mash the fruit.

Add cherries and an equal amount of sugar. Add just enough rum to cover.

Then add black and red raspberries and sugar. Add just enough rum to cover.

Then add blueberries and sugar—but not too many blueberries as they can become rubbery. Add rum to cover.

Then blackberries and sugar, and rum to cover.

Remember to add the equal weight of sugar each time with fruit. And always add just enough rum to cover. Be careful not to add too much rum as this will cause the syrup to become weak.

Let the jar stand about 30 days before serving.

—PAM WILLIFORD

THE WIZARD'S SWEET DREAMS FLOAT

"And oh, what happened then was rich!"

Scant ¼ cup instant regular or
decaf coffee
7   cloves
2   sticks cinnamon
3½   cups boiling water
¼   cup sugar
1½   cups vanilla ice cream
¼   cup heavy cream, whipped

In a saucepan combine the instant coffee, cloves, and cinnamon. Pour boiling water over all. Cover and bring to a boil. Remove from the heat and let stand for 5 to 8 minutes.

Strain, add the sugar to the liquid, and stir until dissolved. Chill. Serve in tall glasses topped with ice cream and whipped cream.

MAKES 4 SERVINGS.

The 1973 Tournament of Roses Parade Oz float (sponsored by FTD) featured three original Munchkins from the movie: Billy Curtis, Hazel Resmondo, and Jerry Maren. The float won the coveted Governor's Award.

The first parade float ever to feature characters from the MGM movie version of The Wizard of Oz, *in the Pasadena Tournament of Roses Parade, January 1939—months prior to the release of the motion picture. (Photo by Ruth Duccini)*

YELLOW BRICK ROAD PUNCH

6   ripe bananas
1   6-ounce can frozen lemonade, thawed
1   12-ounce can frozen orange juice, thawed
1   46-ounce can pineapple juice
3   cups water
2   cups sugar
1   64-ounce bottle 7-Up
     Orange slices

The 1993 Tournament of Roses parade included an Oz entry sponsored by Lions Club International. The float won the Lathrop K. Leishman trophy for most beautiful entry from a noncommercial sponsor. (Beyond the Rainbow Archive)

In a blender combine the bananas and fruit juice concentrates (do half at a time). Blend until smooth.

In a large mixing bowl combine the banana mixture, pineapple juice, water, and sugar, and mix well. Pour into plastic freezer containers (fills 4 quarts). Freeze the containers.

To serve, thaw until mushy. Add the 7-Up. Garnish with orange slices.

Fills an average-size punch bowl twice.

MAKES 1 ½ GALLONS.

—MICHAEL CARSON, The OzCot Restaurant,
Walnut Ridge, Arkansas

The 1954 Tournament of Roses Parade in Pasadena, California, featured this Oz-themed float. (Robert A. Baum Collection)

Soups and Salads and Sauces, Oh My!

SOUPS

Avgo Lemono Soup

1	4-pound chicken
2	quarts water
1	onion
½	cup chopped celery
2	teaspoons salt
1	cup rice or ¾ cup orzo
	Sliced carrots (optional)
3	eggs
2	tablespoons cold water
	Juice of 1½ lemons
	Pepper to taste

In a stockpot cover the chicken with water. Add the onion and celery. Heat gradually to boiling, and boil for about 1 hour and 30 minutes. Halfway through, add the salt. Remove the chicken and set aside. Strain the broth, return to a boil, and add the rice or orzo and carrots. Cover and simmer until tender. Allow to cool slightly.

In a separate bowl beat 3 eggs well. Slowly add 2 tablespoons of cold water and the lemon juice, beating constantly all the while. With a ladle, add a small amount of the hot broth to the egg mixture, blending quickly. Pour this into the soup and stir well. Serve at once.

Editor's Note: We tried this recipe and found it to be equally good for several days. The chicken can be eaten as is, fried lightly in butter, or used for chicken salad.

—VIC DIMONDA, Munchkin Coroner in the Royal Shakespeare *Wizard of Oz* Touring Company

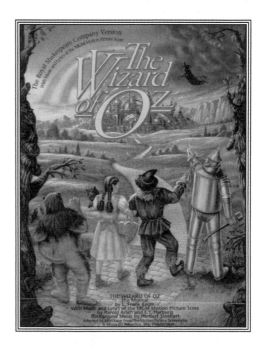

DOROTHY'S MOST DELICIOUS CHILI

1	to 2 tablespoons oil or butter
1	onion, chopped
3	to 4 cloves garlic, chopped
	Mushrooms, chopped (optional)
1	pound tofu, diced (optional)
2	21-ounce cans kidney beans, drained
1	small can salsa (mild)
1	medium can corn, drained
1	28-ounce can stewed tomatoes
1	16-ounce can tomato sauce
	Chili powder to taste
1	tablespoon Bragg's seasoning (or soy sauce)
	Grated cheese
	Sour cream

In a skillet heat the oil or butter and sauté the onion, garlic, mushrooms, and tofu until the onion is tender.

In a large pot combine the kidney beans, salsa, corn, tomatoes, tomato sauce, sautéed vegetables, chili powder, and Bragg's seasoning. Bring to a boil, reduce the heat, and simmer at least 20 minutes.

Serve with grated cheese and a dollop of sour cream.

MAKES 6 TO 8 SERVINGS.

—GITA DOROTHY MORENA, great-granddaughter
of L. Frank Baum

FLOWERPOT GUMBO

¾	cup vegetable oil
1	cup all-purpose flour
1	large onion, chopped
2	green bell peppers, chopped
3	celery stalks, chopped
1	teaspoon salt
	Cayenne pepper
2	whole boneless chicken breasts, cut into squares
3	cloves garlic, minced
1	pound smoked sausage, cut into ¼-inch slices
½	teaspoon hot sauce (optional)
8	cups beef stock or broth
	Cooked white rice

In a saucepan heat the oil and flour together, stirring constantly, over medium heat for about 30 minutes until the mixture turns dark brown.

Add the onion, peppers, celery, salt, and cayenne pepper. Cook for 8 to 10 minutes until soft, stirring throughout.

Add the raw chicken and garlic and continue cooking for 5 to 7 minutes.

Add the sausage, hot sauce, and beef stock, and bring to a boil. Reduce the heat and simmer uncovered for 1 hour. Skim off any fat and discard. Serve hot over white rice.

MAKES 6 TO 8 SERVINGS.

—JIM AND NANCY POORE, Chittenango, New York, Oz Foundation

GEORGIANA'S SPLIT PEA SOUP

This is a recipe that was served in the Lahr household almost weekly. We loved it. Georgiana Motts came to work for Dad slightly before the making of The Wizard of Oz. *She had been cooking for the great filmmaker Eric Von Stroheim. She stayed with Dad and the family for the rest of her life. She was a great cook! Once when I was a teenager, my boyfriend invited me to dine with him and his parents at The Pavilion—the best restaurant in New York at that time. I noticed that the food was no different from what I dined on every day at home! That was Georgiana. Dad loved her cooking. She was born in New Orleans. A fair-skinned black woman, she had witnessed blacks being lynched as a youth. Her childhood was a challenge. Today she would be the toast of the town—she certainly was the toast of our family.*

½   cup dried split peas
1   quart cold water
1   ham bone
2   tablespoons butter
1   tablespoon all-purpose flour
½   teaspoon salt
   Pinch pepper
1   cup milk

This chic pose is one of Jane Lahr's favorite photographs with her father; it was the last photo taken of them together, a year before he died in 1967. (Courtesy of Jane Lahr)

   Green peas for garnish
   Croutons

Soak the peas overnight or for several hours. Drain. Add the cold water and ham bone. Simmer for 3 to 4 hours until soft. Discard the ham bone.

Rub the peas through a sieve. In a skillet melt the butter and add the flour to make a roux. Season with salt and pepper. Add the milk. Blend in the peas. Add a few whole green peas and croutons as a garnish.

MAKES 6 TO 8 SERVINGS.

—JANE LAHR, daughter of Bert Lahr

JERUSALEM ARTICHOKE SOUP

This is a hearty, smoky soup, very good for cold winter evenings. And particularly good for using up holiday leftovers like turkey, chicken, or ham. It is also especially "Ozzy," since Jerusalem artichokes do not come from Jerusalem and have nothing to do with artichokes!

1	10½-ounce can condensed split pea soup
1	13¾-ounce can condensed chicken stock
1	pound Jerusalem artichokes*
½	pound leftover cooked chicken, turkey, or ham
1	cup whole milk
2	cups water
4	cloves garlic
	Olive oil
¼	cup sherry
¼	lemon
¼	cup vinegar
1	heaping tablespoon brown sugar
	Marjoram
	Salt & pepper

In a large stockpot combine all ingredients. Bring to a boil, and boil until the desired consistency.

Jerusalem artichoke is a tall sunflower with an edible tuber that has a sweetish, watery taste. This tuber can be boiled, like a potato, or eaten raw, like a radish. Its name is a corruption of the Italian word girasole, *meaning "sunflower," added to the word* artichoke.

MAKES 6 SERVINGS.

—WALTER MURCH, Director of Disney's
Return to Oz

KABUMPO'S CHICKEN-BROCCOLI CHOWDER

3	cups water
2	cups milk
1	package sour cream 'n' chive potatoes
1	teaspoon instant chicken bouillon
1½	cups sliced carrots
1	10-ounce package frozen chopped broccoli
⅓	cup chopped onion
2	cups cut-up cooked chicken
1½	cups shredded Swiss cheese

In a 3-quart saucepan mix all of the ingredients except the chicken and cheese. Heat to boiling, stirring frequently. Reduce the heat, cover, and simmer, stirring occasionally, for 20 to 25 minutes until the potatoes are tender.

Stir in the chicken and cheese. Cover and cook until hot, about 5 minutes longer.

MAKES SIX 1⅓-CUP SERVINGS.

—BILL BEEM

VEGETABLE SOUP FROM THE HEART

1	quart water
2½	pounds chuck roast (cut into cubes)
1	46-ounce can tomato juice
2	tablespoons chicken stock (not bouillon cubes)
2	tablespoons beef stock (not bouillon cubes)
⅓	cup barley
1	cup mushrooms, sliced
1	bunch asparagus, sliced
1	medium potato, diced
1½	10-ounce packages frozen peas, corn, etc.

In a large soup pot with lid combine the water, chuck roast, tomato juice, chicken stock, and beef stock. Bring the soup to a boil. Reduce the heat to low and simmer for 35 minutes.

Add the barley. Wait approximately 10 minutes, then check the meat to see if it's tender. If it is, add the mushrooms, asparagus, potato, peas, corn, etc. After another 35 minutes, taste to determine if salt and pepper are needed. Add to taste.

MAKES 6 SERVINGS.

—HAL RAYLE, voice of Tin Man in DIC *Oz* cartoon series

VEGETARIAN SOUP

"Become a vegetarian. Your body will respect you for your wisdom, and the animals will love you for your compassion."

2	cups water
1	10-ounce box frozen (or ¾ pound fresh) green beans
½	large or 1 whole small cauliflower, cut into flowerets
3	large chopped carrots
4	large chopped zucchini
6	stalks sliced celery
1	16-ounce can peeled tomatoes
2	to 4 large yellow onions (or a 12-ounce bag frozen chopped onions)
1	46-ounce can V-8 juice
½	teaspoon thyme

In a large stockpot mix all of the ingredients. Bring to a boil, reduce the heat, and simmer for 15 minutes.

This recipe makes a large pot of soup that will keep for two weeks in the refrigerator, covered.

MAKES 8 SERVINGS.

—CASEY KASEM, voice of Shaggy in cartoon series *Scooby-Doo*

Scrappy, Shaggy, and Scooby-Doo visit the Land of Oz in an animated Saturday morning mystery adventure in the 1980s. (Courtesy of Hanna-Barbera, Inc.)

WHO PUT THE *BULL* IN BOUILLABAISSE?

½ cup butter or margarine
2 leeks, trimmed and sliced
1 onion, diced
2 cloves garlic, chopped
1 cup white wine
1 28-ounce can tomatoes, chopped
2 10-ounce cans condensed chicken broth
½ teaspoon saffron
1 bay leaf
2 pounds assorted fish: red snapper, cod,
    flounder, haddock, sea bass, shrimp
1 9-ounce package frozen rock lobster tails
18 mussels or littleneck clams
1 10-ounce package frozen peas
    Salt
    Cayenne pepper

In a large kettle melt the butter. Add the leeks, onion, and garlic, and sauté until golden. Add the wine, tomatoes, chicken broth, saffron, and bay leaf. Bring to a boil. Reduce the heat.

Cut the fish into 2-inch pieces and slice the frozen rock lobster, shell and all, into 1-inch crosswise slices. Add the fish and rock lobster to the soup. Simmer for 10 to 15 minutes until the fish becomes white. Scrub the mussels or clams, removing the beards from the mussels. Add to the soup. Add the peas. Cover and simmer until the mussel or clam shells open, about 10 minutes.

Season to taste with salt and cayenne pepper. Remove the bay leaf. Serve with slices of garlic French bread.

MAKES 6 SERVINGS.

—MICHAEL PATAKAS

SALADS

CITRUS-ENDIVE SALAD

For the sour cream dressing:
7   tablespoons salad oil
3   tablespoons dairy sour cream
1   tablespoon wine vinegar
    Salt to taste
    Freshly ground pepper to taste

2   ruby red grapefruits
2   large oranges
2   heads endive
    Several sprigs fresh mint, chopped

In a medium bowl add the salad oil to the sour cream 1 tablespoon at a time. Mix well. Add the vinegar, blending well. Season with salt and pepper. Set aside.

Peel and section the grapefruits and oranges, removing the outer skin. Wash the endive carefully and shake well in a salad basket to dry thoroughly. Discard any discolored leaves. In a large salad bowl arrange the grapefruit and orange sections and endive. Pour the sour cream dressing over all. Garnish with mint. Serve at once.

Makes 4 servings.

—TED ROSS, Cowardly Lion in Broadway and motion picture version of *The Wiz*

CORN BREAD SALAD

1   medium pan corn bread (1½ packages Jiffy mix), crumbled
½   pound bacon, fried and crumbled
2   bell peppers, finely chopped
4   tomatoes, chopped
1   onion, chopped
1   cup chopped sweet pickles

In a salad bowl combine all the ingredients and toss well.

Can be made ahead and kept in the refrigerator until ready to serve.

Makes 4 to 6 servings.

—MARY LAND

This rare shot captures some of the motion picture cast of The Wiz *relaxing during a break in location filming at Brooklyn's Hoyt-Schermerhorn subway station (November 1977). Nipsey Russell portrayed the Tin Man, Michael Jackson played the Scarecrow, and Ted Ross—who also starred in the original Broadway production—was the Cowardly Lion. On being cast in* The Wiz, *nineteen-year-old Michael Jackson said, "It's the most incredible experience I've ever had. It's something I've always wanted to do and I'm thankful to be a part of it. It was one of my dreams that came true."*

The stars of Radio City Entertainment's touring production of The Wizard of Oz in 1998. (Photo by Cooper)

COURAGEOUS WARM BRIE SALAD

A refreshing salad to impress your friends back at the Lion's Den. This recipe comes from a restaurant in Aspen, Colorado, called Charlemagne . . . and since I'm the "King of the Forest," I thought it would be apropos.

¼   pound Brie cheese
1   tablespoon olive oil
1   bulb shallot, chopped fine
1   tablespoon Grey Poupon mustard
      Romaine lettuce, chopped for salad
      Croutons

Cut the cold Brie into cubes and leave at room temperature. In a saucepan heat the olive oil and add the shallot. Stir until light brown, and then remove from the heat. Add the Grey Poupon and Brie, and mix until the Brie is melted. Add the mixture to the romaine and toss. Add the croutons. Serve with "pride" and "courage!"

MAKES 4 SERVINGS.

—FRANCIS RUIVIVAR, Cowardly Lion in *The Wizard of Oz* National Tour, 1999

EMERALD CITY LAYERED SPINACH SALAD

½   cup grated Romano cheese
3   crisply cooked bacon slices, crumbled
1½   quarts torn spinach
2   cups mushroom slices
1   cup red onion rings
1   10-ounce package frozen peas, cooked and drained
½   cup mayonnaise
½   cup dairy sour cream
1   teaspoon sugar

In a medium bowl combine the cheese and bacon, and mix well. In a 2½-quart bowl layer the spinach, cheese mixture, mushrooms, onions, and peas. In a separate bowl combine the mayonnaise, sour cream, and sugar, and mix well. Spread over the salad to seal. Sprinkle 2 tablespoons of cheese over the top. Cover and refrigerate overnight.

MAKES 8 SERVINGS.

—FAY PATAKAS

GATE TO EMERALD CITY SALAD

1   9-ounce carton Cool Whip
1   20-ounce can crushed pineapple with juice
1   11-ounce can mandarin oranges, drained
1   3-ounce box instant pistachio pudding
1   cup miniature marshmallows (optional)
1   cup chopped nuts (optional)

In a large bowl mix all of the ingredients together and chill.

MAKES 6 TO 8 SERVINGS.

—LEE ANN COLEMAN

Son of a Witch

Margaret Hamilton's son, Hamilton Meserve, was just three years old when his mother was still gleaming green each evening when she returned home from her work as a witch. The actress, a former kindergarten teacher and a divorced mother of one, told a *St. Louis Globe-Democrat* reporter in 1957 that she hadn't planned on showing Hamilton *The Wizard of Oz* until he was at least ten, for fear he might have nightmares.

One day when he was six, Hamilton went to a birthday party where a 16mm print of the film was shown to the kids for the entertainment. Margaret Hamilton got a call from the hostess saying young Hamilton had left the room shortly after the film started and returned just before it ended. The hostess was not aware her little party guest had not seen his mother's most famous movie.

"When Ham got home, I didn't say anything to him," the actress recalled. "Finally he told me he had seen the movie . . . he hadn't liked it much. For a while he didn't say anything else. Then suddenly he said, 'Mother, what did you do with those men?' I asked him what he meant and he said the men in the movie who were prisoners. I explained to him that it was only playing as he played Cowboys and Indians and that they were real people, just like I was a real person."

"He said, 'Yes, Mother, but what did you DO with them?' So then I explained to him that in the play I was a witch who had put a spell on them. When I was melted, they were all free and went back to living. That seemed to answer his question."

GLINDA'S "GOOD" POTATO SALAD

With love and respect I dedicate this recipe to our Dorothy, Jessica Grové, who at the tender age of 17 is a vegetarian, and has been for as long as I have known her.

2½   pounds "good" red potatoes
4   "good" eggs, hard boiled
½   cup diced "good" celery
¼   cup "good" raisins
½   cup "good" red grapes
½   cup "good" walnuts, coarsely chopped
    "Magic" poppy seed dressing (your favorite version)
    Fresh "good" dill, chopped

Boil and cool the potatoes. Dice 3 of the eggs; quarter 1 for garnish. In a large bowl combine the diced eggs, potatoes, celery, raisins, grapes, and walnuts. Toss lightly and add "Magic" poppy seed dressing. Add dill to taste. Let set in the refrigerator—DO NOT let munchkins open for 1 hour.

MAKES 6 SERVINGS.

—JUDITH MCCAULEY, Glinda in *The Wizard of Oz* National Tour, 1998–1999

HAMILTON'S WILTED LETTUCE SALAD

    Lettuce or spinach
2   tablespoons water
⅓   cup vinegar
2   tablespoons sugar
½   teaspoon salt
¼   cup minced onion
1   egg, beaten
5   slices bacon, cooked and drained

Shred the lettuce or spinach and place on salad plates. In a small saucepan combine the water, vinegar, sugar, salt, and onion, and heat on low. Do not boil. Remove from the heat, and whisk in the beaten egg. Crumble the bacon on top of the lettuce or spinach. Pour the heated dressing over the salads.

MAKES 6 SERVINGS.

—HAMILTON MESERVE, son of Margaret Hamilton

Margaret Hamilton and her son, Hamilton Meserve, pose for a photographer, circa 1944. Hamilton was the actress' maiden name, and Meserve was her married name; she combined them when christening her son. (Courtesy of Ham Meserve)

Sneaking Lunch to Judy

I was fifteen when *The Wizard of Oz* was being made, and as L. Frank Baum's granddaughter I was able to visit the set as often as I wanted. Because of my grandmother, I had complete access. My mom and dad drove us in, but they didn't always go in with me. Both my brother and I visited MGM more than a dozen times in a year's period while the film was being made.

My little autograph book was filling up and I wasn't afraid to go up to the stars and talk to them. We'd get on the trams and ride around and see all the other stuff, like Mickey Rooney, Clark Gable, and Jackie Cooper making movies. *The Wizard of Oz* had several huge sets in a row and I remember watching "The Jitterbug" being filmed, and I thought it was good; they worked very hard on that, and it ended up cut out of the movie. And the Munchkins, that was something to watch, to behold. They were all over the set. They were quite brash and cute.

I remember the studio always kept Judy Garland on a very strict diet and she was always hungry. Those stories about Judy being on pills for a weight problem, it's true. I think they told her she was taking vitamins, but she was taking pills to control her appetite. Ask Mickey Rooney, he'll tell you it's true. When she was younger, I never thought she was that heavy, but she wasn't skin and bone. Well, Judy and I had gotten to be friends and of course, I was her devoted slave, I just adored her. I was starstruck and I would've done anything for her. I don't even remember what we talked about when we visited, but she used to say, "I'm hungry." About three or four times I went to the studio commissary and I'd get a double order of mashed potatoes and gravy and sneak it to her; we'd meet at a certain place away from the filming and I'd hand it to her.

—*Florence Baum Hurst*

HORSE OF A DIFFERENT COLOR PEPPER MEDLEY

2	yellow bell peppers
2	red bell peppers
1	purple onion
⅓	cup vegetable oil
2	tablespoons tarragon vinegar
1	tablespoon Dijon mustard
2	teaspoons sugar
1	teaspoon salt
¼	teaspoon freshly ground pepper
1	jalapeño pepper, minced
2	teaspoons caraway seeds
1	teaspoon grated lime rind

Cut the peppers and onion into julienne strips and set aside. In a large bowl combine the oil, vinegar, mustard, sugar, salt, and pepper. Beat with a wire whisk until thickened. Add the reserved vegetables and jalapeño pepper, caraway, and lime, tossing gently. Cover and refrigerate for 3 hours.

MAKES 6 SERVINGS.

—TINA CASSIMATIS

"IF I ONLY HAD A HEART" OF PALM SALAD

¼   cup salad oil
1   tablespoon vinegar
1   tablespoon lemon juice
1   tablespoon chopped parsley
¼   teaspoon salt
⅛   teaspoon dry mustard
    Lettuce
1   14-ounce can hearts of palm, chilled, drained, and cut into strips
1   red onion, sliced
1   hard-cooked egg, sliced
1   tablespoon chopped pimiento

In a small bowl combine the oil, vinegar, lemon juice, parsley, salt, and dry mustard. Mix well to blend. Line salad plates with lettuce, top with hearts of palm, and garnish with onion and egg slices. Pour the dressing over each serving. Sprinkle chopped pimiento on top.

MAKES 6 SERVINGS.

—TINA CASSIMATIS

JIMMI'S BASIL POTATO SALAD

½   cup olive oil
¼   cup Hellmann's Dijonnaise
¼   cup wine vinegar
½   teaspoon seasoned pepper
½   teaspoon sea salt
3   pounds boiled new potatoes, cubed
1   cup chopped celery (strings removed)
½   cup chopped Vidalia onion
½   pound steamed shrimp, chilled
½   pound steamed scallops, chilled
6   leaves basil, chopped

In a bowl stir together the olive oil, Dijonnaise, wine vinegar, pepper, and salt and set aside. In a bowl combine the potatoes, chopped celery, and onion, then add the shrimp, scallops, and basil. Toss with the dressing. Chill for 1 hour before serving.

MAKES 6 SERVINGS.

—JIMMI WILLINGHAM

Someone from the Hollywood Citizen-News didn't see the movie. This newspaper clipping was pasted in Maud Baum's scrapbook. (Robert A. Baum Collection)

JAMES BOLGER, (left) who enacts the role of the Scarecrow in the film version of "The Wizard of Oz," and FRED STONE, who created the role in the stage version many years ago, are shown above as they were photographed last night at Grauman's Chinese Theater, where the picture opened, standing before a real straw man.

LIONS AND TIGERS AND BEARS BEAN SALAD

½   cup sugar
½   cup vinegar
½   cup vegetable oil
1   teaspoon salt
1   16-ounce can green beans
1   16-ounce can yellow beans
1   16-ounce can kidney beans
1   16-ounce can chick peas (garbanzos)
1   medium onion, sliced

In a large bowl combine the sugar, vinegar, oil, and salt, and mix well. Drain the beans and add to the dressing. Add the onion. Refrigerate overnight.

Stir and serve.

Makes 6 to 8 servings.

—KEN FORD

PINEAPPLE CHEESE SALAD

3   20-ounce cans pineapple chunks, drained and juice reserved
2   eggs
2   cups sugar
6   tablespoons all-purpose flour
    Longhorn cheese, grated

In a saucepan combine the pineapple juice, eggs, sugar, and flour. Cook and stir over low heat until a custardlike consistency. Cool slightly. Layer pineapple, grated cheese, and sauce.

Very good served with a ham dinner.

Makes 6 to 8 servings.

—RUTH DUCCINI, Munchkin in *Oz,* MGM

Ruby Slipper Strawberry Salad

2   3-ounce packages (or 1 6-ounce pack-
      age) strawberry gelatin
1½   cups boiling water
1   10-ounce package frozen strawberries,
      partly thawed
1   20-ounce can crushed pineapple
2   bananas, mashed
1   16-ounce carton sour cream

In a large bowl dissolve the gelatin in boiling water. Add the chopped frozen strawberries, pineapple, and bananas. Pour half (3½ cups) of the mixture into a 2-quart casserole dish. Refrigerate until set.

Spread sour cream evenly over the top. Gently pour the remaining gelatin and fruit mixture over the sour cream. Refrigerate until set.

MAKES 6 SERVINGS.

—MYRNA AND CLARENCE SWENSEN, Munchkin soldier in *Oz*, MGM

This rare snapshot was taken on a chilly December 1938 morning while a group of Munchkin actors boarded an MGM studio tram to ride across the lot to their destination.

Introducing the 1962 CBS telecast of The Wizard of Oz *were Dick Van Dyke and his kids, Barry (age twelve), Stacey (age eight), and Chris (age thirteen).*

SHRIMP SALAD

1	cup mayonnaise
½	cup Italian salad dressing
1	teaspoon dill weed (fresh or dried)
1	teaspoon salt
⅛	teaspoon pepper
1	pound bay shrimp, steamed and chilled
1	8-ounce bag curly noodles, cooked
2	cups cucumbers, peeled, quartered, and thinly sliced
½	cup diced tomatoes
½	cup chopped celery
¼	cup chopped green bell pepper
¼	cup chopped onions

In a medium bowl whip together the mayonnaise, salad dressing, dill weed, salt, and pepper until smooth.

In a large bowl combine the shrimp, noodles, cucumbers, tomatoes, celery, green pepper, and onions. Pour the dressing over the salad. Refrigerate for 1 hour.

MAKES 6 SERVINGS.

—BARRY VAN DYKE, cohost, *Wizard of Oz*
CBS telecasts, 1961–62

THE LION'S COURAGEOUS CURRY CHICKEN SALAD

2   teaspoons lemon juice
1   apple, pared and cut into bite-size pieces
4   cups chicken, cooked and cut up
½   cup sliced celery
⅓   cup slivered almonds
½   teaspoon salt
1   cup mayonnaise or salad dressing
½   teaspoon curry powder
1   to 2 tablespoons milk

In a large bowl sprinkle lemon juice over the apple. Add the chicken, celery, and almonds. Sprinkle with salt. In a small bowl mix the mayonnaise, curry, and milk. Toss the two together and refrigerate. Great with Cyclone Popovers (see page 146).

MAKES 6 SERVINGS.

—TINA CASSIMATIS

THE OZCOT SUPREME SALAD

A light summer salad for any occasion.

1   cup mixed fruit (large chunks), drained
1   tablespoon vanilla instant pudding powder (dry)
¼   head lettuce, chopped
4   ounces grilled chicken breast
2   tablespoons raisins
1   tablespoon slivered almonds

In a medium bowl mix the drained mixed fruit and the vanilla pudding together. (For better taste, chill this mixture for 1 hour.)

Place the lettuce in a large individual salad bowl. Cut the grilled chicken into small bite-size pieces. Place the chicken around the outside perimeter of the lettuce, and the remainder on top. Place the fruit mixture on top of the lettuce bed. Sprinkle raisins and almonds over the entire salad. Serve with hot bread stix.

MAKES 1 SERVING.

—DIANNA AND MICHAEL CARSON, The OzCot Restaurant, Walnut Ridge, Arkansas

TUNA NAVY BEAN SALAD

Best if made at least a day ahead of serving.

1   cup dry navy beans
3   cups cold water
1   teaspoon salt
¼   cup olive oil
¼   cup white wine vinegar
½   teaspoon dry English mustard
½   teaspoon salt
     Dash pepper
1   6½- to 9½-ounce can tuna, drained and chilled
1   small red onion, thinly sliced and separated into rings
1   tablespoon snipped parsley

Rinse the beans. Cover with cold water and soak overnight.

Add 1 teaspoon of salt to the beans and soaking water. Cover and bring to a boil. Reduce the heat and simmer for about 1 hour until tender. Drain and chill.

In a jar combine the olive oil, wine vinegar, mustard, ½ teaspoon of salt, and the pepper. Cover and shake well to blend. Chill. Shake again before using.

In a salad bowl combine the chilled beans, tuna, and onion rings. Drizzle the dressing over, and toss lightly. Sprinkle with snipped parsley.

MAKES 4 SERVINGS.

—BLANCHE COX

WORLEY'S WICKED RICE AND SPICE SALAD

1   9-ounce package frozen green beans
2   cups quick-cooking rice, uncooked
1   13-ounce can chicken broth
1   cup sliced fresh mushrooms
¾   cup bottled Italian dressing
3   tablespoons chopped pimiento
¼   teaspoon onion salt

In a saucepan combine the beans, rice, and broth. Bring to a boil. Cover and cook over low heat for about 5 minutes or until all of the liquid is absorbed.

In a large bowl combine the rice mixture and remaining ingredients. Chill.

MAKES ABOUT 5 CUPS.

—JOANNE WORLEY, W.W.W. in *The Wizard of Oz*
National Tour, 1999

YUMMY POTATO SALAD

6   Idaho potatoes, boiled with skins on
       until tender (do not overcook); when
       done place in cold water to cool; remove
       skins and cut into bite-size cubes
6   hard-boiled eggs, chopped
¾   jar India pickle relish
1   teaspoon Dijon mustard
¾   cup mayonnaise
       Pinch sugar
       Salt and pepper to taste
       Paprika

In a bowl large enough to eventually hold the potatoes, mix together the eggs, relish, mustard, mayonnaise, sugar, and the salt and pepper. Add the cooled, cut-up potatoes and mix well. Taste to adjust seasonings—it may need a tad more of the relish and/or mayonnaise. Place in serving bowl and sprinkle with the paprika for color. Refrigerate until time to serve—this will allow the flavors to blend together.

MAKES 6 SERVINGS.

—BILL COSBY, Wizard Host for TV
premiere of *Journey Back to Oz*

Bill Cosby in Journey Back to Oz, *December 5, 1976.*

SAUCES

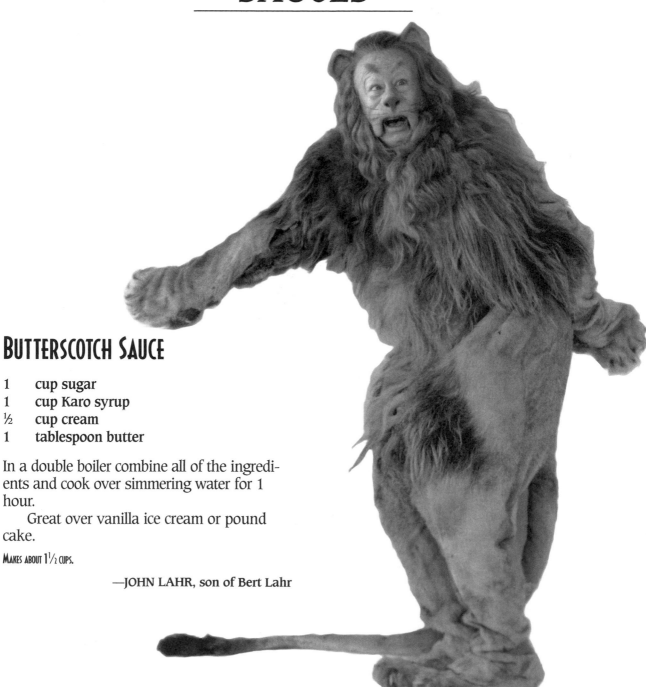

BUTTERSCOTCH SAUCE

1   cup sugar
1   cup Karo syrup
½   cup cream
1   tablespoon butter

In a double boiler combine all of the ingredients and cook over simmering water for 1 hour.

    Great over vanilla ice cream or pound cake.

MAKES ABOUT 1½ CUPS.

—JOHN LAHR, son of Bert Lahr

Fresh Peach Salsa

3½   cups peeled ripe peaches (about 2½ pounds)
¼   cup diced red onion
2   tablespoons finely chopped fresh cilantro
1   tablespoon minced seeded jalapeño pepper
2   tablespoons rice vinegar
1   teaspoon lemon juice
1   garlic clove, minced

In a bowl combine all of the ingredients and stir well. Cover and chill for several hours before serving.

Serve with pork tenderloin or chicken.

Makes about 3 cups.

Highly Superior Hollandaise Sauce

2   tablespoons butter
2   tablespoons all-purpose flour
1   cup milk
1   cup mayonnaise
2   tablespoons lemon juice
      Salt and pepper to taste

In a small saucepan melt the butter and blend in the flour. Blend in the milk to make a white sauce. Gradually add the mayonnaise and lemon juice. Heat thoroughly but do not boil. Season with salt and pepper.

Makes about 2 cups.

—KEN FORD

Julius Caesar Salad Dressing

. . . this is the same genuine, magic, authentic recipe used by the priests of Isis and Osiris in the days of the pharaohs of Egypt, in which Cleopatra first dined with Julius Caesar and Marc Antony, and so on and so on.

1   clove garlic, peeled and sliced
1   stalk celery, scraped and sliced
½   medium onion
1   2-ounce can flat anchovies, drained
1   teaspoon freshly ground black pepper
1   heaping teaspoon Accent
½   teaspoon sugar
2   tablespoons salad mustard
1   tablespoon lemon juice
3   eggs
2   cups salad oil

In a blender combine the garlic, celery, onion, anchovies, pepper, Accent, sugar, mustard, and lemon juice. Blend for a few seconds. Add the eggs and blend again. Add the oil ¼ cup at a time, blending between additions.

This dressing is best on romaine lettuce with croutons. Also a good dip for raw vegetables.

Makes about 2½ cups.

—TINA CASSIMATIS

The Rankin/Bass "Return to Oz" Special

Arthur Rankin and Jules Bass—the creative team who gave us such tele-vised holiday gems as "Rudolph the Rednosed Reindeer," "The Little Drummer Boy," and "Santa Claus Is Coming to Town"—actually began their collabora-tion on the yellow brick road.

"Return to Oz," which premiered in 1964, was the first network TV special produced by Rankin/Bass. Although famous for their stop-motion animation (puppetry they called "Animagic"), this zealous musical adventure was a sixty-minute cel-animated cartoon special whisking Dorothy back to the Land of Oz for more fun with her friends—Socrates the Scarecrow, Dandy Lion, and Rusty the Tin Man. The animated characters, very minimalistic in style, were similar to those from Jay Ward's *Rocky and Bullwinkle* and *Fractured Fairytales.* Rather than re-create the MGM movie in animated form, Rankin/Bass relied more on Baum's stories coupled with their own inventive touch for inspiration. New twists were introduced: Munchkinland became Munchkinville. Instead of a house caught in a cyclone, Dorothy is lured back to Oz via a flying fruit tree.

Prior to this special, Rankin/Bass had produced a syndicated series of brief *Oz* cartoons, *Tales of the Wizard of Oz,* for television in 1961; however, all of the voices were provided by adults. "Along came this special and they wanted to have a real child's voice," says Susan Conway Mitchell, "and I was fortunate enough to get the role."

Oz was a theme that came back to young Susan Conway several times in her life. "This was almost mystical for me," says the actress, now forty-six. "I wanted to be an actress from the age of five. When I was seven, I went to

Young Susan Conway (inset) provided the voice of Dorothy in the Rankin/Bass prime-time animated special, "Return to Oz." (Courtesy Jay Scarfone/William Stillman Wizard of Oz Collection)

camp, and I was very homesick. They were doing the production of *The Wizard of Oz* at the time and I was going to be cast as a Munchkin if I had stayed, but I ended up going home early. Later, in third grade, I played the part of the witch in a school production. And a few years later, there I was playing the role of Dorothy in this animated special. It was a dream come true for me since I was connected with it since I was lit-tle. I had seen the movie, but I hadn't read the books at that time."

Susan Conway Mitchell was the only child to voice a character in the special. As she vividly recalls the recording sessions that took place in Toronto, it's obvious the actress put her entire heart and every ounce of enthusiasm she had into her performance. "It was nice and simple, in a small studio with a microphone. I can see myself back there doing it, standing in front of the microphone," she says. "The other actors were so kind. I remember being completely in awe of the other actors who were doing these magical voices and different roles; I've never laughed so hard in my life as I did when those guys did the animals in the forest and the monkeys. I remember Larry Mann especially. I laughed so hard there were tears pouring down my face."

The musical special aired on NBC as an installment of the *General Electric Fantasy Hour* on Sunday evenings. Even though Mitchell was forewarned that her musical numbers were redubbed with another girl's singing voice, she was excited to see the finished special months after she recorded her lines. "We all crowded around the television when it aired," says Mitchell, who lived in Canada with her family. "My dad had an appliance store so we had our color TV."

"Bunny Cowan, one of the producers, basically found me for this special. He became a dear, lifelong friend. His family came over and watched it with us in our living room. It was live, seen everywhere. I even took a little audiotape machine and put it next to the TV and recorded the sound. That's all we had back then to preserve it."

Rarely seen since its original telecast thirty-five years ago, the program has become a rare visual gem. Because the story and the characters stray from Baum's original versions, some critics dismissed "Return to Oz" as an oddity. But if you can locate an underground copy on videotape, you may be surprised at how well it holds up and how enchanting it really is.

Mitchell, now a wife and mother of two daughters, still resides in Canada and remains sentimental about the program, but not necessarily because it was one of her earliest professional experiences. "I remember this one little speech toward the end," she says, "It was something like, 'Don't you know you should never give up hope? Even a little robin popping out of its nest in the middle of May . . . what's that but magic? Magic is everywhere.' That whole theme of believing in nature as something magical has been a recurring message in my life and how I perceive life now. It's a beautiful message, the whole essence of life. That idea has stayed with me."

The cast of the Rankin/Bass animated special, "Return to Oz," recording in Ontario. From left: Carl Banas (Dandy Lion/Wizard), Pegi Loder (Glinda), Susan Conway (Dorothy), Larry Mann (Rusty the Tinman), and Alfie Scopp (Socrates the Strawman/Wicked Witch). (Photos courtesy of Susan Conway Mitchell)

The cast rehearses musical numbers along with sound engineer Bernard "Bunny" Cowan (in tie), and coproducer Jules Bass (at the piano). Susan Conway Mitchell added, "The blue gingham dress was one that I owned before I got the part of Dorothy. My mom realized it was the perfect dress to wear for the production stills and henceforth referred to it as 'your Dorothy dress,' or 'the Oz dress.' Believe it or not, I still have it."

Mama Susie's Vegetarian Spaghetti Sauce

1   package frozen tofu, thawed
1   green bell pepper
2   to 3 carrots
1   to 2 zucchini
    Oil
1   700-ml. jar pasta sauce
1   680-ml. can tomato sauce
    Basil
    Oregano
    Salt and pepper to taste
1   cup mushrooms, sliced

The secret to this sauce is: freezing the tofu!

Allow the tofu to thaw and it will have a spongelike consistency. With your hands, break the tofu into chunks, and squeeze out as much water as possible. Set aside. In a food processor chop the bell pepper, carrots, and zucchini into fine pieces using an on-off motion of the processor. In a large pot heat a little oil and sauté the vegetables for a couple of minutes.

Chop the tofu into fine pieces in the processor, again using an on-off motion. Add the tofu to the pot, and continue stirring for a few more minutes. Add the pasta sauce, the tomato sauce, basil, oregano, salt, pepper, and mushrooms and simmer for 15 to 30 minutes. Serve with your choice of pasta and top with Parmesan cheese if desired.

MAKES 6 SERVINGS.

—SUSAN CONWAY MITCHELL, voice of Dorothy
in Rankin/Bass "Return to Oz"

Derek Loughran is the Tin Man, John Ritter is L. Frank Baum, and Courtney Barilla is the sickly child cheered by Baum's fanciful tales in the NBC-TV movie, The Dreamer of Oz. *(Courtesy of Derek Loughran)*

Oil Can Marinade

"Oil can marinade what?"

¾   to 1 cup olive oil
3   teaspoons lemon juice
½   teaspoon dried oregano
    Salt and pepper to taste
2   tablespoons Worcestershire sauce
1   teaspoon garlic powder

In a jar combine all of the ingredients. Shake thoroughly. Pour over the meat you are going to grill. (The lemon juice serves as a tenderizer.)

MAKES ABOUT 1 CUP.

—DEREK LOUGHRAM, the Tin Man
in *The Dreamer of Oz*

Popular singer Michael Feinstein beautifully covered a range of songs, including a medley from Oz, on his CD collection of hits from MGM musicals.

STEAK MARINADE

12   pieces jalapeños
1   cup garlic cloves
¼   cup black pepper
2   cups lime juice
6   bunches cilantro
5   cups vegetable oil
2   tablespoons salt
15   pounds meat

In a food processor combine the following ingredients in complete order: the jalapeños and garlic, scraping down the sides from time to time. Next add the black pepper and lime juice. Scrape down the sides again, making sure everything is mixed together. Next add the cilantro little by little, then blend until

smooth. Slowly add the vegetable oil and salt. Pour the mixture onto the meat and marinate for at least 24 hours.

SERVES A CROWD.

—MICHAEL FEINSTEIN

THE SCULPTOR'S SPAGHETTI SAUCE

1   pound ground beef
½   pound ground hot Italian sausage
2   tablespoons olive oil
1   large onion, finely chopped
1   small green bell pepper, finely chopped
2   stalks celery, finely chopped
2   to 3 garlic cloves, finely chopped
2   28-ounce cans tomatoes, cut up
2   8-ounce cans tomato paste
1   teaspoon sugar
2   teaspoons beef bouillon granules
1   tablespoon oregano
½   teaspoon red pepper flakes

In a skillet brown the ground beef and Italian sausage. Drain. In a stockpot heat the oil and sauté the onion, pepper, celery, and garlic until tender. Add the tomatoes, tomato paste, browned meat, sugar, bouillon, oregano, and red pepper flakes. Simmer for 1 hour and 30 minutes.

Refrigerate overnight.

Note: If necessary, dilute with red wine or tomato sauce.

MAKES 6 SERVINGS.

—MICHAEL ROCHE, *Oz* figures sculptor

YELLOW BRICK ROAD SALAD DRESSING

2   cups olive oil
½   cup red wine vinegar
1   egg
2   garlic cloves, pressed
2   teaspoons Dijon mustard
½   teaspoon dried oregano
½   teaspoon dried dill weed
     Salt and freshly ground pepper

In a 1-quart jar combine all of the ingredients. Shake thoroughly. Chill for 2 hours before serving.

MAKES ABOUT 2½ CUPS.

—ELIZABETH AND TOMMY COTTONARO,
Munchkin in *Oz,* MGM

ZUCCHINI RELISH

10   cups ground zucchini
4   cups ground onion
¼   cup salt
1   ground green bell pepper
1   ground red bell pepper
2¼   cups white vinegar
4½   cups sugar
1   teaspoon grated nutmeg
1   teaspoon dry mustard
1   teaspoon turmeric
2   teaspoons celery seed
½   teaspoon black pepper
1   teaspoon cornstarch

In a food grinder grind the zucchini and onions. Measure. Add the salt and mix. Let stand overnight. Rinse and drain. Add the remaining ingredients. Transfer to a large stockpot, stir together, and simmer for 30 minutes. Jar and seal immediately.

Note: Mix with mayonnaise for a great tartar sauce. Mix with ketchup to make a great barbecue sauce or add to macaroni or potato salad.

MAKES 6 PINTS.

—DAVID WILCOX

Vegetables with Vim and Verve

Artichokes à la Munchkin

       Italian breadcrumbs
       Salt and pepper to taste
       Garlic cloves, chopped
1   or 2 tablespoons olive oil
4   artichokes

In a bowl combine the breadcrumbs, salt, pepper, garlic, and olive oil.

Cut off the ends of all artichoke leaves. Cut the stems, leaving 1 inch. Soak the artichokes in water. Pull out some center leaves to form a cavity and fill with the bread mixture. Place the artichokes upright in a saucepan. Be sure they are standing straight. Fill the pan with water halfway up the sides of the artichokes. Boil uncovered for 20 minutes. Cover and simmer for 1 hour and 30 minutes.

To eat, pull off the leaves, one at a time. Scrape off the edible flesh with your teeth. Some of the breadcrumb mixture will be on the leaves. After the leaves have been discarded and the filling eaten, eat the delectable heart of the artichoke with a fork.

(Mickey says the more garlic and olive oil, the better.)

Makes 4 servings.

—MICKEY CARROLL, Munchkin in *Oz,* MGM

Special guest, Munchkin Mickey Carroll, samples the gigantic sheet cake at MGM during a fiftieth anniversary celebration for the film in 1989. (Photo by Steve Cox)

BILLINA'S BAKED DEVILED-EGG CASSEROLE

6	to 9 hard-boiled eggs
1	cup plus 3 tablespoons sour cream
2	teaspoons prepared mustard
¼	teaspoon salt
2	teaspoons butter
½	cup chopped green bell pepper
⅓	cup chopped onion
¼	cup chopped pimiento
1	10½-ounce can cream of mushroom soup
½	cup shredded Cheddar cheese

Cut the eggs in half. In a bowl mash the egg yolks with 3 tablespoons of sour cream, the mustard, and salt. Refill the eggs. In a skillet melt the butter and sauté the green pepper and onion until tender. Remove from the heat. Stir in the pimiento, soup, and 1 cup of sour cream. Place half of the mixture in a shallow 1½-quart casserole dish. Add the deviled eggs, cut sides up. Pour the remaining sauce over the top. Top with shredded cheese. Bake at 350° for 20 minutes.

MAKES 6 SERVINGS.

—JIM AND GLENNA HAYWOOD

BILLY BARTY'S BAKED BUTTER BEANS

3	1-pound cans baby butter beans
½	cup ketchup
3	teaspoons liquid smoke
2	tablespoons minced onion (fresh or dried)
¾	cup firmly packed brown sugar
½	cup dark Karo syrup
12	drops Tabasco (hot sauce is fine)
3	slices bacon, cut into 2-inch pieces

Spray a 9 x 13-inch baking dish with cooking spray. Drain 1 can of beans. Pour all of the beans in the prepared baking dish. Stir in the ketchup, liquid smoke, onion, brown sugar, corn syrup, and Tabasco. Lay the bacon on top to cover. Bake at 350° for 1 to 2 hours.

It will look saucy; it thickens as it cools.

MAKES 8 SERVINGS.

—BILLY BARTY, star of *Under the Rainbow*

DOROTHY'S CYCLONE POTATOES

¼ green bell pepper
¼ red bell pepper
¼ yellow bell pepper
4 large russet baking potatoes, well scrubbed
1 quart salted boiling water
2 cloves garlic, whole, peeled
¼ cup butter
¼ cup heavy cream
   Salt and pepper to taste

Dice the bell peppers into quarter-inch squares. Score the skins on the potatoes so that they are crisscrossed with squares about a quarter-inch across. Slice the potatoes into disks. Place in the boiling water along with the other vegetables and boil 15 to 20 minutes (until the potatoes are just cooked: they should be firm rather than mushy).

Drain the potatoes and peppers well. Mash lightly with a potato masher. Add butter, cream, salt, and pepper and mash with a masher until fairly smooth. The potatoes taste better if they're not completely smooth. The colorful mixture of the other ingredients resembles the swirling debris in Dorothy's cyclone as it whisked her to Oz.

MAKES 4 SERVINGS.

—PETER E. HANFF, President, The International Wizard of Oz Club

EASY VEGETABLE CALZONE

     Refrigerated pizza dough
     Olive oil spray
     Olive oil
1   zucchini
1   yellow squash
1   small can sliced mushrooms
¼   cup sliced black olives
1   small can Italian-style tomato sauce
     with seasonings
¼   cup crumbled feta cheese
3   tablespoons freshly grated Parmesan
     cheese

Unroll the pizza dough and stretch across an olive oil–sprayed cookie sheet. Drizzle the pizza dough with 2 tablespoons of olive oil. Slice the vegetables. In a skillet heat 2 tablespoons of olive oil and sauté the vegetables over medium heat; do not overcook. Set the vegetables aside.

Cut the dough in half (widthwise). Top half of each piece of pizza dough thinly with Italian tomato sauce (lengthwise). (Do not take the sauce to the edges of the crust, so you can fold them later.) Spoon sautéed vegetables on top of the tomato sauce and then top the vegetables with feta cheese. Fold the empty half over the half with all the ingredients. (You should now have 2 loaflike calzones.) Pinch the edges of the dough to seal. Drizzle the top of the dough with olive oil and freshly grated Parmesan cheese. Bake at 400° for 15 to 20 minutes until light golden brown.

MAKES 2 CALZONES.

—FRANCINE MURPHY

EGGPLANT PARMIGIANA

1   or 2 medium-size firm eggplants
3   to 5 large eggs
     Italian-seasoned breadcrumbs
     Light vegetable oil
     Tomato sauce with basil
     Romano cheese

Peel the eggplant and slice about ⅛ inch thick. In a bowl soak the slices in cold salt water to cut the bitterness. Drain and lay on a paper towel to absorb the excess water.

In a bowl beat 2 or 3 eggs. Dip individual eggplant slices into the egg and coat with breadcrumbs. Save the leftover beaten egg and beat in 1 or 2 more eggs, depending on the amount of eggplant. Set aside. In a frying pan lightly brown the breaded eggplant slices in hot oil.

Coat the bottom of a round casserole dish with a layer of sauce. Set in one layer of browned eggplant slices. Lightly drizzle some of the leftover beaten egg over the eggplant, then cover with a layer of sauce and Romano cheese. Repeat, layering 3 more times (for a total of 4 layers).

Preheat the oven to 350°. Bake the casserole for 30 to 45 minutes, until it bubbles.

Let stand 15 minutes before serving.

MAKES 10 TO 12 SERVINGS.

—JAY SCARFONE, coauthor of *The Wizard of Oz Pictorial History, The Wizard of Oz Collectors Treasury,* and *The Wizardry of Oz*

EMERALD SPINACH SOUFFLÉ

2   10-ounce packages frozen chopped
     spinach
2   eggs, well beaten
1   scant cup mayonnaise
1   cup condensed cream of celery soup
1   cup shredded Cheddar cheese

Place the spinach in a colander Pour hot
water over to thaw. Drain well.

In a bowl mix the eggs, mayonnaise, soup,
and cheese together. Mix well. Add the
spinach and spoon into a 1½-quart soufflé
dish. Bake at 325° for 40 minutes or until
golden.

MAKES 4 SERVINGS.

—WILMA WILLINGHAM

(Above) Judy in her kitchen in
1942. Years later, after her three
children were born, Garland told a
reporter, "My mother (Ethel Gumm)
was a hell of a cook. She never
seemed to want us to be successful
in the kitchen, so I sorta sneaked
around and learned a little. I can
now cook for thirty-six people, and
I'm prouder of that than anything
else I do! I can't eat certain foods.
And I can't eat at least three hours
before show times or for several
hours afterwards." (Left) Judy
Garland having dinner at home
with her first husband, David Rose,
and their pet schnauzer, in 1942.
(Beyond the Rainbow Archive)

FAT-FREED VEGGIE MELT

As an Oz historical buff, I dedicate my low-cal, low-fat, cholesterol-free recipe to the late Arthur Freed. It may not be widely known, but Arthur Freed was responsible for the making of MGM's The Wizard of Oz. *In 1938, he was an established studio songwriter, and in that same year he convinced his boss, Louis B. Mayer, to buy the film rights to L. Frank Baum's children's classic from Samuel Goldwyn, for $20,000. Freed then convinced Mayer that a young MGM studio contract player named Judy Garland should play the role of Dorothy. Later, in 1939, after* The Wizard of Oz *had its first preview, it was decided by some that the song "Over the Rainbow" should be removed from the film. Again, Freed prevailed. The song remained and won an Oscar for best song, and Judy Garland received a special Oscar for her performance. MGM's* The Wizard of Oz *was Freed's brainchild, and the first production assignment for which he was given the title of associate producer—but he received no screen credit. He did, however, later become one of MGM's most honored producers with such productions as* An American in Paris *and* Singin' in the Rain. *For more information about* The Wizard of Oz *and Arthur Freed, read* The World of Entertainment: Hollywood's Greatest Musicals, *by Hugh Fordin.*

½   cup vegetable primavera pasta sauce, super chunky (Healthy Choice)
¾   cup soy crumble veggie-burger (Harvest Burgers), refrigerated or frozen
¼   cup chopped onion
3   tablespoons low-fat margarine (Smart Beat)
1   tablespoon mustard
2   slices sandwich bread, whole grain
      Several cut strips of soy melting "cheese" substitute

In a microwavable bowl place the pasta sauce, the soy crumble veggie-burger, and onions.

Stir, cover, and heat on high for 1 minute. Leave covered bowl in microwave.

Coat a large Teflon frying pan with 1 tablespoon of margarine and place on low heat. Spread 1½ teaspoons of margarine on one side of both slices of bread. Place margarine side down on the frying pan and toast that side of bread. Place the bread toasted side up on a dinner plate. Turn the heat off under the skillet.

Heat the veggie-burger mixture on high for another minute. Spread half of it on one slice only. Place the strips of soy melting "cheese" substitute on top. Spread with mustard, then spread on the remainder of the veggie-burger mixture. Place the other slice of bread, toasted side down, on top. We now have a veggie sandwich melt ready for grilling.

Spread 1½ teaspoons of margarine onto the center of the warm skillet, carefully place the sandwich in the skillet, and turn the burner on low. Immediately spread the remaining ½ tablespoon of margarine on top of the remaining piece of bread. Grill the sandwich melt by carefully turning it over, until it's brown on both sides. Serve sliced in half, with a fruit salad.

—BYRD HOLLAND, *Oz* historian

Lorna Luft on *Oz*

Judy Garland's daughter recounts the first time she consciously remembers watching her mother in *The Wizard of Oz*. Lorna was seven at the time, and watched intently with her brother, Joey, who was four.

We had this well-intentioned nanny who said to us kids, "There's a movie on tonight with your mother and we're going to watch it." My mother was in New York at the time. We watched The Wizard of Oz that night and our nanny kept saying, "That's your mother. That's your mother." When the Witch came and the Winged Monkeys came down and picked up our mother we wondered why they carried her off to New York. We got hysterical. Joey was crying and I was crying. We didn't know what to think.

Mother knew the movie was on that night and she called from New York when she thought we might be watching. It was about three hours ahead, there. She told us the Monkeys didn't carry her off to New York and she talked to us and assured us she was okay. From then on, I think, she decided she would watch it with us and she did—and she loved it. She had pleasant memories of making the movie. She would tell us what a sweet woman the Witch really was and how her green makeup would get in her tea. And how wonderful the three guys were, and what fun it all was. After all, this was her first really big, extravagant picture.

"I'LL BIDE MY" THYME NOODLES

¼ cup butter or margarine, softened
2 tablespoons snipped parsley
1 teaspoon crushed dried thyme (or 1 tablespoon fresh)
⅛ teaspoon pepper
1 8 ounce package cream cheese, softened
½ cup boiling water
8 ounces fettuccine or medium noodles
¾ cup shredded Romano or Parmesan cheese, divided

In a saucepan combine the butter or margarine, parsley, thyme, and pepper. Blend in the cream cheese; stir in the boiling water. Blend well. Keep warm.

Cook noodles in large amount of boiling salted water till just tender; drain. Turn into mixing bowl. Sprinkle with ½ cup of the cheese; toss well. Place noodles in serving dish and top with hot herbed cheese sauce. Serve with remaining cheese.

MAKES 6 SERVINGS.

—BLANCHE COX

IMPOSSIBLE BROCCOLI PIE

2	10-ounce packages frozen chopped broccoli
3	cups shredded Cheddar cheese
⅔	cup chopped onion
1⅓	cups milk
3	eggs
¾	cup Bisquick
¾	teaspoon salt
½	teaspoon pepper

Preheat the oven to 400°. Grease a 10-inch pie plate. Rinse the broccoli under running cold water to thaw; drain thoroughly. Mix the broccoli, 2 cups of the cheese, and the onion in the plate. In a blender beat the milk, eggs, Bisquick, salt, and pepper until smooth for 15 seconds on high or for 1 minute with hand beater. Pour into plate. Bake for 25 to 35 minutes until a knife inserted in the center comes out clean.

Top with the remaining cheese. Bake 1 to 2 minutes longer until the cheese is melted. Let stand 5 minutes. Garnish with tomato slices if desired.

MAKES 6 SERVINGS; 405 CALORIES PER SERVING.

—ADRIENNE HALEY BECKER,
Granddaughter of Jack Haley

Gets the Red Out

Jack Haley paid his dues in his career, especially for the jewel that immortalized him. Haley detested aspects of the workaday *Oz*, but as time went by, the grudge lessened and he eventually embraced the motion picture as the classic it had become in his own lifetime. The adulation from fans around the world was a pleasant sedative for the old nightmares.

Don't be mistaken: Haley and his contemporaries in *Oz* were unanimously grateful and proud to have been blessed with an icon on their résumé. Jack Haley, Ray Bolger, and Margaret Hamilton—those three in particular—lived to experience the esteem, and in return, patiently pleased fans at every opportunity. For years, the surviving three stars of the film happily pumped out autographs and made personal appearances until they could no longer do so. Ray Bolger occasionally sent fans actual strands of straw, directly removed from his original costume, with his personal note of authenticity. But for those actors who breathed Technicolor life into the tale of *Oz* in 1938 and 1939, the fame had a price.

Jack Haley's oldest child, daughter Gloria, was a teenager when her father was coping on the Yellow Brick Road for six months. "He hated making the movie," she says. "He couldn't sit down in a chair, he had to lean on a board. He said it was the most miserable time."

Things turned caustic when Jack Haley developed an infection in his eyes. The condition flared up unbearably during the movie's production and he was confined to home. Something in his silver makeup was deemed the cause. Makeup artist Jack Dawn applied a silver aluminum paste with a dash of ordinary bluing—the kind used in washing clothes—to achieve just the right metallic sheen on Haley's skin. It was so smooth, it could have been buffed. After repeated tests, Jack Dawn concocted a recipe for the daily applications. (Studio press releases boasted, "For every day Jack Haley worked, fifty-cents worth of real silver went into his makeup.")

"My father was living in the house that he gave me, on Walden in Beverly Hills," remembers Gloria Haley, "and he woke up one morning in a lot of pain. For two weeks he had to stay in a darkened room and he couldn't go to work. Right in the middle of the movie. They called in a specialist, that's where we met Dr. Haar. He came in and treated him every day so he wouldn't go blind from that silver paint. A little ray of light in the room and he'd scream with pain. All the drapes had to be drawn and we couldn't even put on a light."

It was a long, painful road for the actor, but ol' iron eyes Haley waited it out— and returned to the set of *Oz* for more punishment.

I guess we are the lucky ones.

Bert Lahr in a popular Lay's potato chip TV commercial, 1966. (Courtesy of Frito-Lay, Inc.)

JUST A DANDY-LION

    Dandelion greens
    Water
    Olive oil
    Lemon juice
    Salt and pepper

Wash greens several times, drain, and place them in salted boiling water, enough to cover greens. Boil for 30 minutes to 1 hour until tender. Remove from the water and drain most of the water. Place in a bowl and serve with olive oil and lemon juice. Season to taste with salt and pepper.

    Dandelion greens are available at most international grocery stores as well as health food stores. You can plant your own from seed or pick them from a nice clean empty lot. You pick them before the flower appears. They are an excellent source of iron and many other nutrients and are said to be very beneficial. They can also be made into a salad.

                   —TINA CASSIMATIS

Lunch on the Set of *Oz*

Ray Bolger, Bert Lahr, and Jack Haley found solace at lunch, a brief recess that allowed them to shed the enemy: their costumes. Bolger's itched, Lahr's was sweltering, and Haley's was constraining. And that just describes the costume, not to mention the misery caused by the extensive makeup. Restricted in ways they had never before experienced, the actors attempted to relieve their respective oppressions. Bert Lahr frequently removed the lion's skin to cool himself and dry off. Bolger sat still and smoked cigarettes, wary of matches and stray ashes the entire time. Haley resorted to a leaning board, on which he could rest upright. (More than once, Haley tripped in his costume, and like a turtle on its back, lay there until somebody would right him.)

    The lunch break meant the actors retreated to their dressing rooms or another area for some relaxation, retaining the makeup, but donning nothing but their well-worn bathrobes. Occasionally, the actors spent their time off together, receiving reporters, like Hedda Hopper, who described her visit in an August 1939 newspaper column:

    Bert Lahr had to keep a stiff upper lip. He says he now knows what that means. Because he had a false piece over his own. And the false lip pulled his nose up into that retrousse effect that makes a lion look so silly. When he ate lunch he couldn't nibble or munch, but had to sip through a straw. For months all the strange folk in Wizard of Oz *ate their lunch together on the second floor back in the property department, so as not to frighten the other dears who were working on the same lot. Imagine going through a dark corridor and suddenly coming upon a lion sipping through a straw! One day Bolger got tired of being pushed out of sight and persuaded Jack Haley and Bert to go to a country club for luncheon. All three went in their outlandish get-ups. They frightened the other members right out of their food, and were asked never to come back again. Some people have no sense of humor.*

LENA HORNE'S "BITEY" BEANS

2   cups (1 pound) large black beans
    About 5 cups water
1   teaspoon salt
½   cup olive oil
2   large garlic cloves, pressed
1   onion, peeled and sliced
8   small, fresh tomatoes, peeled and
    chopped
    Freshly ground black pepper to taste
    Smoked ham hocks

Pick over the beans carefully and soak in water overnight. Drain. Place the beans and ham hocks in a large saucepan with water to cover the beans by about 1½ inches. Add the salt, cover, and cook for about 1 hour and 30 minutes until the beans are "bitey."

Meanwhile, prepare the sauce: In a skillet heat 2 tablespoons of olive oil. Sauté the garlic and onion until tender. Add the tomatoes. Cook slowly over low heat to form a thick soft sauce. Place the cooked drained beans in a casserole. Spoon the sauce over the top and heat until piping hot. Drizzle the remaining olive oil over the top and sprinkle with pepper to taste. Serve with sliced cooked ham hocks to complete the meal.

Note: Salt pork or ham bone gives an excellent smokey flavor to beans. For a meatless version, use herbs like coriander, bay leaf, thyme, or sage to flavor the beans. Govern the seasonings according to the use of ingredients. Ham or hocks will give a natural saltiness to the beans without adding excess amounts of salt and pepper. Cook by "feel" and "taste"!

MAKES 6 SERVINGS.

—LENA HORNE, Glinda in the motion
picture *The Wiz*

PREMIERE

THE WIZ

A Filmex Society Benefit for
The Los Angeles International Film Exposition

Wednesday, October 25, 1978, 7:30 pm
Plitt's Century Plaza Theatre
ABC Entertainment Center
Century City

ADMIT ONE $10.00

Section	Row	Seat
RIGHT	GG	20

IT'S A TWISTER Who would guess that one day Dorothy's daughter would marry the Tin Man's son? But it happened. Liza Minnelli and Jack Haley Jr. were married in 1974. Here, the pair (with Haley Sr.) are at a party in New York following Minnelli's Broadway opening in The Act, *October 1977. Haley and Minelli divorced in 1979 but remained good friends.*

LIZA'S POTATO SHELLS

4   small long slender baking potatoes
     4 teaspoons unsalted butter
     Salt and freshly ground pepper to taste
1   cup dairy sour cream (more if needed)
¼   cup caviar
1   jigger vodka

Preheat the oven to 425°. Scrub and dry the potatoes. Rub the skins lightly with butter. Bake for about 1 hour and 30 minutes or until the inside is soft and the skin is crunchy. Cut the potatoes in half lengthwise and remove about half of the potato. Put ½ teaspoon of butter in each shell with a light sprinkling of salt and freshly ground pepper. Fill each shell with sour cream. Top with 1 tablespoon of caviar and sprinkle with vodka. Serve at once as finger food to go with cocktails.

Note: Liza's potato shells can be made as a dinner accompaniment by removing all the potato, flavoring it with butter, salt, and pepper, then restuffing and double baking it before adding sour cream, caviar, and vodka.

MAKES 8.

—LIZA MINNELLI, daughter of Judy Garland

Evillene

Evillene was my favorite character in the Broadway production of *The Wiz*. I'll never forget how she rolled around the stage; there must have been a rolling piano stool hidden under her dress. But the funniest thing I remember was her costume; it looked all dark until she did her evil laugh and pulled two cords which hung from her midriff. To the surprise of the audience, it created two bulging blinking eyes on her bosom. It was hysterical!

—Elaine Willingham

chunks of cheese, and a few shakes of paprika together. Last add the evaporated milk. The mixture should be thick, but not slushy. Cut the second block of cheese into strips and place on top of the casserole. Sprinkle a little more paprika on top. Place some pieces of butter on top. Bake for 20 minutes until the top bubbles and gets golden brown.

Let it cool before cutting with a spatula into wedges like a piece of pie. It's delicious reheated the next day.

MAKES 6 SERVINGS.

—MABEL KING, Evillene in *The Wiz*

MAMA'S MACARONI PIE

This was one of my mama's holiday or Sunday specials. Her name is Rosalie Washington, and she loved making this, and we loved having it. We call it macaroni pie because that's what it looks like.

2   blocks Cracker Barrel mild Cheddar cheese
1   pound elbow macaroni, boiled and drained
3   eggs
6   tablespoons (¾ stick) margarine or butter
     Paprika
1   12-ounce can evaporated milk

Preheat the oven to 350°. Cut one block of the cheese into small chunks.

In a round casserole dish mix the macaroni, eggs, margarine, small

Mabel King, as Evillene in the motion picture The Wiz, *appeared on the November/ December 1978 cover of* Theatre Crafts *magazine. In the film, King re-created her menacing role of the Wicked Witch from the original Broadway production, performing the number "Don't Nobody Bring Me No Bad News." Television audiences in the late '70s knew her as Mama on the sitcom* What's Happening! *on ABC-TV. (Tod Machin Collection)*

MARGARET'S OLD-FASHIONED HOPPING JOHN

2   cups dried black-eyed peas
4   cups water
1   cup coarsely chopped onion
1   tablespoon bacon drippings
1   cup long-grain rice
1   teaspoon salt
½   teaspoon pepper
¼   pound thickly sliced bacon, cooked

Wash and sort the peas. In a medium saucepan combine the peas and 4 cups of water, and bring to a boil. Reduce the heat, cover, and simmer for 45 minutes. Drain the peas, reserving the liquid. Set both the peas and the liquid aside.

In a Dutch oven sauté the onion in the bacon drippings until golden. Add water to the reserved liquid from the peas to make 4 cups. Add the water, peas, rice, salt, and pepper to the onions and bring to a boil. Reduce the heat, cover, and simmer for about 35 to 40 minutes, until the peas and rice are tender and the liquid is absorbed. Crumble the bacon and stir into the Hopping John.

MAKES 8 SERVINGS.

—MARGARET PELLEGRINI,
Munchkin in *Oz,* MGM

MARGARET'S SOUTHERN-STYLE SWEET POTATO PONE

4   cups sweet potatoes, peeled and shredded
     Rind of 1 orange, grated
1   cup milk
2   eggs, lightly beaten
1½ cups firmly packed brown sugar
1   teaspoon ground cinnamon
½   teaspoon salt
¼   teaspoon grated nutmeg
¾   cup butter, softened
½   teaspoon pepper

In a large mixing bowl combine the sweet potatoes and orange rind. Add the remaining ingredients and blend thoroughly. Spoon the mixture into a greased 8-inch square baking dish. Bake at 325° for 1 hour and 30 minutes. Serve hot or cold.

MAKES 10 TO 12 SERVINGS.

—MARGARET PELLEGRINI, Munchkin
in *Oz*, MGM

MUNCHKINLAND FRESH VEGETABLE PIZZA

Colorful and delicious!

2	8-ounce cans refrigerated crescent dinner rolls
1	cup sour cream
2	tablespoons prepared horseradish
¼	teaspoon salt
⅛	teaspoon pepper
2	cups chopped fresh mushrooms
1	cup chopped tomatoes
1	cup small broccoli florets
½	cup chopped green bell pepper
½	cup chopped green onions

Preheat the oven to 375°. Separate the dough into 4 long rectangles. Place the rectangles crosswise in an ungreased 10 x 15-inch jelly-roll pan; press over the bottom and 1 inch up the sides to form crust. Seal the perforations. Bake at 375° for 14 to 19 minutes or until golden brown. Cool completely.

In a small bowl combine the sour cream, horseradish, salt, and pepper; blend until smooth. Spread evenly over the cooled crust. Top with mushrooms, tomatoes, broccoli, green pepper, and onions. Cut into appetizer-size pieces. Refrigerate leftovers.

MAKES 60 APPETIZERS.

—BLANCHE COX

Producer Mervyn LeRoy, Judy Garland, and director Victor Fleming (holding Toto) are surrounded by Munchkins in this delightful publicity photograph. Now, sixty years later, of the 124 little people who worked in the movie, only 12 survive. (Courtesy Mickey Carroll Collection)

CRISS CROZ

Although their most famous roles, their career zeniths, were of course in *The Wizard of Oz*, the film's main actors all had sizable careers in the entertainment industry stretching well beyond *Oz*. Did you know that most of them already knew each other, having crossed paths in motion picture work? They were friends and acquaintances, having socialized or worked together, long before they accepted roles in the movie that launched Judy Garland to new heights.

After *Oz*, this special fraternity of actors continued to bump into each other, in stage productions, motion pictures, and in television appearances. For more of your favorites, check out these flicks:

PRIOR TO OZ *Margaret Hamilton and Frank Morgan in a scene from the 1934 film* By Your Leave.

By Your Leave (1934) with Margaret Hamilton and Frank Morgan
Piccadilly Jim (1936) with Billie Burke and Frank Morgan
The Great Ziegfeld (1936) with Frank Morgan and Ray Bolger
Pigskin Parade (1936) with Jack Haley and Judy Garland
Everybody Sing (1938) with Billie Burke and Judy Garland
Listen, Darling (1938) with Charley Grapewin and Judy Garland
Broadway Melody of 1938 (1938) with Buddy Ebsen, Judy Garland, and Charley Grapewin
Babes in Arms (1939) with Judy Garland and Margaret Hamilton
Twin Beds (1942) with Margaret Hamilton and Toto
Sing Your Worries Away (1942) with Bert Lahr and Buddy Ebsen
The Harvey Girls (1948) with Judy Garland and Ray Bolger
People Are Funny (1948) with Clara Blandick and Jack Haley
The Daydreamer (1966) with Margaret Hamilton and Ray Bolger

MY BEAUTIFUL WICKEDNESS BROCCOLI "THING"

The reason former President George Bush hates broccoli is because the cook at his home (he was a rich kid) simply boiled it, put it on his plate, and said: "Eat it!" Broccoli needs a little selling and a lot of dressing up. This delicious southwestern dish appeals to everyone, even George, because it is irresistibly delicious. It can also be served as a dip.

⅔   cup margarine
2   10-ounce packages frozen chopped broccoli, thawed and drained
4   green onions, chopped
4   ribs celery, chopped
2   3-ounce cans sliced mushrooms
2   10¾-ounce cans cream of mushroom soup
1   6-ounce roll garlic cheese
     Worcestershire sauce
     Tabasco sauce
     Salt and pepper
     Breadcrumbs

In a skillet melt the margarine over medium-high heat and sauté the broccoli, onions, and celery for 10 to 15 minutes. Add the mushrooms, soup, cheese, and seasonings, and stir until the cheese melts. Pour into a 2-quart casserole. Top with breadcrumbs. Bake at 350° for about 30 minutes. May be frozen before baking.

MAKES 6 SERVINGS.

—PHYLLIS DILLER, W.W.W. in 1991
Oz stage musical

Witch and Famous

Broomstick in hand, the wacky Phyllis Diller eclipsed box-office records at the ostentatious, open-air Starlight Theatre in Kansas City, Missouri, when she starred in a 1991 summer stage production of *The Wizard of Oz*. It was literally standing room only and the show drew more than fifty-five thousand people for Diller's one-week run—an all-time attendance record for the forty-year-old theater. Many noted the success of the show was due to an energetic performance by Diller, who was seventy-five at the time. In a surprising curtain call, Diller didn't walk out and take a bow . . . she descended from above, situated on a huge half-moon, dressed as herself in a glittery gown and fright wig. The *Kansas City Star* proclaimed: "The star, of course, is veteran stand-up comic Phyllis Diller, who taps into the fundamental fun of the show with an amusing turn as the Wicked Witch of the West. Her airborne broom-riding, her diabolical laughter, her deliciously malicious dialogue, occasional ad-libs, and a delightfully grotesque vocal performance she delivers when 'melting' all add up to a memorable, just-for-laughs performance." (Photo by Troy Thomas)

OZZIE PASTA WITH EMERALD SPINACH SAUCE

½   cup olive oil
¼   cup butter
1   large onion, sliced
2   cloves garlic, crushed
1   10-ounce package frozen spinach, thawed and drained
½   teaspoon salt
1   teaspoon basil
½   cup Parmesan cheese
1   8-ounce package linguine

In a skillet heat the oil and butter. Add the onion, garlic, and spinach. Reduce the heat, cover, and simmer for 10 minutes. Add the salt and basil. Simmer 5 minutes more. Stir in the Parmesan cheese.

Cook the linguine pasta for 12 to 15 minutes in boiling salted water. Drain. Pour the spinach mixture over the linguine. Serve with more Parmesan cheese. A yummy way to end the day! Great for those Oz parties. No muss, no fuss—light and bright!

—KATIE FLEMING

Hyperion Animation's The Oz Kids, *released by Paramount Home Video. Originally a popular series in Japan and several European countries in the mid-1990s, the animated adventures focused on the second generation of the famous Oz citizens; the series included additional Oz characters such as the Ork, the Hammerheads, the Mangaboos, and the Jackdaws. (Courtesy of Hyperion Animation, Inc.)*

PASTA NORMA

3   pounds Roma tomatoes
1   large ripe eggplant
1   cup plus 1 tablespoon extra-virgin olive oil
3   cloves garlic, chopped
1   brown (or large yellow) onion, chopped
1   pound penne rigate pasta
2   cups chopped basil

Dunk the tomatoes in boiling water for 30 seconds. Cool slightly, then peel, and roughly chop. Season with salt and pepper.

Slice the eggplant into ½-inch squares. In a skillet heat 1 cup of olive oil and brown the eggplant until crisp. Drain and wrap in paper towels.

In a skillet cook the chopped garlic and onion in 1 tablespoon of olive oil until the onion is translucent. Add the tomatoes and cook on medium-high heat about 20 minutes until liquid is just evaporated. Meanwhile, cook the pasta in salted water (white sea salt is always best for pasta). Drain the pasta and toss with the cooked tomatoes, eggplant, and basil. Serve immediately.

MAKES 6 TO 8 SERVINGS.

—WILLARD CARROLL, creator and producer, *The Oz Kids* series; coauthor, *100 Years of Oz*

SAUSAGE, CORN, AND POTATO CASSEROLE

1	pound ground pork sausage
3	cups sliced uncooked potatoes
1	16-ounce can cream-style corn
1	cup sliced onions
½	teaspoon salt
6	to 8 green bell pepper rings

Preheat the oven to 350°. Meanwhile cook the sausage, drain, and layer the sausage with the potatoes, corn, and onions in a 2-quart casserole. Sprinkle with salt. Top with green pepper rings. Cover and bake for 45 minutes. Remove the cover and bake for 15 minutes more. If too moist, bake another 15 minutes.

MAKES 6 SERVINGS.

—MARY LAND

This is a rare photo from the scrapped footage of Oz, directed by Richard Thorpe in 1938. Sets, costumes, and makeup were yet to be altered drastically.

". . . I won't be any trouble, because I don't eat a thing."

SCALLOPED PINEAPPLE

3   well-beaten eggs
2   cups sugar
1   cup melted butter, cooled
1   cup milk
1   18- to 20-ounce can crushed pineapple
     with juice
4   cups soft bread cubes

In a large bowl mix together the eggs, sugar, butter, milk, pineapple, and bread cubes. Transfer to an ungreased 1½-quart dish. Bake at 325° for 45 minutes until nicely browned. Serve warm.

MAKES 6 SERVINGS.

—LEE ANN COLEMAN

SUPER, DUPER FRENCH-FRIED ONION RINGS

Crisp and brittle, they are great with steaks or as an appetizer.

2   large Spanish* onions
     Ice water
1   egg
1   cup buttermilk
1   cup all-purpose flour
½   teaspoon salt
½   teaspoon baking soda
     Oil for frying

Slice the onions about ¼ inch thick, separate them into rings, and soak them in ice water for several hours. Drain and dry thoroughly. In a medium bowl beat the egg and buttermilk. In a separate bowl sift together the flour, salt, and baking soda. Add the dry ingredients to the liquid mixture and blend well. Dip the onion rings into the batter.

Fry in deep fat or oil heated to 375° until brown. Drain well on paper towels, then place in a 350° oven for added crispness.

A Spanish onion is a large yellow onion.

—BLANCHE COX

TIN MAN'S TIN CAN SURPRISE

½   can evaporated milk
1   10¾-ounce can cream of mushroom soup
2   21-ounce cans green beans
1   14-ounce can artichoke "hearts"
1   6-ounce can sliced mushrooms
1   tall can French-fried onions

In a bowl mix together the milk and mushroom soup. Drain the green beans, artichoke hearts, and mushrooms and add to the soup mixture. Add half of the fried onions and mix together. Transfer to a 1½-quart baking dish. Bake at 350° for 25 minutes.

Remove from the oven and add the remainder of the fried onions. Bake for 5 more minutes.

MAKES 4 SERVINGS.

—DIRK LUMBARD, Tin Man in *The Wizard of Oz* National Tour, 1998–1999

UNCLE HENRY'S AU GRATIN POTATOES

1   10¾-ounce can cream of mushroom soup
¾   cup milk
6   cups sliced potatoes
    Dash salt
    Dash pepper
1   red onion, thinly sliced
1   cup grated Cheddar cheese
1   tablespoon butter, melted

Butter a 2-quart casserole. In a small bowl blend the soup and milk. Alternate layers of potatoes, salt, pepper, onion, cheese, and soup mixture, and then repeat. Dot with melted

Jessica Grové is Dorothy and Mickey Rooney is the Wizard/Gatekeeper in the 1998–1999 touring company of The Wizard of Oz, *produced by Radio City Entertainment. (Photo by Katie Grové)*

butter. Cover and bake at 375° for 1 hour.

Remove the cover and bake 15 minutes more or until golden and tender.

MAKES 6 SERVINGS.

—WILMA WILLINGHAM

VEGAN (STRICT VEGETARIAN) PIZZA

This recipe is contributed on behalf of my favorite charity, Pet Hope, Inc.

Fresh Pizza Dough:
2½   cups flour, half whole wheat and half all-purpose
1   cup water
2   tablespoons active dry yeast

Dash salt
1 tablespoon molasses (optional)
½ teaspoon dried rosemary
1 teaspoon sesame seeds (optional)
Cornmeal

Toppings:
2 cups tomato sauce
Dried or fresh Italian spices
Chopped vegetables and other toppings to taste
Grated VeganRella* (optional)
1 cup alfalfa sprouts (optional)

In a large bowl mix all dough ingredients except the cornmeal and knead (or let a bread-making machine do this work). Let sit and rise for an hour in a warm, dark place. Scatter a bit of cornmeal into a 9-inch pizza pan and press the dough into the pan.

Add the vegetables and other toppings. Top with VeganRella (*a soy-based substitute for cheese available in many groceries and natural foods stores). Bake at 350° for about 20 minutes or until the VeganRella has melted and starts to brown around the pizza's edge. Serve hot, topped with alfalfa sprouts (optional).

Note: Many health food stores sell dry mixes for preparing vegetarian "sausage"; vegetarian Canadian bacon can be found in health food store dairy cases, with the imitation meat products. Not all of these products are vegan, but they are vegetarian.

Note: Pizza dough, boxed mixes, and pre-baked crusts can be purchased at many grocery stores. However, these are often made with eggs, milk, or whey, making them far from vegan.

MAKES 4 SERVINGS

—BILLIE HAYES, Witchiepoo in TV series *H. R. Pufnstuf*

Sid & Marty Krofft's Saturday morning answer to Oz: the inimitable Witchiepoo, portrayed by actress Billie Hayes on TV's H. R. Pufnstuf *(1969–1973). Admittedly, co-producer Sid Krofft drew heavily from* The Wizard of Oz, *a favorite that inspired and fascinated him as a youth. (He eventually worked with Judy Garland in her concert tours.) Pufnstuf incorporated many Oz parodies and parallels: talking trees, swarms of little characters—even a hopping, singing frog named "Judy Frog," clearly patterned after Garland.*

Yes, Witchiepoo and the Wicked Witch of the West appeared together on a Paul Lynde Halloween TV special in the early 1970s. Billie Hayes and Margaret Hamilton reprised their famous cackling characters—this time as sister witches—in a hilarious comedy sketch. The actresses became close friends. Both ladies were immense fans of each other. "I couldn't believe Margaret actually watched H. R. Pufnstuf," *says Hayes, "but she told me she loved it because she wished she had been allowed to be funny as the witch in the movie, but of course, they didn't allow her that." (Author's Collection; Photo courtesy Billie Hayes/Kay Hobday Collection)*

VI'S ZUCCHINI DINNER

1   pound lean ground beef
1   clove garlic, crushed
1   large white onion, chopped
1   each large green, red, and yellow bell
     peppers, chopped
2   20-ounce cans whole tomatoes, cut up
6   cups sliced zucchini
1   tablespoon Italian seasoning
     Salt and pepper to taste
3   tablespoons sugar
     Parmesan cheese

In a skillet brown the beef with the garlic, onion, and chopped peppers. Add the cut-up tomatoes with juice, zucchini, seasonings, and sugar. Simmer covered until the zucchini is tender. Add ½ cup of cheese. Serve over pasta, rice, or mashed potatoes. Top with Parmesan cheese.

You may also use broccoli in this recipe, if desired.

MAKES 6 SERVINGS.

—VIOLA WHITE BANKS, Child Munchkin
in *Oz*, MGM

WICKED GARLIC TURNIP MASHED POTATOES

5   russet potatoes
1   turnip
1   rutabaga
1   onion, diced
¼   cup garlic, diced
¼   cup chicken broth
     Butter (optional)
¼   cup milk or plain yogurt

Salt and pepper to taste
Parmesan cheese

Peel (optional) and cut the potatoes, turnip, and rutabaga into chunks. In a saucepan cover with water and boil until tender. Drain. In a skillet sauté the onion and garlic. Add to the vegetables. Add the chicken broth, butter, milk or yogurt, salt, and pepper. Whip until smooth. Sprinkle with Parmesan cheese.

MAKES 4 TO 6 SERVINGS.

—DENISE MOSES, W.W.W. in Energizer Bunny
TV commercials

Denise Moses provided a wickedly perfect impression of Margaret Hamilton's witch for a popular "Energizer Bunny" battery TV commercial in 1993. "How 'bout a little fire, Bunny?" (Photo by Andrea Stern)

ZEKE'S ZESTY CHEESE-TOMATO PIE

Pastry for a single-crust pie (refrigerated, frozen, or homemade)
4   or 5 tomatoes
2   to 3 tablespoons chopped fresh basil
2   to 3 tablespoons chopped fresh oregano
2   to 3 tablespoons chopped fresh chives
4   ounces (1 cup) shredded mozzarella cheese
4   ounces (1 cup) shredded Provolone cheese
4   ounces (1 cup) shredded Asiago cheese
1   sweet onion (such as Vidalia), thinly sliced
1½   teaspoons garlic powder, divided
1   teaspoon freshly ground black pepper, divided
½   cup grated Parmesan cheese, divided
2   tablespoons seasoned dry breadcrumbs
4½   teaspoons butter

Preheat the oven to 375°. Fit the pastry into a pie plate and prick with a fork. Bake for 10 to 15 minutes or until the pastry is firm.

Remove from the oven; reduce the heat to 350°.

Meanwhile, wash the tomatoes, cut into thick slices, and place on paper towels to drain. In a small bowl combine the basil, oregano, and chives; set aside. In a bowl combine the mozzarella, Provolone, and Asiago cheeses; set aside.

Pat the tomatoes dry. In a pie shell layer half the tomatoes, half the onions, and half the cheese mixture. Sprinkle with half the herbs, ¾ teaspoon of garlic powder, and ½ teaspoon of pepper. Sprinkle with ¼ cup Parmesan cheese. Repeat layers.

Sprinkle breadcrumbs on top; dot with butter.

Bake for 30 minutes or until the cheese melts.

MAKES 4 TO 6 SERVINGS.

—NANCIE AND ART GUARIGLIA

ZUCCHINI À LA BILLIE BURKE

My mother, Billie Burke, was not a cook by any stretch of the imagination! But she loved zucchini so much that she learned to cook it. She said she would never starve if she had a couple of pieces of whole wheat toast, slathered in butter, and a plate of zucchini! Here is her recipe:

5   or 6 (4- to 6-inch) shiny zucchini, cut into ½-inch slices
5   or 6 large cloves garlic, peeled and thinly sliced
1   cup water
1   tablespoon chopped fresh parsley
1   tablespoon chopped fresh dill
2   tablespoons butter
    Salt and pepper to taste (optional)
½   teaspoon dry hot mustard (Coleman's)
    Pinch salt and pepper
1   teaspoon firmly packed brown or raw sugar
½   cup olive oil
    Juice of ½ lemon
1   ice cube

In a large saucepan place the zucchini, garlic, and water. Bring to a boil. Cover and boil for 5 minutes. Turn off the heat and let stand for 15 minutes. Drain well. Add the parsley, dill, butter, salt, and pepper.

Prepare BB's French dressing: In a large bowl mix the mustard with the pinch of salt and pepper and the sugar. Add the oil slowly; mixing well. Add the lemon juice and then the ice cube. Mix together thoroughly. Bon appetit!

Should you want to eat the zucchini cold on some lettuce, chill well and add ½ cup of BB's French dressing.

MAKES 6 SERVINGS.

—PATRICIA ZIEGFELD STEPHENSON,
daughter of Billie Burke

Billie Burke, widow of Florenz Ziegfeld, with daughter Patricia in 1935.

Billie Burke in 1959, autographing copies of her book, With Powder on My Nose, *in St. Louis. (Beyond the Rainbow Archive)*

An *Oz* Exhibition

There are scarce few truly rare glimpses of *Oz* left in the world, and we are proud to have a few of them right here for you. Unseen *Oz*. Keep in mind that after six decades, this motion picture has been universally proclaimed an object of art, a treasure considered worthy of dissection. *The Wizard of Oz* has been studied, exploited, mined, and explored in most every way possible. And although several documentaries and profusely illustrated books have been produced about the making of the classic, Production 1060, every now and then some precious photographic images surface and offer yet another unexpected peek at a lost moment in time. These rare behind-the-scenes set stills were photographed on MGM soundstages for the benefit of a variety of personnel: set designers, lighting technicians, prop men. With credit due to the generosity of film historians Ron Borst and Eric Daily, we proudly unveil a few recently discovered gems.

Dorothy's bedroom wallpaper featured a design of poppies—a foreshadowing of the story. Notice the picture of Dorothy and Aunt Em propped up on the table, the same keepsake discovered by Professor Marvel when he rummaged through Dorothy's basket.

Although the slate indicates Victor Fleming as director, the Gale farmhouse scenes (including Dorothy's "Over the Rainbow" solo) were actually completed by director King Vidor when Fleming left Oz to direct Gone with the Wind.

In the film, audiences never get a good look at the gothic and exotic decorations in Professor Marvel's wagon; notice the shrunken head hanging from the ceiling.

Pay no attention to that man on the left; finally we can examine the great and powerful gadgetry that is Oz.

Victor Fleming (far left, in background) rehearses the scene in which the Winkies are crushed by a falling chandelier. Near Fleming, you'll notice the moving image of a set worker dressed in white overalls and cap.

THERE'S NO PLACE LIKE HOME—FOR DINNER

ANDRÉ'S WHOLE-FOOD, SOUL-FOOD DINNER

As I prepare to ease on down the road into the twenty-first century, I am reminded of the solid emerald advice given by Dorothy, the Scarecrow, the Tin Man, and the Lion: "Don't you carry nothin' that might be a load." That refers to emotional baggage. Well, Mr. Wiz has a suggestion for making your nutritional load a little lighter—Whole-Food, Soul-Food. So when you think of home, consider these two comforting, delicious, and nutritious recipes.

WHOLE-FOOD CORN BREAD

(Whenever possible ingredients should be organic.)

1½	cups whole grain yellow cornmeal
¼	cup whole grain brown rice flour
¼	cup whole grain wheat flour
½	teaspoon sea salt
¼	cup evaporated cane juice
4	teaspoons non-aluminum baking powder
¼	cup plus 1 teaspoon unrefined canola oil
1	cup creamy original Vita-Soy non-dairy beverage
1	portion egg substitute, beaten

André De Shields is The Wiz, *in the original Broadway production at the Majestic Theatre. (Photo by Martha Swope)*

Preheat the oven to 425°. Oil an 8- or 9-inch cast-iron skillet with 1 teaspoon of unrefined canola oil.

In a large bowl combine the cornmeal, flour, and salt, and blend together. In a medium bowl combine the egg substitute, cane juice, canola oil, and Vita-Soy, and blend vigorously with a wire whisk. Pour the liquid mixture all at once into the dry ingredients. Blend with a wooden spoon, using as few strokes as possible. Pour the batter into the skillet. Place in the oven on the middle rack and bake about 25 minutes until yellow-brick-road golden brown, or until a wooden toothpick inserted in the center comes out dry. Cool on a rack for 5 to 10 minutes. Serve from the skillet.

WHOLE-FOOD LIMA BEANS

1   pound white lima beans
1   gallon or more distilled water
1   strip kombu (sea vegetable)
2   bay leaves
12   whole black peppercorns
2   teaspoons Herbamare
4   cloves garlic

Place the lima beans in a colander or sieve. Rinse under running cold tap water. Pick over to remove foreign particles and discolored beans. Place the rinsed beans in a cast-iron pot. Add distilled water to cover. Cover and refrigerate overnight.

The next day (the beans will have largely absorbed the water), add the kombu, bay leaves, peppercorns, Herbamare, and garlic. Add more distilled water to cover. Bring to boil over high heat. Reduce the heat and simmer for several hours, stirring occasionally with a wooden spoon and adding water to cover as necessary. The beans are done when they surrender readily to the back of the wooden spoon and the contents reach a thick stew consistency. Remove the bay leaves and any large pieces of kombu. Let the beans rest 5 to 10 minutes before serving.

Together the beans and bread are sufficiently awesome to stop a tornado. Just click your heels together three times and enjoy.

—ANDRÉ DE SHIELDS, *The Wiz* in the original, Tony Award–winning Broadway hit

Tony Award nominee André De Shields today. (Photo by Princess Lia Chang)

BAKED CHICKEN SALAD PIE

1   deep-dish 9-inch pie crust
2   tablespoons all-purpose flour
2   tablespoons mustard
2   eggs, slightly beaten
½   cup condensed cream of chicken soup
½   cup mayonnaise
½   cup sour cream
½   cup finely chopped celery
¼   cup finely chopped onion
¼   cup finely chopped water chestnuts
¾   cup snow peas
2   cups diced cooked chicken breast
¾   cup shredded Cheddar cheese

In a 9-inch pie plate place the crust, prick slightly, and bake at 350° for 7 to 10 minutes.

In a small bowl place the flour and gradually stir in the mustard to form a paste. In a large bowl stir together the eggs, soup, mayonnaise, sour cream, and mustard paste. Add the celery, onion, and water chestnuts, stirring well to combine. Mix in the snow peas, chicken, and Cheddar cheese. Spread the mixture into the prepared pie crust. Bake at 350° for 45 to 50 minutes until slightly browned.

MAKES 6 SERVINGS.

—LOIS GROTHMAN

BAKED HAM WITH CHERRY SAUCE AND YAMS

6   medium yams (or sweet potatoes)
     Salad oil
1   1-inch-thick fully cooked ham slice
     (about 1½ pounds)
½   cup firmly packed dark brown sugar (or light brown sugar)

⅛   teaspoon grated nutmeg
3   thick orange slices
1   17-ounce can pitted Bing cherries, drained
½   cup sherry wine
1   tablespoon brandy
     Butter (or margarine)

Scrub and dry the yams. Rub each with a little salad oil. Arrange on one side of the oven rack, leaving room for the ham dish to be placed later. Bake at 350° for 45 to 50 minutes or until fork-tender.

Once the yams have been placed in the oven, place the ham slice in a 12 x 8 x 2-inch baking dish. Cover with brown sugar and then sprinkle with nutmeg. Place the orange slices on top of the ham. In a small bowl combine the drained cherries, sherry, and brandy. Pour the mixture around the ham slice.

When the yams have been baking for 15 minutes, place the prepared ham slice in the oven and bake with the yams for at least 30 minutes. When the ham and yams are done, remove from the oven. Cut a 1½-inch cross in the top of each yam. Using oven mitts, knead the bottom and sides of each yam until the tender interior partially bursts through cross. With a fork, break up the interior of each potato lightly; then lay a piece of butter on top. Place around the edge of a heated platter. Cut the ham slice into 6 servings and place in the center of platter. Divide each orange slice in half and place one piece on top of each ham serving. Pour the cherry sauce into a serving bowl and serve alongside.

MAKES 6 SERVINGS.

—BLANCHE COX

The United States Postal Service went Hollywood in 1990, issuing a se-tenant (or attached block) of first-class stamps honoring motion picture classics. The brilliant paintings on the stamps, by artist Thomas Blackshear, were also featured on posters, T-shirts, and a myriad of accompanying postal merchandise. Blackshear's artistry also graced the Fiftieth Anniversary Oz Commemorative Plate Collection and Portraits From Oz series, both produced by The Hamilton Collection. The plates, trimmed with a twenty-three-carat-gold "yellow brick road" border, beautifully captured memorable scenes and characters from the MGM film.

BLACKSHEAR'S BAKED SALMON

"Ever since I was a kid, I have loved The Wizard of Oz *and have been thrilled at the way the movie has become a part of my illustration career."*

Salmon
Cooking sherry to cover
Salt and pepper to taste
Lemon juice
Butter

Marinate the salmon overnight in sherry (or at least 2 hours). When ready to bake remove the salmon from the marinade. Season with salt and pepper. Place the salmon in a shallow pan and pour the remaining marinade into the pan. Cover with aluminum foil. Bake at 400° for about 15 to 20 minutes. Remove the foil. Squeeze fresh lemon juice over the fish. Place the pan under the broiler for about 7 to 10 minutes until golden brown. Remove from the oven and spread butter over the salmon, and enjoy!

—THOMAS BLACKSHEAR, *Oz* illustrator

BILLINA'S CHICKEN ADOBO

12   chicken thighs, skinless
1   cup apple cider vinegar
1   jigger rice wine (or splash)
1   cup soy sauce (Golden Mountain or low salt)
3   cloves garlic, minced
3   quarter-size slices gingerroot
1   tablespoon black peppercorns
1   bay leaf
2   to 3 cups hot steamed rice (jasmine rice preferred)

In a medium nonreactive saucepan place the chicken. Add the vinegar, wine, and soy sauce. Stir in the garlic, gingerroot, peppercorns, and bay leaf. This mixture can be covered and allowed to marinate for 1 hour in the refrigerator if desired. Place the saucepan on stove and bring to a boil. Cover, reduce the heat, and simmer for 1 hour, turning the chicken after 30 minutes. Serve on rice.

MAKES 6 SERVINGS.

—NANCY K. ROBINSON, Dorothy's House, Liberal, Kansas

CABBAGE ROLL-UPS

1   large head cabbage
2   quarts water
2   cups water
2   cups rice
2   teaspoons salt
¼   cup oil
1   medium onion, finely chopped
1   cup chopped mushrooms
1   tablespoon chopped parsley
2   tablespoons finely chopped celery
     Salt and pepper to taste
1   10¾-ounce can cream of mushroom
     soup

Prepare the cabbage by cutting the core out and removing the outer leaves. In a large saucepan bring 2 quarts of water to a boil. Place the cabbage in boiling water and simmer until the leaves pull apart easily. Rinse with cool water. Remove the leaves, cutting off all the thick parts.

In a large saucepan boil 2 cups of water. Add the rice and salt. Return to a brisk boil and cook 1 minute. Cover, turn off the heat, and allow the rice to stand until the water is absorbed. In a medium sauté pan heat the oil and cook the onion until tender. Add the mushrooms, parsley, and celery. Sauté for approximately 5 minutes. Add these vegetables to the rice. Mix well. Season with salt and pepper to taste.

Place a generous spoonful of rice filling in each leaf. Bring in the sides and roll. In a buttered baking dish arrange the rolls. Salt and pepper each layer. In a small bowl mix the soup with 1 can of water and pour over the rolls. Protect the top layer with extra leaves to prevent scorching. Cover the pan and bake at 350° for 1 hour to 1 hour and 15 minutes.

Variation: Also delicious with beet or spinach leaves, which should be washed and rinsed well. Place in a colander and pour boiling water over them until well wilted. Handle gently. If the leaves are small use 2 or 3 together to make a larger surface for the filling. Reduce baking time to 1 hour.

MAKES 6 SERVINGS.

—ANNA CUCKSEY MITCHELL, wife of Frank Cucksey, Munchkin in *Oz*, MGM

Several of the little men who worked in Oz slid directly into employment with the Sunshine Biscuit Company; the tiny bakers promoted Sunshine's crackers in an elaborate exhibit at the 1939 New York World's Fair.

CARNEY'S CREAMY MUSHROOM CHICKEN

3 whole chicken breasts, skinned, split, and boned
1 10¾-ounce can cream of mushroom soup
2 cups sour cream
1 8-ounce can chopped mushrooms, drained
3 cups hot cooked white and wild rice, combined
   Chinese noodles or buttered bread-crumbs for garnish

In a medium saucepan boil the chicken breasts. Cut into bite-size pieces. In a medium bowl combine the soup, sour cream, and mushrooms. Gently stir in the chicken. Pour into a 9 x 12-inch casserole dish. Bake at 350°until heated through. Serve over hot rice. Top with buttered breadcrumbs or Chinese noodles.

MAKES 5 TO 6 SERVINGS.

—JEAN AND ART CARNEY

Following his popularity as Norton on TV's The Honeymooners, *Emmy Award–winning actor Art Carney starred in several family-oriented programs, such as a TV adaptation of the play* Harvey. *In 1958, Carney hosted an ABC-TV special, "Art Carney Meets Peter and the Wolf," and narrated children's albums, including the tale of Oz.*

CATACLYSMIC CACCIATORE

1	pound beef
1	pound pork
1	pound veal
1	cup oil
3	onions, cut into eighths
1	fresh garlic clove, minced
2	stalks celery, diced
1	green bell pepper, diced
2	carrots, diced
1	2-ounce jar pimiento
1	20-ounce can crushed tomatoes
1½	teaspoons Lawry's seasoned salt
1½	teaspoons garlic salt
½	teaspoon onion salt
½	teaspoon oregano
1	teaspoon dried marjoram
1	teaspoon chili powder
1	teaspoon dried thyme
1	tablespoon mixed dried Italian herbs (unseasoned)
1	teaspoon dry mustard
1	1-pound package vermicelli (Butoni) Grated Parmesan cheese

Prepare the beef, pork, and veal by trimming all fat and cutting into small bite-size pieces. In a large heavy Dutch oven brown the prepared meat in oil. Add the onions and garlic and cook until the onions are slightly golden. Add the celery, green pepper, carrots, pimientos, and tomatoes, including juice. Stir in the seasonings and spices. Cover and simmer until done.

While the cacciatore is cooking, prepare the vermicelli according to package directions. Drain, rinse, and add butter. Keep hot.

Serve cacciatore over hot vermicelli and top with Parmesan cheese.

MAKES 6 TO 8 SERVINGS.

—PHYLLIS DILLER, W.W.W. in 1991
Oz touring production

CHANTERELLE CRÊPE LASAGNE

¼	cup olive oil
1	pound chanterelles (or 32 ounces pre-cooked)*
	Salt and pepper to taste
10	crêpes, plain
2	cups marinara sauce
1	pound broccoli florets, blanched (or 32 ounces precooked)
1	10-ounce package fresh spinach
8	ounces Parmesan cheese, grated
20	slices mozzarella cheese
2	cups Alfredo sauce
2	cups pesto sauce

In a medium sauté pan heat the olive oil and cook chanterelles until crispy. Drain, add salt and pepper, and set aside.

Spray a 15½ x 10½ x 2-inch chef's pan with nonstick coating. Into the prepared pan place 2 crêpes. Over the crêpes spread marinara sauce, then chanterelles, broccoli, spinach, and 1 tablespoon of Parmesan cheese, and top with 4 slices of mozzarella cheese. For the second layer, repeat using Alfredo sauce instead of the marinara. For the third and fourth layers, use pesto sauce. Repeat layers until all the crêpes are used, ending with 4 mozzarella slices. On the top spoon a strip of each sauce and sprinkle with Parmesan cheese. Bake at 350° for about 20 minutes. Then increase the oven temperature to 400° and cook until golden brown. If it starts to burn, cover with aluminum foil.

Chanterelles are edible mushrooms that are trumpet shaped and are yellow to orange in color.

—MICHAEL FEINSTEIN

For the Record

Harold Arlen, composer of some of America's most popular and enduring songs, worked magic with music in the timeless film, The Wizard of Oz. In 1996, the U.S. Postal Service featured Arlen on a 32-cent stamp, along with other legendary songwriters.

Judy Garland considered her signature song, "Over the Rainbow," a sacred lullaby, more than once labeling it "the best song ever written." She sang it often in concert as the finale or her encore, and she offered it in private, like the time she softly sang it into the telephone for a friend's sickly child. Liza Minnelli has yet to take on the tune in concert; however, during a 1997 concert tour, Minnelli departed from the norm. During a year that would've marked her mother's seventy-fifth birthday, she reneged on an old "promise" and performed her mother's standard, "You Made Me Love You." Variety noted, "Sung a cappella with obvious inspiration, it was beautifully rendered with a genuine sentiment that transcended any vocal flaws."

Garland's contemporaries, however, didn't hesitate covering her tunes, because they instantly fell in love with them, just like the public. "Over the Rainbow" was no exception. More than a few performers have recorded songs from the unforgettable *Oz* score. Some remain exquisite versions, and then there are some you wouldn't believe.

Did you ever hear Bing Crosby's version of "Ding Dong the Witch Is Dead"? Harry Connick Jr.'s track of "If I Only Had a Brain"? Or the Chipmunks singing "We're Off to See the Wizard"? It's one thing to hear Barbra Streisand belt out "Ding Dong . . ." (on a Harold Arlen album), but it's another to endure the Del Rubio Triplets warbling the same tune, clanking on guitars for background music.

Believe it or not, the composer and lyricist, Harold Arlen and Yip Harburg respectively, both stepped up to the microphone and recorded their own versions of "Over the Rainbow" on albums. Here's a smidgen of the list of diverse performers who have recorded "Over the Rainbow," the most popular selection from the soundtrack of *The Wizard of Oz*. There's a reason Judy Garland's original performance earned it an Academy Award.

Tony Bennett	Ella Fitzgerald	Patti LaBelle	Henry Nilsson
Benny Carter	Aretha Franklin	Jerry Lewis	Mandy Patinkin
Ray Charles	Kathy Lee Gifford	Liberace	Doc Severinsen
Perry Como	Tom T. Hall	Melissa Manchester	Frank Sinatra
Michael Crawford	Sam Harris	Henry Mancini	Barbra Streisand
Doris Day	Neal Hefti	Hugo Montenegro	Tiny Tim
Bo Diddley	Jewel	Willie Nelson	Joe Utterback
Billy Eckstine	Bert Kaempfert	Olivia Newton-John	Sarah Vaughan

CHARLEY'S BEEF STEW

3   pounds beef stew meat, cut into 1½-inch
       cubes
       All-purpose flour
¼   cup peanut oil
2   10½-ounce cans condensed beef broth
1   cup water
2   bay leaves
1   onion, chopped
       Pinch thyme
2   cloves garlic, chopped
6   whole allspice
1   tablespoon chopped parsley
3   cups either carrots, peas, lima beans,
       tomatoes, potatoes, or presoaked lentils
       (your choice)
       Salt and pepper to taste

Roll the meat in flour and shake off excess. In a Dutch oven heat the oil and brown the meat. Cover with broth and water. Add the bay leaves, onion, thyme, garlic, allspice, and parsley. Cover and simmer for at least 2 hours or until the meat is tender. A half-hour before serving, add 3 cups of any of the vegetables listed (or use canned or frozen vegetables). Simmer until the vegetables are tender. Season with salt and pepper.

MAKES 8 SERVINGS.

Judy Garland looks as if she doesn't know what to think of this rotund Mayor of Munchkinland (Charley Becker) and the rest of the City Fathers gathered around her. (Beyond the Rainbow Archive)

Hizzoner, the Chef

What most of the surviving midget actors from *Oz* recall about the Mayor Munchkin, Charley Becker, is that he ruled in the kitchen as well. A German-born midget who stood three feet, nine inches when he portrayed the rotund Munchkin Mayor, Becker didn't aspire to be a performer. As a youth he was trained by his father to be a butcher. The task was difficult for him because of his size—he could barely wield the cleavers and butchers' knives. Discouraged, Charley eventually joined Leo Singer's troupe of European midgets and came to America for wider opportunities. He never looked back.

Months before *Oz*, Becker portrayed a chef, complete with white apron and little chef's hat, in the all-midget musical western film, *The Terror of Tiny Town*. In the bizarre flick, which has become a cult classic, Becker spastically chases around a sly goose he's trying to prepare for dinner. (In fact, he has a dual role, also portraying a whiskered musician in the saloon musical numbers.)

"Charley cooked for everybody in the whole troupe," says Karl Slover, the last surviving member of the famed Singer Midgets. "When we'd be traveling, he would fix fried chicken, cucumber salad, and he'd put it in a cooler and we'd have it over the run, on the train. He made stews and goulash. Mostly we'd have breakfast in the hotels, in his room. Whatever he fixed was pretty good.

"Sometimes for dinner, he'd cook at the theatre," recalls Slover. "He'd get a big dressing room where he could cook. He had pots and pans that he brought along. When we would first get into a town, say in New York, he'd invite newspaper men and he'd cook for maybe twenty or thirty newspaper men at the theatre."

Although there have been more than a few reported little impostors who claimed to be the Mayor of Munchkinland in *The Wizard of Oz*, only one man bore the oversized pocketwatch and welcomed Dorothy with such glee. Charley Becker retired from show business when Singer Midgets disbanded in the 1940s; he died in Sacramento, California, on December 28, 1968, at age eighty.

Charley and Jessie Becker in their Wichita, Kansas, home in 1962. Inset: Jessie Kelley Becker in Munchkin wardrobe. (Courtesy of Margaret Pellegrini)

Some of the Singer Midgets troupe out for beer and pretzels with one of their managers in 1929. Charley Becker (in glasses) was the superb cook of the bunch. (Nita Krebs Collection)

The Munchkins are snappin', cracklin', and poppin' with the famous Kellogg's mascots during a 1995 promotion at the company's home offices and plant in Battle Creek, Michigan. From left: Margaret Pellegrini, Lewis Croft, Clarence Swensen, Jerry Maren, and Meinhardt Raabe. (Courtesy of Lewis Croft)

CHICKEN AND DRESSING CASSEROLE

1　frying chicken (or 2 cups cooked turkey)
　　Salt to taste
1　cup sour cream
1　10¾-ounce can condensed cream of
　　mushroom soup
½　teaspoon poultry seasoning
½　cup melted butter
1　6-ounce bag corn bread stuffing mix

In a large saucepan or Dutch oven cook the chicken in lightly salted water to barely cover until tender, about 35 minutes.

　　Remove the chicken from the broth, reserving 1 cup for later use. Cool the chick-en. Break apart into bite-size pieces and discard skin and bones. Grease a 9 x 13-inch casserole dish. Place the chicken pieces in an even layer over the bottom of the prepared dish. In a small bowl blend the sour cream, soup, and poultry seasoning together and pour over chicken. In a medium bowl stir together the chicken broth, butter, and dressing mix. Spoon over the sour cream layer. Bake uncovered at 350° for 30 minutes.

MAKES 6 SERVINGS.

—MYRNA AND CLARENCE SWENSON,
Munchkin in *Oz*, MGM

CHICKEN AND RICE

1   10½-ounce can onion soup
1   10½-ounce can cream of mushroom soup
1   soup can water
1   6¾-ounce package original wild rice (uncooked)
1   chicken, cut into pieces (or 3 to 4 chicken breasts)
    Salt and pepper to taste

In a large bowl combine the soups, water, and rice mix. Spread the mixture into a 2½-quart baking dish. Season the chicken pieces and place them on top of the rice mixture. Cover. Bake at 350° for 1 hour and 15 minutes to 2 hours.

MAKES 6 SERVINGS.

—PATTY MALONEY, Munchkin in
Under the Rainbow

CHICKEN BÉARNAISE

¼   cup olive oil
6   skinless boneless chicken breasts
1   cup sliced mushrooms
24 sun-dried tomatoes
½   cup white wine (optional)
1   package Knorr Béarnaise sauce mix
2   tablespoons chopped fresh basil

In a large skillet heat the olive oil over medium heat. Fry the chicken breasts until golden brown on both sides. Lower the heat and add the mushrooms and sun-dried tomatoes. Cover and steam until the mushrooms are done. Add white wine if desired.

Prepare the Knorr Béarnaise sauce according to the package directions. Place the chicken in a serving dish and ladle on the sauce. Top with chopped basil and serve.

Serving suggestion: Delicious served with asparagus and any type of rice dish.

MAKES 6 SERVINGS.

—ELAINE WILLINGHAM

Under the Rainbow, *a 1981 film, was a wild parody about the little people's legendary behind-the-scenes mischief.*

CHICKEN KIEV

1   cup butter, softened (or margarine)
1   clove garlic, crushed
½   teaspoon chopped rosemary
1   tablespoon minced parsley
1   tablespoon finely chopped chives
1   teaspoon Worcestershire sauce
½   teaspoon salt
⅛   teaspoon pepper
3   large whole chicken breasts, with small
     wing bones attached
½   cup all-purpose flour
2   eggs, beaten
2   cups fine soft breadcrumbs
     Vegetable oil
     Parsley for garnish (or watercress)

In a medium bowl blend together the butter, garlic, rosemary, parsley, chives, Worcestershire sauce, salt, and pepper. Form into a 6-inch roll. Wrap in waxed paper and chill until firm.

Cut the chicken breasts in half. Bone each portion, leaving the wing bone attached. Pound the chicken breasts to flatten to ¼-inch thickness. Divide the chilled butter-and-seasonings roll into 6 equal portions. Center a portion on each breast half. Tuck the ends in and roll up tightly, letting the wing bone protrude. Fasten with skewers or string. Dredge the rolls in flour. Dip in beaten egg, then in breadcrumbs. In a large skillet fry the chicken rolls in 2 inches of hot oil for about 12 minutes, turning occasionally. Drain on paper towels. Garnish with parsley or watercress.

MAKES 6 SERVINGS.

—FLORENCE BAUM HURST, granddaughter
of L. Frank Baum

CHICKEN TANDOORI

5   skinless boneless chicken breasts
     Canola oil
1   cup cooked rice
2   tomatoes, chopped
2   green bell peppers, chopped
2   onions, chopped

A rare family snapshot of a frail L. Frank Baum, near the end of his life, at the dinner table with his family, circa 1917. (Robert A. Baum Collection)

Salt to taste
2   tablespoons curry powder
1   tablespoon cumin
½   teaspoon ground cinnamon
½   teaspoon garlic powder
2   cups water
Peanuts for garnish (or coconut)

Cut the chicken into 1-inch pieces. In a large sauté pan cook the chicken in oil until almost done. In a large mixing bowl combine the chicken with the rice, tomatoes, peppers, onions, seasonings, and water. Grease a 2½-quart baking dish and ladle in the chicken-rice mixture. Bake at 375° for 50 minutes. Serve with peanuts or coconut sprinkled over the top.

Note: You can prepare this dish in a microwave. It saves time and is just as delicious.

—JUNE FORAY, voice of Dorothy in
Off to See the Wizard

Chinese Chicken Salad

3   3-ounce packages Top Ramen Noodles (oriental chicken flavor)
1   12-ounce can Valley Fresh chicken in broth (or 2 chicken breasts, cooked & shredded)
6   green onions, chopped
1   16-ounce package salad greens (lettuce and cabbage)
½   cup plus 2 tablespoons water
½   cup plus 2 tablespoons salad oil
¼   cup sugar
½   cup plus 2 tablespoons Nakano seasoned salad rice vinegar
2   ounces slivered almonds
1   tablespoon sesame seeds

Off to See the Wizard *was a short-lived ABC-TV prime-time series that featured animated* Oz *characters introducing children's stories, nature documentaries, and family movies (*Flipper, Clarence the Cross-Eyed Lion, *and* The Adventures of Huckleberry Finn *among them). Produced by MGM Television, the animated segments were handled by legendary cartoon king Chuck Jones. Versatile voice actress June Foray (Natasha, Rocky the Squirrel) provided the voice of Dorothy. For such a brief broadcast history (one prime-time season), the series spawned a broad and imaginative line of beautifully designed merchandise for kids, including an* Off to See the Wizard *playset, paint-by-numbers set, magic slate, talking glove puppet, Colorforms Kit, stuffed doll, and Scarecrow-in-the-Box.*

In a large bowl break the noodles. Add the chicken, green onions, and salad mixture. Mix all ingredients.

In a medium bowl prepare the dressing by combining the water, salad oil, sugar, and vinegar. Pour the dressing over the salad mixture. Cover and let stand in the refrigerator for 4 hours.

Add the almonds and sesame seeds before serving. Serve with hot rolls or bread.

Makes 8 servings.

—CHARLENE AND ROGER BAUM, great-grandson of L. Frank Baum; author of several *Oz* books

DANNY KAYE'S CHINESE STIR-FRY OYSTERS AND SHRIMP

Note: *The success of this dish depends on the skill and speed of the chef! For this reason, have everything prepared prior to cooking. Do not overcook oysters or shrimp.*

1   cup raw oysters
¼   cup all-purpose flour
         Water
½   pound shrimp, shelled and deveined
1   2-inch piece fresh gingerroot, peeled and finely shredded
5   scallions, trimmed and cut into 2-inch lengths
1   teaspoon light soy sauce
1   teaspoon sesame oil
         Salt and pepper to taste
4½   teaspoons cornstarch
2   tablespoons cold water (more if needed)
2   tablespoons peanut oil (or vegetable oil)

In a medium mixing bowl combine the oysters, flour, and enough water to cover. (Flour will cleanse and plump oysters.) Stir the oysters in the liquid. Drain well, then run under several changes of cold water. Drain well again.

In a small saucepan heat water to a simmer and drop in the oysters carefully. Turn off the heat and let stand 1 minute. Drain and set aside in a small bowl. Again heat water to a simmer and repeat with shrimp, placing them in another small bowl, and set them aside.

In a small bowl place the ginger and scallions. In another small bowl combine the soy sauce, sesame oil, and salt and pepper.

In a final small bowl combine the cornstarch and cold water and set aside. Heat peanut oil in a medium wok (or skillet) over high heat. Add the ginger and scallions. Cook, stirring, 5 seconds. Add the oysters and shrimp, stirring rapidly. Cook 15 seconds. Add the soy sauce mixture, stirring constantly. Stir the cornstarch paste into the wok or skillet. Cook 12 seconds. Serve at once.

This was one of Danny Kaye's favorites.

MAKES 8 SERVINGS.

—DANNY KAYE, host for CBS telecasts of *The Wizard of Oz,* 1960s

DANNY THOMAS'S LAMB PIES

1   ¼-ounce package active dry yeast
         Dash sugar
2½   cups lukewarm water, or more
8   cups all-purpose flour
1   tablespoon salt
3   tablespoons olive oil
3   pounds ground lean lamb
4   medium onions, minced
⅔   cup yogurt
⅔   cup fresh lemon juice
¾   cup pine nuts, sautéed lightly in butter
2   teaspoons salt
¼   teaspoon freshly ground pepper
         Dash allspice

In a small bowl sprinkle the yeast and sugar over ½ cup of the lukewarm water. Stir until dissolved. Set aside for 5 minutes. In a large bowl mix the flour and salt. Make a well in the center. Add the yeast mixture, olive oil, and remaining water. Mix well, adding more water or flour if needed. The dough should be rather stiff. On a lightly floured surface knead the dough until smooth and elastic. Oil the inside surface of a large bowl. Place the dough in the bowl, then turn over dough to oil all sides and cover with damp towel. Let rise in warm place until doubled in bulk, about 1 hour and 30 minutes.

While the dough is rising prepare the lamb filling. In a large bowl combine the ground lamb, onions, yogurt, lemon juice, pine nuts, seasonings, and spice. Chill for the remaining time while the dough is rising.

Divide the risen dough into four parts. On a lightly floured board roll out each part until it is about ⅛ inch thick. Cut the dough into 3-inch rounds. Place a heaping tablespoon of lamb filling in the center of each round. Wet the edge of the dough with water, bring the dough up over meat filling, and pinch the edges together to form a triangle. Leave a small opening on top. Oil foil-lined baking sheets. Place the meat pies on the sheets. Brush the pie tops with oil. Bake at 375° for 40 minutes or until golden brown. Serve warm.

Note: The dough may be re-rolled if it's first allowed to rise again. If there is any lamb filling left, shape into balls and brown in butter or vegetable oil.

This was one of comedian Danny Thomas's specialties.

MAKES 6½ DOZEN.

—**DANNY THOMAS, voice of the Tin Man**
in the animated *Journey Back to Oz*

Danny Kaye loved The Wizard of Oz *and adored fellow entertainer Judy Garland even more. Kaye hosted "wrap-around" segments for CBS's 1964–1967 telecasts of the movie.*

DOROTHY AND BUDDY'S CABBAGE ROLLS

1	pound ground veal
½	cup cooked rice
1	small onion, finely chopped
2	tablespoons breadcrumbs
1	egg, beaten with a little milk
1	teaspoon ground marjoram
½	teaspoon ground oregano
3	teaspoons chopped parsley
2	teaspoons paprika
	Salt and pepper to taste
1	large green cabbage
1	jar sauerkraut, drained and rinsed
2	tablespoons caraway seeds
2	whole bay leaves
1	instant chicken bouillon cube
1½	cups hot water
1	tablespoon oil
1	tablespoon all-purpose flour
1	16-ounce can tomato sauce
1	tablespoon sugar
2	Hungarian smoked sausages
1	8-ounce carton whipping cream

In a medium bowl combine the veal, rice, onion, breadcrumbs, egg, marjoram, oregano, parsley, paprika, salt, and pepper. Mix together with hands so everything is smooth. Set aside.

In a large saucepan of boiling water plunge the head of cabbage so the leaves become soft but do not break. Remove from the pan and separate the leaves, cutting out the thick membrane at the base of each leaf. Have 10 to 12 leaves ready to stuff. If necessary, plunge the cabbage again in boiling water to loosen the leaves. Place about a tablespoonful of filling at the base of each cabbage leaf and tucking sides in, begin to roll. Set on a platter.

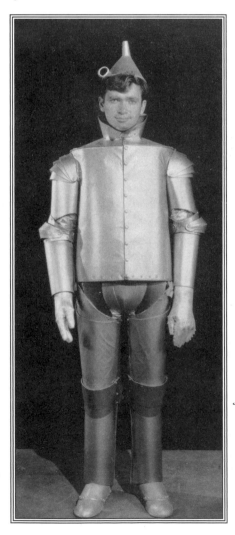

EXITUS OZIMUS This rare costume test photo of Buddy Ebsen as the Tin Man hardly reflects the horror he experienced. In an October 26, 1938, newspaper column, Hedda Hopper described the original Tin Man's toil: ". . . Buddy Ebsen as the Tin Man really had the miseries. His hair was completely covered with a silver cap. Over his face is a layer of soft wax, sprinkled with a half a pound of silver dust, and he has a stationary chin strap from ear to ear. He relaxes against a huge leaning board with rests for his arms— supposed to ease the burden of cumbersome pants, which flare up in front like hoops of steel and prevent him from sitting." During a few weeks of filming, Ebsen ingested a damaging amount of the pure aluminum dust that was repeatedly powdered over his face, which landed him in the hospital; he was replaced by Jack Haley, whose silver makeup was altered to an aluminum paste. (Photo courtesy of Eric Daily Collection)

The remaining cabbage is to be chopped and mixed with the sauerkraut. In the bottom of a large Dutch oven place the sauerkraut mixture, caraway seeds, and bay leaves. Place the cabbage rolls on top. Dilute the chicken bouillon in 1 cup of hot water and pour over the cabbage rolls. Cover and simmer for 45 minutes. Make sure the juice almost covers the rolls.

While the rolls are simmering prepare the sauce. In a small saucepan heat the oil. Add the flour and stir. When the flour starts to brown, add ½ cup of hot water, the tomato sauce, and sugar. Mix well and set aside.

When the cabbage rolls have simmered for 45 minutes, pour the sauce over the rolls and cook for about 20 minutes longer. Cut sausages 3 to 4 inches in length and place on top of the cabbage rolls. Cook a little longer, so the sausages are hot. Then take out a little juice and mix with cream. Pour over the rolls and heat up again.

This is a wonderful dish to prepare one day before serving. Excellent served with boiled potatoes. Guten Appetit!

MAKES 10 TO 12 ROLLS.

—DOROTHY AND BUDDY EBSEN,
original Tin Man in MGM's *Oz*

Buddy Ebsen, Bert Lahr, and Ray Bolger emerge from a rehearsal stage for a newsreel story in 1938. (Courtesy of Buddy Ebsen; Photo by Gabi Rona)

EMERALD CITY CHICKEN CHESAPEAKE

4	boneless chicken breasts
¼	cup all-purpose flour
½	cup butter, divided (or margarine)
1	clove garlic, minced
2	cups fresh spinach, washed and chopped
8	ounces fresh mushrooms, sliced
1	cup crabmeat (6 ounces)
4	to 6 slices mozzarella cheese

Pound the chicken breasts flat with a meat mallet and lightly flour. In a large skillet melt ¼ cup of butter and sauté the chicken breasts for about 4 minutes or until nicely browned. Remove from the skillet and place in an 8-inch square baking dish. Set aside. Add the remaining butter to the skillet and sauté the garlic, spinach, and mushrooms for 3 to 5 minutes. Remove from the heat. Top the chicken with crabmeat. Cover the crabmeat with the spinach mixture and top with mozzarella cheese slices. Bake at 400° for 7 to 8 minutes.

MAKES 4 SERVINGS.

—KEN FORD

EUROPEAN MEATBALLS

(WITH OR WITHOUT TOMATO SAUCE)

1	tablespoon butter
1	cup chopped onion
2	pounds ground beef
2	eggs, beaten
2	cups soft breadcrumbs
3	tablespoons chopped parsley
3	tablespoons chopped mint leaves
1	tablespoon salt
½	teaspoon pepper
1	cup all-purpose flour
1	cup oil

In a small sauté pan melt 1 tablespoon of butter and fry the onion until golden brown. Remove to a large mixing bowl. Add the ground beef, eggs, breadcrumbs, parsley, mint leaves, salt, and pepper. Mix well by hand. Roll the meat mixture into balls about the size of an egg and roll lightly in flour. In a large skillet in very hot oil fry the meatballs until brown. Do not fry more than 10 to 12 meatballs at a time.

Can be served as is with a salad or in Tomato Sauce (recipe follows).

TOMATO SAUCE

3	tablespoons butter
½	cup chopped onion
1	6-ounce can tomato purée
1	cup water
1	teaspoon dried parsley flakes
1	teaspoon sugar
1	bay leaf
	Dash ground cinnamon
	Salt and pepper to taste

In a medium saucepan heat the butter and sauté the onion until tender. Add the tomato purée, water, parsley flakes, sugar, bay leaf, cinnamon, salt, and pepper. Simmer for 10 to 15 minutes or until thickened. Serve over meatballs.

MAKES 4 TO 6 SERVINGS.

—FELIX SILLA, Munchkin in
Under the Rainbow

Gene's Greens

I have a picture in my manager's office of Ray Bolger and me on the set of Fame. *I remember [Bolger] was impressed that I was playing the Scarecrow. The executive producer on the show invited him to watch the number that I did and he loved it; he went around and met everybody on the show. It was great. That was one of my favorite episodes. We were filming our show at MGM's soundstages because it was an MGM show, which is now the Sony lot. We were on the soundstages where they filmed some of* The Wizard of Oz, *so it was spectacular to redo* Oz *right there.*

2	smoked turkey legs
1	green bell pepper
1	red pepper
1	onion
4	bunches collard greens or 5 bunches mustard greens
	Seasoned salt to taste
	Salt to taste
⅓	cup vinegar

Place the turkey legs in a pot filled halfway with water and bring to a boil. Boil for about 45 minutes.

Finely dice the green pepper, red pepper, and onion. Wash the greens, stack, and chop them. Add the greens, peppers, and onion, seasoned salt, salt, and vinegar to the pot and simmer for about 1 hour. Serve in a bowl.

—GENE ANTHONY RAY, cast of TV's *Fame*

Ray Bolger dropped by the set of the TV drama Fame *and thrilled the cast when they filmed an Oz-themed episode, January 1983. Here, Bolger poses with dancer Gene Anthony Ray, who wore the straw in the episode.*

Glinda's Good Sandwitch

1	1- or 2-pound round rye bread loaf (whole unsliced)
	Sandwich spreads (horseradish sauce, Dijon mustard, mayonnaise, etc.)
	Pickle relish, well drained
	Variety of deli-style lunch meats (turkey, salami, corned beef, etc.)
	Variety of cheeses (Swiss, Monterey Jack, Colby, etc.)

Cut the bread horizontally, making 4 or 5 round slices. Beginning with the bottom slice, spread with a selected spread, sprinkle with pickle relish, then layer with meat and cheese. Spread the bottom of the next slice with another spread and lay on top of cheese. Continue spreading and alternating until all bread slices are used.

Wrap in foil and refrigerate overnight before slicing to serve.

Makes 6 to 8 servings.

—BLANCHE COX

Baum's Paradise: The Hotel del Coronado

Although L. Frank Baum spent many years in the East and the Midwest, he preferred to winter in the warm and welcoming sunshine of Coronado, California, a picturesque community on the Pacific Coast, just across the bay from San Diego. In 1904, during Baum's first visit, he stayed at the Hotel del Coronado, which was then—and still is today—a magnificent turn-of-the-century seaside resort. Between 1904 and 1910, Baum traveled to Coronado repeatedly, where he usually resided at the hotel for months at a time, although in later years he and his wife, Maud, rented a house nearby.

According to the heritage department at the Hotel del Coronado, a local newspaper article published during those years reported, ". . . the noted author has long ago discovered that he can do his best work in the sunny clime of Coronado." The article went on to reveal Baum's habit of working from early morning until noon. "In the afternoon he generally spends in realizing that he is truly again in Coronado."

Baum's love of the Southern California paradise ran deep. In a poem about Coronado ("scratched off," Baum said, in a half-hour while he and his wife were waiting for some dinner companions to arrive), he wrote: "and every day her loveliness / shines pure, without a flaw / new charms entrance our every glance / and fill our souls with awe!" So inspired, Baum wrote four books in the *Oz* series during his years in Coronado: *Marvelous Land of Oz* (1904), *Dorothy and the Wizard of Oz* (1908), *The Road to Oz* (1909), and *The Emerald City* (1910).

Today, the historic Hotel del Coronado still stands as a beach-lover's vacation haven. The hotel's unique design has been the backdrop for many films and television programs over the decades, most notably in the Marilyn Monroe/Jack Lemmon/Tony Curtis classic film, *Some Like It Hot* (1959).

Even today, the hotel pays tribute to Baum in its History Gallery display. Says Christine Donovan, director of the hotel's heritage department, "It's impossible to explain the del's history without mentioning L. Frank Baum. Not only is he a respected author, directly tied to our establishment, but he actually designed the crown-shaped chandeliers in our main dining room. "According to Donovan, Baum was critical of the hotel's original lighting fixtures, deciding that they were not grand enough for the Crown Room's extraordinary ambiance and imposing proportions. Baum offered to design new chandeliers, which remain a prominent feature in the dining room to this day. (Baum used a crown motif as a tribute to *Coronado*, which actually means "the crowned one.")

Although some scribes have assumed that the author based his description of Emerald City on the Hotel del Coronado, Baum had already created his fictitious fantasy setting years before visiting the hotel. Still, one can see why he found the hotel so entrancing. With its whimsical design, fanciful red roofs, magical spires, and unusual setting, the del is as close to Emerald City as one can get.

GRILLED SWORDFISH

Dressing:
2	cloves garlic, minced
1	shallot, minced
½	lemon, juiced
3	tablespoons Balsamic vinaigrette
½	cup olive oil
	Salt and pepper to taste

3	ounces mixed greens
3	wedges vine-ripe tomatoes
3	wedges red baby potatoes
1	hard-boiled egg, cut in half
2	ounces Kalamata olives
4	spears blanched asparagus
1	6-ounce fillet grilled swordfish loin

In a medium bowl combine the garlic, shallot, lemon juice, vinaigrette, olive oil, salt, and pepper. Whisk until blended.

Arrange the mixed greens and all other items on a plate, and add dressing.

MAKES 1 SERVING.

—HOTEL DEL CORONADO, courtesy
Joseph Giunta, Executive Chef

This photograph of the Hotel del Coronado's beautiful Crown Room shows the opulence of L. Frank Baum's favorite retreat. Note the crown-shaped chandeliers that Baum himself designed for the hotel.

HALEY'S SHEPHERD'S PIE

3	pounds potatoes, peeled and cubed
½	cup 1% milk
2	tablespoons butter, melted (or margarine)
¼	cup chopped fresh parsley
½	teaspoon ground black pepper
3	pounds extra-lean ground beef (or lamb)
1	clove garlic, pressed or minced
4	tablespoons butter (or oil)
6	large carrots, chopped
8	ounces mushrooms, chopped
2	onions, chopped
1	tablespoon chopped fresh thyme leaves (or 1 teaspoon dried)
2	tablespoons all-purpose flour
2	cups chicken broth
2	10-ounce packages frozen corn, thawed

In a large saucepan cover the potatoes with water. Bring to a boil and then reduce to a simmer. Cover and cook for 25 minutes or until the potatoes can easily be pierced with a fork. Drain and return to the saucepan. Add the milk, 2 tablespoons of butter, parsley, and ¼ teaspoon of pepper. Mash with a potato masher or electric mixer. Set aside.

In a large nonstick skillet over medium-high heat cook the beef and garlic, stirring frequently, until the beef is no longer pink. Remove the meat mixture to a bowl. Set aside.

In the skillet heat 2 tablespoons butter or oil over medium heat. Add the carrots, mushrooms, and onions. Cook, stirring frequently, until the carrots can easily be pierced with a fork. Stir in the thyme and remaining ¼ teaspoon of pepper. (Any leftover vegetables, such as string beans, peas, etc., can be added if desired.)

Place the flour in a small bowl. Gradually add the broth, whisking until smooth. Add to the skillet and mix well. Bring to a boil, stirring frequently. Reduce the heat and simmer, stirring occasionally, for 10 minutes or until slightly thickened.

Add the corn and reserved meat mixture. Stir to mix well.

Coat a 2-quart (or larger) baking dish with nonstick spray. Spread the beef and vegetable mixture in the prepared baking dish. Cover entire top with the mashed potatoes. Bake at 375° for 30 minutes or until bubbly and the potatoes are golden.

MAKES 8 SERVINGS.

—GLORIA HALEY, daughter of Jack Haley

"Why, my little party's just beginning!" Family gathers 'round for papa Jack Haley's seventy-ninth birthday in August 1977, with son Jack Jr., daughter Gloria Haley Parnassus, and Mrs. Florence Haley. (Courtesy of Haley Estate)

HAM-STUFFED PORK CHOPS

1	cup chopped cooked ham
3	cups fresh breadcrumbs
1	egg, beaten
1	teaspoon salt
⅛	teaspoon pepper
¼	teaspoon grated nutmeg
1	10½-ounce can beef broth, divided
6	1½-inch-thick pork chops, with pocket cut in each
¼	teaspoon ground sage
¼	teaspoon dried thyme
	Salad oil
	Water
2	tablespoons cornstarch

In a medium bowl prepare the stuffing by thoroughly combining the ham, breadcrumbs, egg, salt, pepper, nutmeg, and ½ cup of beef broth. Trim the pork chops of excess fat, and rub with additional salt, sage, and thyme. Fill the pockets with stuffing. Brush on all sides with oil. Place side by side in a large baking pan. Bake uncovered at 450° for about 30 minutes or until browned, turning them once.

Reduce heat to 400°. Remove the chops from the oven and drain off the excess fat. Mix 1 cup of water with the remaining beef broth. Pour this around the chops. Cover the pan with aluminum foil. Bake an additional 50 to 60 minutes or until the chops are tender. Arrange the chops on a serving platter and keep warm.

In a small saucepan combine the cornstarch with ¼ cup of water, stirring until smooth. Add the gravy from the baking pan and stir over medium heat, bringing quickly to a boil. Pour the gravy around the chops or pass in a gravy boat.

MAKES 6 SERVINGS.

HOT CHEESE ENCHILADAS

For those with a cast-iron constitution.

20	red pasilla peppers
1½	cups water
4	cloves garlic
1	teaspoon cumin
1	teaspoon salt
1	tablespoon all-purpose flour
	Corn oil
24	small (or medium) corn tortillas
½	medium onion, chopped
½	bell pepper, chopped
¼	cup sliced black olives
½	cup diced tomatoes
1	pound Monterey Jack cheese, grated

Remove the stems and seeds from peppers and rinse with water. In a small saucepan boil the peppers in water for 15 minutes, then set aside, and allow to cool slightly. In a blender combine the undrained peppers, garlic, cumin, and salt. Blend until liquefied. Blend in the flour.

In a small saucepan heat 2 tablespoons of corn oil over medium heat. Add the pepper mixture and stir until heated through. Set aside. In another small saucepan pour oil ½ inch deep and heat until warm. Remove from the heat. Lightly dip each tortilla in the oil, then in the pasilla mixture, coating both sides well. Stuff with onions, bell peppers, olives, and tomatoes (or fillings of your choice). Roll and place on a flat baking pan (or in a slow cooker). Top with grated cheese. Bake at 350° until the cheese is melted.

MAKES 6 SERVINGS.

—HAL RAYLE, voice of Tin Man
in DIC *Oz* cartoon series

Bon Voy-oz! Advertising for the first prime-time television broadcast (November 3, 1956) on CBS . . .

HUNK'S HAWAIIAN SANDWICH

2	8-ounce packages cream cheese
1	16-ounce can unsweetened crushed pineapple, undrained
1	loaf King's Hawaiian bread
¾	pound honey-roast sliced ham
¾	pound honey-smoked sliced turkey
4	chopped green onions

In a medium mixing bowl place the cream cheese. Add the canned pineapple and mix well. Slice the Hawaiian bread horizontally into three or four layers. Beginning with the bottom slice, spread each slice with the cream cheese mixture and alternate layers of ham and turkey. Sprinkle each layer with green onions as you reassemble the layers. Chill for 1 hour in the refrigerator. Cut into wedges and serve.

Serving suggestion: Fried sliced bananas are great on the side!

—ELAINE WILLINGHAM

"IF I ONLY HAD A BRAIN" SANDWICH

½	pound brains, washed
	Vegetable oil or butter for frying
4	eggs, scrambled
	Salt and pepper to taste

In a large pot cover the brains with salted water. Bring to a boil and cook until done. Cool slightly and remove the membrane. Chop in small pieces. In a skillet heat a small amount of oil and brown the brains lightly. Add the scrambled eggs and heat through. Serve on toast.

MAKES 2 SERVINGS.

—ANN AND JOHN VENARDOS

. . . and the final network broadcast (May 8, 1998) on CBS.

JUDY GARLAND'S SHEPHERD'S PIE SUPREME

This was one of Judy Garland's specialties. She described it once in a newspaper article, saying: "It's beautiful. . . . It comes out looking like a birthday cake, all fluffy and delicious. Be sure to give yourself lots of time."

5	pounds leg of lamb, bone in
2	large chicken breasts (1¾ pounds)
1	10¾-ounce can chicken broth
1	10¾-ounce can beef broth
3	tablespoons minced fresh dill
½	teaspoon salt
⅛	teaspoon freshly ground pepper
1	10½-ounce can cream of mushroom soup
2	teaspoons Worcestershire sauce
½	teaspoon onion juice
1	cup water
½	cup milk
2	tablespoons butter
2½	cups instant potato flakes
1	cup sour cream
1	tablespoon minced chives
½	teaspoon caraway seeds (or sesame seeds)
	Salt and freshly ground pepper to taste

Judy Garland is caught sneakin' a snack out of the "fridge" at her home on Stone Canyon Drive—the residence she lived in while making The Wizard of Oz, *circa November 1939. (Beyond the Rainbow Archive)*

In a roasting pan with a rack place the leg of lamb. Insert a meat thermometer, being careful not to touch the bone. Roast uncovered in a 300° oven for 2 hours and 15 minutes or until a meat thermometer registers 170° for rare meat. Cool slightly. Trim and discard the outer skin, fat, and cartilage. Grind the meat, using the coarse blade of the meat grinder.

While the lamb is roasting, prepare the chicken. In a medium saucepan cover the chicken with the chicken and beef broths. Cover and simmer for about 45 minutes or until tender. Cool on a plate. Reserve the stock to be divided later. Skin and debone the cooled chicken. Grind the chicken meat through the coarse blade of the meat grinder.

In a large mixing bowl combine the ground lamb and chicken meats, dill, salt, and pepper. Mix well with hands. In a small bowl combine the mushroom soup with 1 cup of the reserved chicken stock, Worcestershire sauce, and onion juice. Combine with the meat mixture and mix well. Butter two 2-quart casserole dishes. Press half the meat mixture into each dish.

In a medium saucepan combine the water and 1 cup of the remaining reserved stock. Heat until boiling. Remove from heat.

Add the milk and butter. Stir in the potato flakes, beating until light and fluffy. Add the sour cream, chives, caraway seeds, salt, and pepper. Blend well. Top the meat in each casserole with the whipped potato mixture. Bake at 450° for 20 to 25 minutes. Place under the broiler to brown. Reserve the second casserole for encores, or cover tightly and freeze.

EACH CASSEROLE MAKES 8 TO 12 SERVINGS.

—JUDY GARLAND, contributed by
her son, Joe Luft

Young Judy Garland celebrates her thirteenth birthday in this rare candid photo. (Beyond the Rainbow Archive)

KING RANCH CHICKEN

2   chickens
1   10½-ounce can cream of mushroom soup
1   10½-ounce can cream of chicken soup
1   10-ounce can Rotel tomatoes
20 tortillas
1   cup chopped onion
1   green bell pepper, chopped
    Dashes of salt, pepper, garlic salt, and chili powder
2   cups grated cheese

In a large Dutch oven boil the chickens in enough water to almost cover. Cook until tender. Remove the chickens from the broth and place on a platter to cool. Reserve the broth. When the chickens are cool enough to handle, skin and debone them. Chop the meat.

In a small bowl combine both soups and stir in the Rotel tomatoes.

Coat a 13 x 9-inch pan with nonstick spray. Wilt the tortillas in the reserved broth. In the prepared pan layer the tortillas, chicken, soup mixture, onions, green pepper, seasonings, and grated cheese. Repeat layers, ending with cheese. Sprinkle the top with chili powder. Bake at 350° for 30 minutes.

MAKES 8 TO 10 SERVINGS.

—MYRNA AND CLARENCE SWENSEN,
Munchkin in *Oz*, MGM

LITTLE OSCAR'S PINEAPPLE HAM "BURGER"

8   slices canned pineapple, drained
1   pound cooked ham, ground
4   maraschino cherries

Coat an 8-inch square baking pan with non-stick spray. In the prepared pan place a layer of 4 pineapple slices. Divide the ground ham into four portions. Shape each portion into a patty about the same size as a ring of pineapple. Place a patty on top of each pineapple ring. Press down in the center of each patty slightly to anchor inside each pineapple ring hole. Top with another pineapple ring, pressing down just enough for a small portion of ground ham to ooze up into the top hole of the pineapple. Bake at 300° just long enough to warm the ham and brown the pineapple around the edges. Place a cherry on top.

Makes 4 servings.

—MEINHARDT RAABE, coroner Munchkin in *Oz,* MGM

Meinhardt Raabe as "Little Oscar" and his wife, Marie, demonstrating in-store food preparations along with "Teddy Snow Crop" in the 1950s. (Tod Machin Collection)

Munchkins Gus Wayne, Margaret Pellegrini, and Fern Formica promoting the "Munchkin" donut holes at Dunkin' Donuts in 1989.

MARGARET'S DOWN HOME CHICKEN AND DUMPLINGS

1   plump hen, cut up
       Salt and pepper to taste
2   cups sifted all-purpose flour
2   teaspoons baking powder
1   teaspoon salt
¼   cup cold shortening
⅔   cup cold milk
1   tablespoon butter
¼   cup all-purpose flour
½   cup milk

In a large pot simmer the chicken pieces in seasoned water until the chicken is tender. While the chicken cooks prepare the dumpling batter. In a large bowl sift 2 cups of flour, the baking powder, and salt together. Cut in the shortening with 2 knives or a pastry blender. Add ⅔ cup of milk and mix quickly. Knead for a few seconds on a lightly floured board. Pat out into ½-inch thickness and sprinkle with pepper. Cut into strips about 1 inch wide.

When the chicken is tender add the butter. Drop the dumpling strips over the chicken in a crisscross pattern. Cover the pot tightly and simmer for 12 minutes without peeking (steam pressure makes the dumplings tender and fluffy). Open the pot and lift out the dumplings and chicken pieces.

In a small cup or bowl place ¼ cup of flour and gradually stir in ½ cup of milk a little at a time until a smooth paste is formed. Then combine a small portion of the hot chicken stock to the paste to prevent lumping. Then combine the paste with the hot broth in the saucepan and heat, stirring until mixture thickens. Serve over the chicken and dumplings.

MAKES 4 TO 6 SERVINGS.

—MARGARET PELLEGRINI, Munchkin
in *Oz*, MGM

MEXICAN CHICKEN ROLLS

½　cup dry breadcrumbs
¼　cup gated Parmesan cheese
1　teaspoon chili powder
¼　teaspoon ground cumin
¼　teaspoon pepper
8　skinless boneless chicken breast halves
1　8-ounce package Monterey Jack cheese with peppers
⅓　cup butter, melted (or margarine)
1　jar salsa
1　envelope dry taco seasoning

In a shallow dish combine the breadcrumbs, Parmesan cheese, and seasonings. Set aside.

Place each chicken breast between 2 sheets of plastic wrap. Using a meat mallet (or rolling pin) flatten each to ¼-inch thickness. Divide the package of cheese slices in half crosswise to make 8 equal slices. Place one slice on top of each flattened chicken breast and roll up from the short side. Secure each roll with wooden picks. Lightly grease an 11 x 7 x 1½-inch baking pan. Dip the rolls in butter and dredge in the breadcrumb mixture. Place the rolls seam side down on the prepared pan. Bake at 400° for 30 minutes.

In a small saucepan mix together the salsa and taco seasoning mix. Heat through and pour on top of the chicken breasts.

MAKES 8 SERVINGS.

—RAMONA SMITH THOMPSON

INTERNATIONAL FLAVOR A vintage Mexican lobby card for El Mago de Oz, *circa 1939. (Eric Daily Collection)*

The cast of TV's Fame *staged a fantasy segment that paid tribute to Oz in the episode "Not in Kansas Anymore" (1983).*

MUSTARD CHICKEN

2   cut-up chickens
    Seasoned salt to taste
    Garlic salt to taste
    Pepper to taste
    Paprika
16 pats of butter
4   tablespoons Grey Poupon mustard
1   cup water

Cover a baking pan completely with aluminum foil. Place the chicken on the foil in the baking pan and season with seasoned salt, garlic salt, pepper, and paprika. (Cover the chicken thoroughly with paprika, making it red.) Place a pat of butter on each piece of chicken.

In a bowl mix the mustard and water to make a pourable sauce. Pour over the chicken, covering well. Cover the entire pan with another piece of foil and vent by poking holes in the foil. Bake at 350° for about 45 minutes.

Remove the foil on top. Baste with some of the sauce and bake an additional 20 minutes. Should be brown and crispy.

MAKES ABOUT 8 SERVINGS.

—GENE ANTHONY RAY, cast of TV's *Fame*

OXTAILS EN CHILE COLORADO WITH TORTAS DE COLIFLOR

2   pounds oxtails
1   medium onion
3   laurel leaves
8   garlic cloves
       Salt and pepper to taste
6   dry seedless California chilies
2   medium-size ripe tomatoes
1   teaspoon ground cumin
1   tablespoon olive oil
1   medium cauliflower
4   eggs, beaten
½   cup canola oil

In a large saucepan combine the oxtails with enough water to cover, ¾ of the onion, laurel leaves, 5 garlic cloves, and salt to taste. Boil about 2 to 3 hours until the oxtails are soft. While the meat is cooking prepare the sauce. Wash the chilies. In a small saucepan boil the chilies and tomatoes until chilies are soft. Let them cool. In a blender pulverize the chilies, tomatoes, remaining garlic and onion, cumin, salt, and pepper. Strain the sauce.

In a large nonstick frying pan warm the olive oil on medium heat. Add the sauce and oxtails. Let simmer for 30 minutes. While the oxtails and sauce are simmering prepare the Tortas de Coliflor. In a large saucepan boil the cauliflower until tender. Drain, pull the florets apart and sprinkle with salt, pepper, and flour.

In a large nonstick frying pan heat canola oil. When the oil is hot, dip the florets in the beaten eggs and carefully add to the frying pan. Fry until they are golden brown. Place them on a big platter and cover them with paper towels to blot up the excess oil.

Serve with oxtails and pour the sauce on top.

—RICHARD PRYOR (and Ana M. Perfecto); Pryor played *The Wiz* in the 1978 film

Comedian Richard Pryor was The Wiz *in the 1978 motion picture directed by Sidney Lumet, with music adapted and supervised by Quincy Jones.*

PARTY CHICKEN WITH CLING PEACHES

¼   cup oil
6   chicken breasts
1   cup rice
2   cups chicken broth
4   ounces sliced mushrooms
2   tablespoons chopped parsley
¾   teaspoon salt
⅛   teaspoon curry (or thyme)
3   tablespoons orange marmalade
1½ teaspoons lemon juice
    Dash ground cloves
6   cling peach halves

Prepare a 2-quart baking dish by lining it with foil. In a large skillet heat the oil and brown the chicken breasts. Place the chicken breasts on a platter. In the same skillet combine the rice, chicken broth, mushrooms, parsley, salt, and curry. Heat to boiling and turn into the prepared dish. Place the chicken over the rice mixture. Fold and seal the foil. Bake at 350° for 50 minutes.

In a small bowl combine the orange marmalade, lemon juice, and cloves. Spread on the cut side of 6 drained peach halves. Arrange around the chicken. Bake, uncovered, for 10 to 15 minutes more.

MAKES 6 SERVINGS.

—BLANCHE COX

PARTY ENCHILADAS À LA MUNCHKIN

As a good friend who was a doctor used to say of this dish, "I'll take two and a margarita with both. Don't call me in the morning."

2   10- to 12-count packages tortillas
6   to 10 tablespoons corn oil

Sauce:
2   15-ounce cans tomatoes
2   cloves garlic, minced
2   to 3 jalapeño peppers, finely chopped
¼   teaspoon cayenne pepper
⅛   teaspoon cumin powder
Filling:
4   cups grated Cheddar cheese
1¾ green onions, chopped

In a skillet heat the oil and fry each tortilla for 15 to 20 seconds on both sides and stack with paper towels between to drain. Add extra oil as needed. Set aside.

Preheat the oven to 425°. In a small pan combine the tomatoes, garlic, jalapeño peppers, cayenne, and cumin powder. Bring to a boil, cover, and reduce the heat to a simmer. Simmer for 20 minutes.

Place the sauce in a shallow pan. Dip a tortilla into the sauce and place in a 13 x 9-inch baking dish. Put 2 to 3 tablespoons of Cheddar cheese in the center and 1 teaspoon of onion over the cheese. Roll up and place with the seam side down. Repeat with the remaining tortillas. Cover the enchiladas with the remaining sauce. Sprinkle the remaining Cheddar cheese on top. Bake for 20 minutes. Broil for about 3 to 5 minutes to melt the cheese.

Serve hot on warm plates. Goes well with Spanish rice and black fried beans. Serve on a buffet table with condiments: sour cream, chopped green onions, chopped tomatoes, guacamole, tortilla chips, and medium-hot salsa.

MAKES 8 TO 10 SERVINGS.

—DONNA STEWARD HARDWAY,
child Munchkin in *Oz*, MGM

PROFESSOR MARVEL'S OPEN-PIT BACON-CHEESE CHILI DOGS

"As one dog to another"

10	slices bacon
10	hot dogs
⅔	cup shredded Cheddar cheese
3	tablespoons chili sauce
10	hot dog buns

In a 10-inch skillet cook the bacon over low heat for 2 minutes on each side. Drain. Split the hot dogs lengthwise, not cutting completely through. In a small bowl mix the cheese and chili sauce. Put 2 teaspoons of the cheese mixture in each hot dog. Close and wrap each hot dog with a slice of bacon. Secure with a wooden pick. On a grill, cook the hot dogs 4 inches from medium coals for 12 to 15 minutes, turning occasionally, until the bacon is crisp. Serve on buns with your favorite condiments.

MAKES 5 SERVINGS.

DANCE AND BE MERRY In a nostalgic holiday treat, Ray Bolger dug out his original Scarecrow costume and re-created his famous rubber-legged routine on the ABC-TV series The New Ray Bolger Show, *Christmas Eve, 1954. Years later, Bolger bequeathed his costume to the Smithsonian Institution.*

ROARING HUNGARIAN SHORT RIBS

2	pounds short ribs
	Salt and pepper to taste
¼	cup firmly packed brown sugar
1	8-ounce can crispy sauerkraut
1	8-ounce can stewed tomatoes, mashed

In a large saucepan boil the ribs until tender in seasoned broth. Remove the ribs from the broth and trim the fat. In an 11 x 7-inch baking dish place the ribs in a layer. Sprinkle with brown sugar. Add a layer of sauerkraut and top with a layer of stewed tomatoes. Bake at 350° until bubbly and browned. Serve with sour cream, if desired.

MAKES 2 SERVINGS.

—CHARLIE SCHRAM, Bert Lahr's makeup man in *The Wizard of Oz*

Munchkins Margaret Pellegrini, Jerry Maren, and Ruth Duccini revisit MGM (now Sony) Soundstage #27 where Munchkinland was filmed sixty years earlier. (Photo by Steve Cox)

Ruth's No-Peekie Stew

You can while away the hours.

2   pounds beef stew meat cut into 1½-inch cubes
1   10½-ounce can cream of mushroom soup
1   package onion soup mix
1   cup water

In a 3-quart casserole combine the stew meat, mushroom soup, onion soup mix, and water. Mix well. Bake at 350° for 3 hours. No need to check the meat while it cooks!

Serve with cooked noodles or rice and a tossed salad.

MAKES 8 SERVINGS.

—RUTH DUCCINI, Munchkin in *Oz*, MGM

Sautéed Veal Scaloppine with Lemon Sauce

1   pound veal scaloppine
2   tablespoons vegetable oil
¼   cup butter, divided
¾   cup all-purpose flour
     Salt and pepper to taste
2   tablespoons lemon juice
2   tablespoons finely chopped parsley
½   lemon, thinly sliced

Slice the scaloppine very thin and pound it flat. In a skillet heat the oil and 2 tablespoons of butter over medium-high heat. (It should be quite hot. Thinly sliced veal must cook quickly or it will become leathery.) In a shallow dish place the flour. Dip both sides of the scaloppine in flour and shake off the excess. Slip the scaloppine carefully into the hot skillet, no more than will fit comfortably at one time into the pan. If the oil is hot enough the meat should sizzle. Cook the scaloppine until they are lightly brown on one side, then turn and brown on the other side. If they are very thin, they should be completely cooked in about 1 minute. When done, transfer to a warm platter and season with salt and pepper.

Turn off the heat. Add lemon juice to the skillet, scraping loose the cooking residue. Swirl in the remaining 2 tablespoons of butter. Add parsley, stirring it into the sauce. Add the scaloppine, turning them in the sauce. Turn on the heat to medium very briefly, just long enough to warm up the sauce and scaloppine together. Do not overdo it, because the scaloppine are already cooked. Transfer the scaloppine to a warm platter. Pour the sauce over them. Garnish with the lemon slices, and serve immediately with your favorite pasta.

MAKES 4 SERVINGS.

—JOAN KENMORE, child Munchkin in *Oz*, MGM

Munchkin Rendezvous '97 gathered six of the surviving Munchkin actors for a special Halloween event at the Culver Hotel—where many of the Munchkins were housed when they made The Wizard of Oz. *The extravaganza was later listed in the special year-end issue of* Entertainment Weekly *magazine as one of "The Best of 1997." Forming a conga line are Jerry Maren, Margaret Pellegrini, Mickey Carroll, Ruth Duccini, Clarence Swensen, and Karl Slover. (Beyond the Rainbow Archive; Photo by Andy Cassimatis)*

SAVORY CRESCENT CHICKEN SQUARES

1   8-ounce can refrigerated crescent rolls
2   cups cooked cubed chicken
¼   teaspoon salt
⅛   teaspoon pepper
1   tablespoon chopped chives (or onion)
1   tablespoon chopped pimiento
2   tablespoons milk
1   3-ounce package cream cheese, softened
2   tablespoons margarine, melted
¾   cup crushed seasoned croutons

Separate the crescent rolls into 4 rectangles, sealing the perforations. Place on an ungreased cookie sheet. In a medium bowl combine the cubed chicken, salt, pepper, chives, pimiento, and milk. Stir in the cream cheese and mix well. Spoon ½ cup of the chicken mixture in the center of each rectangle. Pull all 4 corners of dough to the center over the mixture and seal. Brush the tops with melted margarine. In a shallow dish place crushed croutons and roll the chicken squares to coat. Bake at 350° for 20 to 25 minutes until golden brown. Refrigerate any leftovers.

MAKES 4 SERVINGS.

—MYRNA AND CLARENCE SWENSEN,
Munchkin in *Oz,* MGM

SCHNITZEL OZ

6   large veal scallops
     Salt and pepper to taste
     All-purpose flour
1   egg, well beaten
2   cups cracker crumbs (or corn flake
     crumbs)
½   cup butter (divided)
¼   cup cooking oil
1   9-ounce package spinach noodles
6   eggs
12   flat anchovy fillets, drained
2   tablespoons capers, drained
2   tablespoons minced parsley

Pound the veal until paper-thin. Sprinkle both sides with salt and pepper. In a shallow dish dredge the veal in flour, then shake off the excess. In another shallow dish dip the veal into the beaten egg and then dredge in a shallow dish of cracker crumbs. Coat completely, pressing the crumbs firmly until they adhere. Let stand at room temperature for 1 hour to dry.

In a large skillet heat ¼ cup of butter and the cooking oil and brown veal quickly on both sides. Place the meat on a platter and cover to keep warm. In a large saucepan cook the noodles according to the package directions. Drain. In a large skillet melt the remaining butter and fry six eggs until the whites are set but the yolks are still soft. Place an egg on top of each veal scallop, and top each with a crisscross of 2 anchovy fillets. Sprinkle with capers and parsley and place on top of a bed of cooked spinach noodles.

Serving suggestion: Serve with a lettuce cup filled with pickled beets and dill pickles.

MAKES 6 SERVINGS.

SOUTH OF THE BORDER SKILLET DINNER

1   pound ground beef
2   bunches green onions, reserve ½ cup
     sliced onion tops for garnish
6   tablespoons Schilling Mexican
     Seasoning, reserve 1 tablespoon for
     garnish
     Salt to taste
1   teaspoon black pepper
2   cups halved cherry tomatoes
1   16-ounce can chili beans (or kidney
     beans)
1   large green bell pepper, finely chopped
1   large red bell pepper, finely chopped
1   large yellow bell pepper, finely chopped
1   5.5-ounce package instant potato buds

In a large skillet combine the ground beef, onions, 5 tablespoons of Mexican seasoning mix, salt, and pepper. Cook the meat mixture on medium heat until meat is well done. Reduce the heat to low and add the tomatoes, beans, and bell peppers. Cook until the peppers are tender. Meanwhile, prepare the mashed potatoes according to the package directions. Cover the ingredients in the skillet with the mashed potatoes. Garnish with reserved green onion tops and 1 tablespoon of Mexican seasoning. May be served from the skillet.

Note: Schilling Mexican Seasoning comes in a jar. You may substitute 1 package Mexican Chili Mix.

MAKES 4 SERVINGS.

—VIOLA WHITE BANKS, child Munchkin
in *Oz,* MGM

Relishing His Work

Five Questions for the Original "Little Oscar"

Meinhardt Raabe worked for the Oscar Mayer meat company from 1937 through 1970, beginning at their Madison, Wisconsin, plant and eventually transferring to Philadelphia. As the original "Little Oscar" chef, he toured, made commercials, instructed, and in 1938 took leave for a few months to work in *The Wizard of Oz*. In doing so, Raabe, who played the Munchkin Coroner in the film, became the link between the wiener and *The Wizard*. Eventually, three additional tiny chefs were hired to assist in the company's regional advertising—George Molchan, Jerry Maren, and Joe White.

"Little Oscar" was Raabe's concept, inspired by the midget mascot named "Johnny," a sporty hotel bellboy who advertised Phillip Morris cigarettes on radio and in print advertising at the time. "I based the entire concept on the success of Little Johnny," says Raabe. "He did a lot for them and I convinced Oscar Mayer that Little Oscar could do some wonderful personal promotion as well. You see, my grandparents came from Germany, and we made all different kinds of German sausage at home, so I told the company I know what goes into these types of meats; I know what needs to be cooked or cured and stuff like that. Eighty percent of their customers at that time were German butchers and I could sell in two different dialects in German."

Raabe helped make hot dogs a staple of our culture during the past century. Keep in mind, years ago hot dogs were much more popular because pizza had not yet hit the market. "Oscar Mayer wieners were exclusive at Chicago's Wrigley Field for as long as I worked for them," Raabe recalls. Hot dogs are synonymous with Americana, in great part due to Oscar Mayer's success and longevity. You know the saying, "Baseball, hot dogs, and apple pie."

And then there's the other saying: "Oh I wish I were an Oscar Mayer wiener. . . ."

"Little Oscar" was a marketing concept created by Meinhardt Raabe, shown here in an early publicity photograph for the meat company. (Tod Machin Collection)

What did you do as "Little Oscar"?

I wasn't putting out fancy recipes, but I was showing consumers the proper methods of preparing meats and the basic use of Oscar Mayer's meats. I gave a lecture on what should be broiled, what should be steamed, what should be baked, and so forth. When the table-top broilers first came out, I went to different department stores and demonstrated these, showing how nicely bacon laid on a rack and broiled, and how nice and crisp and straight it would be rather than shriveled up in a frying pan.

What do you recall about old man Oscar Mayer, the company's founder?

Oscar Mayer Sr. was still active in the company when I started, but his son, the business head of the company, was the one who hired me. Mr. Mayer (senior) would be sitting at the front desk of his office and every morning I'd come in and he'd have a greeting in German for me; he'd ask what I was doing today or where I was going. He was a homey type, not an aristocrat or a bombastic individual. He was down home. He came to America as a teenager and worked in a meatpacking plant in the late 1800s and first started his business in 1883 peddling his sausage in a little meat market in Chicago and in the German neighborhood, by wagon. He was a cordial man who worked hard. I never went to his house for dinner or anything, it wasn't that type of relationship. He was always dressed distinctively as a businessman. I don't remember when he died; I didn't go to his funeral.

Short Order Cooks: Company founder Oscar F. Mayer poses with his four "Little Oscar" chefs in the early 1950s: George Molchan, Joe White, Meinhardt Raabe, and Jerry Maren. Raabe and Maren (on right) met in 1938 when they both portrayed key Munchkins in The Wizard of Oz. (Jerry Maren Collection)

When did the Wienermobile become part of your presentation?

The Wienermobile was introduced in 1936 and became the Little Chefs' mode of transportation. I thought it was a good idea. We never had any mishaps in the Wienermobile, which was redesigned several times over the years as automobiles changed. We went through rainstorms and windstorms and all that, but we never had any accidents. We had to be careful around kids because they would crowd around when we were parked at a store.

What's the strangest thing you've seen done with a hot dog?

The thing that always made me upset is that you'd go to, let's say a picnic, where they'd be serving Oscar Mayer wieners. And they'd have them in a kettle boiling them to death. A hot dog isn't a hot dog until it's cooked. And if you cook it again, why you're cookin' the hell out of it. They'd split open and you've cooked the juice and flavor right out of them. The trick is not to cook them at all—just heat them. Some people say they eat them raw, but they're never raw. They're not a hot dog until they're completely cooked. A loaf of bread is not bread until it's baked. You wouldn't buy a loaf of bread and rebake it. All lunch meats are completely cooked before they're put on the market.

Do you ever get sick of hot dogs?

Oh, no. But I'm selective as to which ones I enjoy, but I still like them. I rarely buy them because I much prefer little smokey links. Over the years I ate hundreds of (hot dogs), because I'd be eating my samples when I didn't have time for lunch. After many years of that, I don't make a point of going out to buy hot dogs for lunch.

SPINACH ENCHILADAS

1   12-ounce package frozen spinach (drain well)
4   large radishes, sliced thin
¼   cup green onions, chopped
1   cup sour cream
½   teaspoon red chili powder
½   teaspoon coriander
¼   teaspoon salt
¼   teaspoon pepper
¼   cup sliced black olives

Red Enchilada Sauce (or use canned sauce):
1   28-ounce can tomato sauce (or 2 small cans)
2   tablespoons green chilies
¼   teaspoon cumin
1   teaspoon garlic powder
1   teaspoon onion salt
¼   teaspoon cayenne pepper

     Blue corn or flour tortillas
¾   cup grated Cheddar cheese

In a large bowl combine the spinach, radishes, green onions, sour cream, chili powder, coriander, salt, pepper, and olives. Mix well and set aside.

In a bowl combine the tomato sauce, chilies, cumin, garlic powder, onion salt, and cayenne pepper. Dip the corn tortillas in oil for 2 to 3 seconds. Fill the tortillas with ¼ to ½ cup of spinach mixture. Arrange in a baking dish and top with the enchilada sauce. Sprinkle with Cheddar cheese. Bake at 350° for 20 to 25 minutes until the cheese is melted. Garnish with lettuce, chopped tomatoes, green onions, and sour cream. Fills five 10-inch tortillas.

MAKES 5 SERVINGS.

—SUSAN CASSIMATIS

STEINRUCK'S FLANK STEAK

2   pounds flank steak
     Lupo's lemon-garlic marinade (or Italian salad dressing)

In a covered container marinate the steak in the refrigerator for 24 hours. Barbecue on the grill for 2½ minutes on each side, repeating twice more until steak has cooked 15 minutes. Slice steak across the grain in very thin slices.

MAKES 4 SERVINGS.

—KURT STEINRUCK

STEINRUCK'S GRILLED SALMON STEAK À LA HAL

1   8-ounce salmon steak
2   tablespoons butter, melted
1   clove garlic, crushed
1   tablespoon lemon juice

Place the salmon on a large piece of aluminum foil and brush with butter and garlic. Pour lemon juice over the salmon. Seal the foil and place on the grill. Grill for 5 minutes. Unseal and allow the salmon to brown. Grill an additional 3 minutes. Remove from the fire and serve.

—KURT STEINRUCK

SUPPER ON A BREAD SLICE

1½   pounds ground beef
½   cup chopped onion
1½   teaspoons salt
½   teaspoon pepper
1   tablespoon prepared mustard
½   cup cracker meal
1   egg, beaten
⅔   cup evaporated milk
1   loaf French bread
4   American cheese slices

In a skillet brown the ground beef and onion.
Drain. In a large bowl place the drained beef
mixture, salt, pepper, mustard, cracker meal,
and egg. Stir in the evaporated milk.

Cut the loaf of bread in half lengthwise.
Line a cookie sheet with aluminum foil. Cut
a generous piece so it can be folded up on
the sides of the bread but not cover it.
Spread half the meat mixture evenly over
the cut side of each bread slice. Wrap the foil
on each side of the crust. Bake at 350° for
25 minutes. Remove from the oven. Cut the
cheese into strips and lay on top of the meat
mixture crisscrossed or straight. Return to
the oven for 5 minutes or longer until the
cheese is melted. Slice across or diagonally.

MAKES 6 TO 8 SERVINGS.

—ROBERTA BAUMAN

TIN MAN'S CAST-IRON KETTLE POLLO

6   chicken thighs, skinned
6   chicken drumsticks, skinned
1   whole tomato, hollowed out
2   stalks celery, chopped
½   medium onion, chopped
3   cloves garlic, chopped
1   teaspoon salt
3   cups water
1   cup white rice

In a large cast-iron kettle with a lid place the
thighs, drumsticks, tomato, celery, onion, garlic, salt, and water. Cook on high for 20 minutes. Remove the tomato and 2 ladles of
broth and purée in the blender. Return to the
pot and add the rice. Cover, reduce the heat,
and simmer for approximately 20 minutes.
Keep covered and at a constant low boil until
the chicken falls off the bone.

Serving suggestion: Excellent served with
a tossed salad—and remember, the Tin Man
prefers oil on his salad.

MAKES 6 SERVINGS.

—HAL RAYLE, voice of Tin Man
in DIC *Oz* cartoon series

TRIPLE MEAT ROAST

With "that certain air of savoir faire"

1½	pounds ¼-inch-thick round steak
1½	pounds ¼-inch-thick fresh ham steak
1½	pounds ¼-inch-thick veal steak
	Salt and pepper to taste
½	cup snipped parsley
2	tablespoons shortening
1	10½-ounce can condensed consommé
½	cup sliced celery
1	medium onion, sliced
4	whole cloves
¼	cup all-purpose flour

Sprinkle all three steaks with salt and pepper, then generously with snipped parsley. Stack the steaks on top of each other, starting with the round and ending with the veal. Roll up the steaks, jelly roll fashion. Tie gently across and then lengthwise with a cord to keep the shape.

In a Dutch oven over medium heat melt the shortening and brown the meat roll on all sides. Remove from the heat. Pour in the consommé. Add the celery, onion, and cloves. Roast uncovered at 325° for 2 hours and 30 minutes or until tender.

Remove the meat from the oven. Place the meat roll on a cutting board and clip the cords. Strain the gravy. Return to the pan. In a small bowl blend the flour with ¼ cup of water to make a thickening paste. Stir the paste into the gravy. Cook over medium heat, stirring until thickened. Serve the sliced meat hot with the gravy. (Also good served cold.)

MAKES 8 TO 10 SERVINGS.

—THE COX FAMILY

Getting away from it all, twenty-nine-year-old Judy Garland holds a trout she reeled in at Sun Valley Lake, Idaho (August 1950). (Beyond the Rainbow Archive)

TROUT, BY GUMM

6   trout
2   13¾-ounce cans chicken broth
¼   cup cider vinegar
2   tablespoons chopped fresh dill
1   small onion, sliced
2   long thin cucumbers, unpeeled
     Salt
2   ripe tomatoes, chopped
1   cup chopped celery
½   cup chopped sweet pickles
¼   cup French dressing
2   envelopes unflavored gelatin
1   hard-boiled egg, sieved
     Fresh dill sprigs for garnish

Clean the trout and remove the heads. In a 2-inch-deep pan that has a lid place the trout side by side in a single layer. Add the chicken broth, vinegar, dill, and onion. Cover tightly and simmer for 15 minutes or until the trout are firm to the touch. Allow the trout to cool in the broth. Place a rack over a shallow pan. Carefully remove the trout and place them side by side on the rack. Reserve the broth.

Slice the cucumbers paper-thin and sprinkle with salt. Let stand until wilted. Drain and dry the slices on paper towels. Place the cucumber slices over the trout in overlapping rows to resemble scales. Chill the trout. In a medium bowl combine the tomatoes, celery, pickles, and French dressing. Chill.

Strain the reserved broth. Add water to the chicken broth, if necessary, to make 3 cups. Combine ½ cup of broth with the gelatin and soak for 5 minutes. In a small pan place the gelatin mixture over low heat and stir constantly until the gelatin is dissolved. Add to the remaining broth. Chill until slightly thickened. Spoon gelatin over the trout, coating them evenly, catching the drippings in the pan. Chill. Spoon another layer of gelatin over the trout. Chill. Place the coated trout on a serving platter. Surround them with drained vegetables. Sprinkle sieved egg over the vegetables. Garnish with fresh dill.

MAKES 6 SERVINGS.

UNCLE HENRY'S FAVORITE MEATLOAF

1½   pounds ground beef
1   egg
3   tablespoons sour cream
½   cup onion, chopped
1   teaspoon salt
1   teaspoon pepper
½   cup tomato sauce

In a large bowl mix together all of the ingredients except the tomato sauce. Spoon into a loaf pan. Drizzle the tomato sauce on top. Bake at 350° for 50 to 60 minutes or microwave on high for 21 to 25 minutes.

MAKES 4 TO 6 SERVINGS.

—KATHY ANDREWS

Toto Recall

If ever there was a "Dorothy" in the real Toto's life, it probably was Hango Dennison, a niece of Carl Spitz. "Hango" (a nickname) was just a little girl when the Spitzes got Toto. Because her family and the Spitz family all lived together as a two-family household, Hango cuddled the lovable dog any time she wanted.

Hango, now a resident of Alaska, recently reminisced about Toto. She says she is a professed fan of her little pal who became famous in *The Wizard of Oz*.

What's your earliest recollection of Toto?

Terry, as she was first called, was really kind of shy when they got her and they put her in my room where I could give her lots of attention and get her out of her shyness. I believe Toto was brought in as a dog to train and the owners decided they didn't want the dog and our kennel was sort of stuck with her. So Uncle Carl trained her the rest of the way. She went through all the various obedience training courses and cue courses, which was necessary for movies in those days.

How was Toto at home?

She basically became a pet. A housedog. Mainly, Toto was very affectionate, but very afraid of strangers. When my friends were over to the house, I'd coax her out of her little bed, which was at the foot of my bed. And eventually she would play with visitors. She was, by nature, a kind of one-person shy dog. She was very spry. Cairn terriers are active dogs. In fact, they were originally used in Europe and bred for catching mice and rats.

How did Toto, a small dog, interact with say, Buck, who was a very large Saint Bernard?

Fine, because Buck was a male and Toto was a female. No problems there. Generally speaking, with dogs, you don't have a conflict with males and females.

Was Toto "your" dog in one sense?

Well, in that I spent a lot of time with her. I also had a Scottish terrier who was also in films. That was Mr. Binkie. His real name was Whiskers, but we called him Whiskey. His pedigree name was Whiskers of Niles.

Was it *Oz* that made Toto famous?

Toto didn't become active working, really, until after *Oz*. She was not one of the busiest dogs, although she had done several movies. She was the dog with Shirley Temple in *Bright Eyes*. And at the time, none of us thought of how famous any of these dogs would become. For a long time, Buck, the Saint Bernard, was the movie star around the place.

Why did her name change from Terry to Toto?

After *The Wizard of Oz* everybody called her Toto, so the family did too. People would come to the kennel and ask to see Toto and Mom would say, "Okay. Go get Terry!" So we just renamed her and she adjusted fine.

Did you visit the set of *The Wizard of Oz*?

No. I did help on some of the movies when they had several dogs that were working.

*Virginia Weidler and Gene
Reynolds with Toto in the film
Bad Little Angel (1939).*

Did your family see the movies these dogs were in?
Oh yes. All the dogs we had. We always went to see the films as soon
as they were released. Uncle Carl took Toto to the premiere of *The
Wizard of Oz* at Grauman's Chinese Theatre in Hollywood. They didn't
have any stand-ins for [Toto] or any of that. There was only one Toto.

Do you recall when Toto died?
It was toward the end of World War II when she died and I had left
home by then. As I remember, Toto died of just natural old age. One
of our Bucks [there were three] was poisoned at a dog show. But in
Toto's case, she lived out her life to a natural old age. Nothing overly
dramatic about it.

—*Interview Conducted by Steve Cox*

Hango Dennison, age seven, holds onto a wriggling Toto in 1933.

WICKED WITCH'S SLOW-COOK SPARERIBS

"All in good time . . . all in good time."

4   pounds country-style spareribs
1   10½-ounce can condensed tomato soup
½   cup cider vinegar
½   cup firmly packed brown sugar
1   tablespoon soy sauce
1   teaspoon celery seed
1   teaspoon salt
1   teaspoon chili powder
    Dash cayenne pepper

In a crock pot layer the spareribs. In a mixing bowl combine the tomato soup, vinegar, brown sugar, soy sauce, celery seed, salt, chili powder, and pepper. Pour over the spareribs.

    Cover the crock pot and cook on medium or low setting for 8 hours. Skim the fat from the juices before serving.

MAKES 4 SERVINGS.

—GEORGE LILLIE, scenic painter,
The Wizard of Oz, MGM

WINE STEW

This recipe has been cooked by my family as long as I can remember and "Toto" undoubtedly was the beneficiary of a few trimmings of the meat from time to time.

2   pounds round steak, cubed, fat trimmed (or sirloin)
1   package onion soup mix
1   8-ounce can mushroom pieces
2   10½-ounce cans condensed cream of mushroom soup
1   cup cooking sherry

In a 2-quart casserole that has a lid place the meat. Sprinkle with the soup mix. Add the mushrooms and soup. It is not necessary to stir. Cover. Bake at 325° for 1 hour and 30 minutes. Remove from the oven and add the sherry. Stir thoroughly. Cover and return to the oven for 30 minutes. Serve spooned over mashed potatoes, steamed rice, or egg noodles. Enjoy!

MAKES 6 SERVINGS.

—HANGO DENNISON

HOT DOGS *Canine pals Toto and Prince (the great dane who appeared in the film* Little Lord Fauntleroy) *are caught in this rare snapshot taken on a hot summer day at the Carl Spitz kennel property in Southern California, circa August 1941.*

MOTHER GOOSE AND GRIMM   By Mike Peters

THE WICKED WITCH OF THE EAST ALWAYS HATED PLAYING TWISTER.

Mother Goose & Grimm © Grimmy, Inc. Dist. By Tribune Media Services. All Rights Reserved. Reprinted by permission

WITCH'S POPPY SEED HEARTHSIDE LOAF

Wickedly Delicious

1	loaf unsliced buttercrust bread (not French or Italian)
½	cup butter, softened (or margarine)
⅓	cup minced onion
3	tablespoons prepared mustard
1	tablespoon poppy seeds
2	teaspoons lemon juice
12	slices processed Swiss cheese
6	slices bacon
	Dill pickles

Make six diagonal cuts in the bread from the top almost through the loaf. Place the loaf on a baking sheet. In a small bowl combine the butter, onion, mustard, poppy seeds, and lemon juice. Mix well. Reserve 3 tablespoons of this mixture. Spread the remainder on the diagonally cut surfaces of the bread. Place 2 cheese slices in each bread cut; then spread the reserved butter mixture on the top and sides of the loaf. Bake at 350° for approximately 20 minutes, until cheese melts and the loaf is brown. In a skillet cook the bacon until crisp. When the loaf is done, lay bacon slices across top and serve with dill pickles. Enjoy!

MAKES 6 SERVINGS.

—THE COX FAMILY

FIRE IT UP In this rare costume test photo, Ray Bolger cautiously enjoys a smoke. He learned his lesson after twice setting himself on fire when a stray cigarette ash landed on his straw. And so, Margaret Hamilton was not the only one plagued by fire during the production of The Wizard of Oz. Hamilton, whose face and hands were seriously burned during the Wicked Witch's torchy entrance in Munchkinland, was again forced to play with fire— and this time set her costar ablaze. Hollywood magazine's Jessie Henderson was observing the filming that day and described the incident in an article. In the Witch's dim castle, director Victor Fleming instructed a nervous Hamilton. "That's right," he told her, "get your broom aflame and then light him as if he were a cigarette. Go on. What's the matter?" Hamilton told the director she was scared, but nevertheless, she put her broom in the fire and pushed it at Bolger's straw arm, which immediately ignited. The scene was repeated five times to get it right, but not before Fleming finally said firmly, "Let's try it again, and, Miss Hamilton, please look as if you enjoyed it." (Photo courtesy Eric Daily Collection)

HELP!

RAY BOLGER, WHO LIKES TO SMOKE, SET HIMSELF ON FIRE WHILE WEARING HIS "SCARECROW" COSTUME FOR "THE WIZARD OF OZ".

WIZARD'S EASY CHEEZ WHIZ CHICKEN AND RICE

You'll find it is a Wiz of a Whiz . . . if ever a Whiz there was.

1	tablespoon oil
4	chicken breast halves, skinless and boneless
1	14½-ounce can chicken broth
2	cups Minute Rice, uncooked
1	16-ounce package frozen broccoli cuts, thawed and drained
1	14-ounce jar Cheez Whiz Pasteurized Process Cheese Sauce

In a large nonstick skillet heat the oil on medium-high heat. Add the chicken. Cook covered for 4 minutes on each side, or until cooked through. Remove the chicken from the skillet. Add the broth to the skillet and bring to a boil. Stir in the Minute Rice, broccoli, and Cheez Whiz. Top with the chicken and cover. Cook on low heat for 3 minutes. Stir until the cheese is melted.

MAKES 4 SERVINGS.

—ERIC DAILY

"Turkey, I've a feeling we're not in Kansas anymore." Go ahead, spend Thanksgiving in the kitchen with Judy, cooking in Oz. (Beyond the Rainbow Archive)

Jam and Bread

JAM

Bing Cherry Jam

4   cups (2½ pounds) pitted chopped Bing cherries
¼   cup lemon juice
½   teaspoon ground cinnamon
1   package powdered pectin
¼   cup Amaretto liqueur
¼   teaspoon ground cloves
4½   cups sugar

In a large kettle combine all the ingredients except the sugar. Bring the mixture to a boil that cannot be stirred down. Immediately add the sugar. Allow the mixture to return to a boil and continue boiling for 2 minutes. Skim mixture. Pour the hot jam immediately into hot jars, leaving ¼ inch of headspace. Adjust the caps. Process 10 minutes in a boiling water-bath canner.

MAKES ABOUT 5 OR 6 HALF-PINT JARS.

—TINA CASSIMATIS

Blueberry Jam

2   pints fully ripe blueberries, washed
½   teaspoon grated nutmeg or ground cinnamon (optional)
4   cups sugar
2   tablespoons lemon juice
1   pouch Certo fruit pectin

Thoroughly crush the berries, one layer at a time. In a large bowl combine 2 cups of the prepared berries, the spice if desired, and the sugar, mixing thoroughly. Allow the mixture to stand 10 minutes, stirring frequently.

In a small bowl combine the lemon juice and fruit pectin. Stir into the fruit. Continue stirring for 3 minutes. A few sugar crystals will remain. Ladle quickly into containers that have been rinsed in boiling water, leaving ½ inch of headspace. Cover at once with tight lids. Let stand at room temperature overnight, then store in the freezer. Small amounts may be covered and stored in the refrigerator for up to 3 weeks.

MAKES ABOUT 4 HALF-PINTS.

—SONNY GALLAGHER, Judy Garland historian

CERTO RUBY SLIPPER JAM

1   quart fully ripe strawberries, stemmed and washed
4   cups sugar
2   tablespoons lemon juice
1   pouch Certo fruit pectin

To prepare the fruit, thoroughly crush berries, one layer at a time. Into a large bowl measure 1¾ cups of berries. Mix in the sugar thoroughly; allow the mixture to stand 10 minutes, stirring frequently.

In a small bowl combine the lemon juice and fruit pectin. Stir into the berries. Continue stirring 3 minutes. A few sugar crystals will remain. Ladle quickly into containers that have been rinsed in boiling water, leaving ½ inch of headspace. Cover at once with tight lids. Let stand at room temperature overnight, then store in the freezer. Small amounts may be covered and stored in refrigerator up to 3 weeks.

MAKES ABOUT 2 PINTS.

—ANASTASIA ARGER

PEACH JAM

1¼   pounds fully ripe peaches
3¼   cups sugar
3   tablespoons lemon juice
1   pouch Certo fruit pectin

Peel and pit the peaches, then finely chop or grind them. In a large bowl measure 1¼ cups of chopped peaches. Thoroughly mix in the sugar and allow to stand 10 minutes, stirring frequently.

In a small bowl add the lemon juice to fruit pectin. Stir into the fruit mixture. Continue stirring for 3 minutes. A few sugar crystals will remain. Ladle quickly into containers that have been rinsed in boiling water, leaving ½ inch of headspace. Cover at once with tight lids. Let stand at room temperature overnight, then store in freezer. Small amounts may be covered and stored in refrigerator up to 3 weeks.

MAKES ABOUT 1 PINT.

THE LION'S CROCK POT APPLE BUTTER

"Put 'em up, put 'em up!"

5   to 6 pounds apples
3   sticks cinnamon
1   anise star (optional)
2½   cups sugar
½   teaspoon ground cloves

Wash and quarter the apples. In a large saucepan boil the apples until soft. Mash the apples through a sieve and discard the seeds and skins. In a crock pot combine 2½ quarts of the mashed apples and add remaining ingredients. DO NOT PUT LID ON. Cook on low for 24 to 36 hours. Seal in sterilized canning jars or cool and then freeze if desired.

MAKES ABOUT 8 CUPS.

—FRANK PARENTI

"Are you hinting my apples aren't what they ought to be?"

BREAD

AUNT EM'S TWISTER CRULLERS

1   package active dry yeast (or compressed yeast cake)
1   cup scalded milk, cooled
1   teaspoon salt
½   cup sugar
¼   cup melted shortening, divided
1   egg, well-beaten
4   cups all-purpose flour, divided
     Confectioners' sugar

In a large bowl dissolve the yeast by adding the milk slowly, stirring until the yeast is completely dissolved. Stir in the salt, sugar, 2 tablespoons melted shortening, and the well-beaten egg. Add 2 cups of flour and beat until smooth. Add the remaining flour, and after mixing well, stir in the remaining shortening and blend thoroughly. Knead on a floured board until smooth. Place the dough in a greased bowl, cover, set in a warm place, and let rise until double in bulk.

   Roll out on a floured board to ½-inch thickness. Cut in 5 x 1-inch strips. Lay one strip on top of a second strip, pressing together at one end. Twist one on top of the other, pressing together at other end. Again let rise until double in bulk. Then deep-fry in hot fat (365°) until light brown. Drain on paper towels and roll in confectioners' sugar.

Careworn Aunt Em was portrayed by stately actress Clara Blandick, who appeared on Broadway before coming to Hollywood in 1929 to work in motion pictures. Suffering from severe arthritis, the actress took her own life on April 15, 1962, at age eighty.

AUNTIE EM'S CRULLERS

"Here . . . can't work on an empty stomach. Have some crullers . . . just fried."

1   egg, well-beaten
1   tablespoon melted butter
⅛   teaspoon salt
3   tablespoons sugar
¼   teaspoon ground cinnamon
¼   teaspoon grated nutmeg
     All-purpose flour
     Confectioners' sugar (optional)

In a small bowl combine the egg, butter, salt, sugar, and spices. Beat thoroughly. Add enough sifted flour to make a stiff dough. Turn onto a lightly floured board. Roll in a sheet ¼ inch thick. Cut into strips 3 x 2 inches. Plump up with your finger slightly. Drop into hot grease (365°). Fry until brown. Drain on absorbent paper. Sprinkle with sugar if desired.

MAKES ABOUT 4 SERVINGS.

—DENISE ORTH

The *Oz* Movie: Myths, Legends, and Truths

- Don't be fooled by the more recent urban legend . . . something about a person hanging in the background. No suicide, no murder took place on the Yellow Brick Road. It didn't happen. And even if it did, the news would have broken long before the late 1980s, when someone first spread this ridiculous story. One version has a dead Munchkin hanging from the rafters in the haunted forest scene. Watch the movie again and you'll see there is no such nonsense. The only unusual things to spot in the backgrounds are some exotic animals around the Tin Woodman's house, and in the apple orchard. Look for a toucan, a pheasant, and a crane wandering about.

- Despite popular belief, the sinister Miss Gulch does not curse at Aunt Em, threatening to "bring a damn suit that'll take your whole farm!" The words are "damage suit."

- When Frank Morgan reported to the MGM wardrobe department for a fitting for *The Wizard of Oz*, he was handed a black topcoat. He looked inside the pocket and there was a name (or maybe just initials) stitched in: L. Frank Baum. Reportedly, it was the dark coat Morgan wore as Professor Marvel. And so it was a grand coincidence, maybe an omen, verified by Baum's widow, Maud Gage Baum, when one of Metro's wardrobe department showed her the coat. According to Maud, the studio had bought out some 1905 stock from a secondhand dealer, and the dealer had gotten the coat from a tailor who always made Baum's clothes. Another version (from a studio press release) stated the coat's label inside showed the coat was made in Chicago in 1909 for L. Frank Baum. After sixty years, the details are fuzzy; however, members of the cast have maintained over the years that the weird incident assuredly happened.

- How did the word *Oz* originate? Only one man really knew, however, the prevailing story through the decades has described storyteller L. Frank Baum discovering inspiration when he peered over his shoulder at his file drawer. His widow, Maud Gage Baum, refuted that legend several times. In a July 1939 *Syracuse Herald* interview, she told reporter Teet Carle: "The plots would just unfold in his mind, even the names," she explained. "I've often been asked how he evolved the name of Oz. I've read that he looked at a letter file and saw the classification 'O to Z.' That isn't true. The name just popped into his mind as did all others." (Of course, but the question remains . . . did it just pop into his head after unconsciously viewing a file cabinet marked O-Z?)

- Yes, unfortunately it's true. Most of the Munchkin actors earned $50 a week while making *The Wizard of Oz*. Toto took home $125 a week. Quite an expensive bark. The highest salary on *Oz* went to Ray Bolger, who earned $3,600 per week for twenty weeks.

- It's nearly impossible to decipher the writing on the Coroner Munchkin's Certificate of Death. Inspection of a clear, unfaded original publicity still photograph of the Munchkin scene, reveals this data: Inscribed on the certificate, the handwriting lists the death of the Wicked Witch of the East (of The Land of Oz) as having occurred on May 6, 1938, at 12:30 P.M. Signed, W. S. Barristor, M.D., Munchkin City. Hmmm. So the Coroner had a name. What's more bizarre is the fact that L. Frank Baum, creator of *Oz*, died on May 6, 1919.

- Contrary to popular belief, when *The Wizard of Oz* premiered in theaters in August 1939, the reviews were rampant raves. Across the nation, critics loved it and audiences adored it. With the masses, it was an acclaimed hit. Now, if you had asked the studio accountants at the time, they might've labeled it a flop. It's true, the movie did not hit the profit margin until the studio reissued it theatrically ten years later, years after World War II ended.

- Judy Garland frivolously joked about it on TV's *The Jack Paar Show*. But don't take her levity seriously. The actors who portrayed Munchkins with her in *Oz* were definitely not a group of drunkards, and it's taken years for the surviving little people to shake the stale stereotype. Unfortunately, over the years, the cruel Hollywood legend that was created and flourished had the Munchkins throwing wild parties, attending drunken orgies, and wreaking pure havoc in the Culver Hotel, where most were housed during production. Of the 124 midgets brought in from all corners of the country (many were foreign-born), only a few of them were known to drink excessively and party during off-hours—a shadow that haunted all of them.

BILLIE BURKE'S BRAN MUFFINS

1   cup ready-to-eat whole bran cereal
1   cup milk
1   tablespoon molasses
1   tablespoon flaxseed*
½   cup golden raisins
1   large egg
1   tablespoon vegetable oil
½   cup whole wheat flour
1   teaspoon baking powder
1   teaspoon baking soda
1   tablespoon firmly packed dark
     brown sugar

In a small bowl stir together the bran, milk, molasses, flaxseed, and raisins. In another small bowl beat the egg and oil until blended. In a medium bowl stir together the whole wheat flour, baking powder, soda, and brown sugar. Add the bran and egg mixtures to the flour mixture and stir until the flour mixture is moistened. Fill greased muffin pan cups (each ⅓ cup capacity) ⅔ full. Bake in a pre-heated 400° oven for about 15 minutes until a cake tester inserted in the center comes out clean. Loosen the edges and remove; serve hot (or reheated).

*Available at health food stores.

MAKES 12 SMALL MUFFINS.

—BILLIE BURKE; Miss Burke contributed this recipe to a celebrity cookbook (now out of print), as one of her favorites.

CYCLONE POPOVERS

Come up, come up, wherever you are.

1½   cups milk
4½   teaspoons melted butter, cooled
3   eggs, slightly beaten
1½   cups all-purpose flour
¾   teaspoon salt

In a medium bowl combine the milk, melted butter, and eggs. In a small bowl combine the flour and salt. Add the flour mixture to the egg mixture and beat until batter is smooth (not longer than 1 minute). Place in 6 heavily greased custard cups. Bake at 400° for 1 hour.

Great filled with The Lion's Courageous Curry Chicken Salad (see page 46) or Certo Ruby Slipper Jam (see page 143) and butter.

— MARY HENDRICKS

Actor Edward Arnold assists social butterfly Billie Burke with a helping of dinner salad at a Tinseltown gala in 1948.

DANDY BLUEBERRY MUFFINS

1   egg
¾   cup milk
1   cup fresh blueberries
½   cup vegetable oil
⅓   cup sugar
1   teaspoon salt
2   cups all-purpose flour
3   teaspoons baking powder

Preheat the oven to 400°. Grease the bottoms only of 12 medium muffin cups. Beat the egg; then stir in the milk, blueberries, and oil. Stir in the remaining ingredients all at once, just until the flour is moistened (the batter will be lumpy). Fill the muffin cups about ¾ full. Bake about 20 minutes, until golden brown. Immediately remove from the pan.

MAKES 12 MUFFINS.

—SONNY GALLAGHER, Judy Garland Historian

DING-A-DERRY DANISH PUFF

1   cup all-purpose flour
½   cup butter
2   tablespoons ice water
1   cup water
½   cup butter
1   cup all-purpose flour
3   eggs
½   teaspoon almond extract
1   cup confectioners' sugar
1   tablespoon butter
½   teaspoon almond extract
2   to 3 tablespoons milk
¼   cup sliced almonds

In a small bowl mix 1 cup flour and ½ cup butter. Blend with a pastry blender until the size of peas. Sprinkle with ice water. Stir with a fork until mixed. Divide the dough in half and spread each portion on an ungreased cookie sheet into a 12 x 3-inch strip.

In a medium saucepan bring 1 cup of water and ½ cup of butter to boil. Remove from the heat; stir in 1 cup of flour until smooth. Add the eggs one at a time, beating until smooth. Stir in ½ teaspoon of almond extract. Spoon over the first layer. Bake at 350° for 50 to 60 minutes.

In a small bowl combine the confectioners' sugar, 1 tablespoon of butter, ½ teaspoon of almond extract, and the milk. Glaze the pastries when cooled. Sprinkle sliced almonds over the top and cut into slices.

MAKES 6 SERVINGS.

—MICHAEL VANESSE

Veteran character actress Mary Wickes starred as the Wicked Witch in a touring stage production of The Wizard of Oz *(with Cathy Rigby as Dorothy) in the late 1980s. Interestingly, Wickes and Margaret Hamilton were friends, played similar roles, and worked together on a Saturday morning TV show,* Sigmund and the Sea Monsters *(1973–1975). Wickes, a recognizable hatchet-faced actress (with a sizable beak like Hamilton), had a lengthy Broadway, film* (The Man Who Came to Dinner, White Christmas)*, and television career; she enjoyed renewed popularity when she portrayed a nun, Sister Mary Lazarus, with Whoopi Goldberg in the 1992 hit film* Sister Act *and its sequel Wickes was still recording dialogue for a talking gargoyle in the animated Disney feature* The Hunchback of Notre Dame*, when she died in October 1995 at age eighty-five.*

EXTRAORDINARY APPLE FRITTERS

Mary loved these, according to friends.

½   cup milk
1   egg
2   tablespoons margarine
    Grated orange rind (½ orange)
    Juice from ½ orange
½   cup chopped unpeeled apples
½   teaspoon vanilla extract
1½ cups cake flour
¼   teaspoon salt
1   tablespoon baking powder
    Cooking oil

In a medium bowl combine the milk, egg, and margarine. Add the grated rind, orange juice, chopped apples, and vanilla. In a small bowl sift together the flour, salt, and baking powder. Stir into the milk mixture with a spoon just until blended. In a medium frying pan heat ½ inch of oil. Drop the batter by spoonfuls into hot oil. Fry to a golden brown. Drain.

MAKES ABOUT 24 FRITTERS.

—MARY WICKES, W.W.W. in 1980s
Oz touring stage musical

FERN FORMICA'S GARLIC BREAD

This recipe was given to us verbally by Fern as we were enjoying a great dinner at an Italian restaurant in Hemet, California.

1   cup margarine
½   cup Parmesan cheese
1   teaspoon garlic powder
     Italian spices (basil, oregano, thyme, etc.)
1   loaf Italian or French bread

In a medium bowl combine the margarine, Parmesan cheese, and garlic powder. Add Italian spices to taste. Spread generously on one side of sliced Italian or French bread. Place under the broiler until golden brown.

MAKES 6 TO 8 SERVINGS.

—BLANCHE AND JERRY COX

IT'S A CHEESE TWISTER!

1   17¼-ounce package frozen puff pastry (thawed)
1   egg, slightly beaten
⅔   cup grated Parmesan cheese
1   tablespoon paprika

Line two cookie sheets with waxed paper. Roll each sheet of puff pastry into a 12 x 10-inch rectangle. Brush the pastries with egg. In a small bowl combine the Parmesan cheese and paprika. Sprinkle 3 tablespoons of this mix on each pastry. Press in. Turn the pastries over and repeat on the other side. Cut the pastries into ½-inch strips. Turn each end in the opposite direction to form twists. Bake at 425° for 7 to 8 minutes or until golden brown. Serve warm or cool.

MAKES 4 DOZEN.

—ELLEN ARMSTRONG

KANSAS CORN FRITTERS

1   10-ounce can whole kernel corn
     Milk
1½   cups sifted all-purpose flour
3   teaspoons baking powder
¾   teaspoon salt
½   cup sugar
1   egg, beaten

Drain the corn, reserving the liquid. Add enough milk to the liquid to make 1 cup. In a medium bowl sift together the dry ingredients. In a small bowl combine the beaten egg, milk mixture, and corn. Add to the dry ingredients, mixing just until moist. Heat ¼-inch layer of cooking oil in a heavy skillet. Drop the batter by tablespoonfuls into hot grease. Fry until brown. Drain on paper towels.

MAKES 4 TO 6 SERVINGS.

—DAVID WILCOX

NISU—UNKASTUKKE

Nisu is a Finnish sweet bread. The recipe comes from my maternal grandmother, Arlene Hietanen, whose parents arrived in the USA from Finland around the end of the nineteenth century. Nisu in Finland has since developed somewhat different-ly, so this recipe is an American version. Traditionally, the dough is shaped into a braided loaf called unkastukke. We make one for every family member for Christmas.

2	packages active dry yeast
2	cups milk
1	cup sugar
1	tablespoon salt
16	ground cardamom seeds (or 1 teaspoon commercially ground cardamom)
7	to 9 cups all-purpose flour
3	to 4 eggs
½	cup butter, softened
	Confectioners' sugar
	Water

In a large bowl dissolve the yeast in milk. Beat in the sugar, salt, cardamom, and half the flour. Beat in the eggs, one at a time. Add the remaining flour. Knead. While kneading, add the softened butter a little at a time. Cover and set in a warm place to rise until doubled in size.

Punch down the risen dough. Divide the dough into 3 equal parts and form into lengths to be braided together to form 1 loaf. Let rise again to double in size.

Bake at 350° for 25 to 30 minutes.

In a small bowl make a frosting by mix-ing a little confectioners' sugar and water. For a festive touch, add food coloring to the sugar frosting. Cool before spreading frost-ing on top of the braided loaf.

MAKES 1 LOAF.

—ERIC SHANOWER, *Oz* illustrator

A smattering of original Baum books, as well as titles by Ruth Plumly Thompson, who contin-ued his famous Oz stories. First editions with dust jackets are increasingly rare and expensive collector's items. It would be hard to imagine how many bil-lions of readers have enjoyed the original Oz stories throughout the past century; many of the titles are still available in libraries and bookstores around the world. (Beyond the Rainbow Archive)

SAUSAGE ZUCCHINI CORN BREAD

1   pound bulk Italian turkey sausage
1   medium onion, chopped
2   large zucchini, scrubbed and coarsely
      shredded
2   cups all-purpose flour
2   cups cornmeal (stone-ground is
      preferable)
1   teaspoon baking soda
1   tablespoon baking powder
2   cups buttermilk
2   eggs, well beaten
½   cup vegetable oil
1   cup shredded Cheddar cheese

Spray a large skillet with vegetable spray. In a
skillet brown the sausage. Remove from the
pan. In the leftover drippings sauté the
chopped onion, and then add the shredded
zucchini. Cook until the zucchini is slightly
softened. Set aside to cool.

    In a large bowl combine the dry ingredi-
ents. In a medium bowl mix together the
buttermilk, eggs, and oil. Add to the dry
ingredients. Stir in the cooked sausage, vegetable mixture, and shredded Cheddar
cheese. Mix just until blended. Turn into a
greased 10 x 13-inch pan. Bake at 350° for
45 minutes or until the top is golden and
set.

MAKES ABOUT 10 MAIN DISH SERVINGS.

—ANNETTE O'TOOLE, portrayed Maud Baum
in TV-movie *The Dreamer of Oz*

SCARECROW'S CORN BREAD

It's a no-brainer!

¾   cup all-purpose flour
¾   cup cornmeal
2   teaspoons baking powder
¾   teaspoon salt
2   tablespoons sugar
1   egg
¾   cup milk
2   tablespoons bacon drippings
      Butter

In a medium bowl sift the dry ingredients
together. In a small bowl beat the egg, milk,
and bacon drippings together and add to dry

*Annette O'Toole portrays Maud Gage Baum and John
Ritter is* The Dreamer of Oz, *in the NBC-TV movie
about the life of writer L. Frank Baum.*

mixture. Stir only until smooth and pour into a well-buttered 8-inch square pan. Bake at 425° for 25 minutes, or until the top is well browned.

Makes 8 servings.

Scarecrow's Stuffin'

1½   loaves dry sourdough bread (or French or Italian)
2   pounds bulk Italian sausage (hot or sweet)
2   cloves garlic, minced
      Olive oil (optional)
1   onion, diced
4   to 5 celery stalks, halved and thinly sliced
1   small can almonds, finely chopped (garlic or hickory flavor is good)
      Basil, oregano, rosemary, and crushed red pepper to taste
1   to 2 cups chicken broth (or stock)

Cut the bread into small cubes. Spread on a baking sheet and bake at 250°, turning the cubes periodically until dry, but not crunchy. Set aside.

In a heavy skillet brown the sausage with garlic. Use a little olive oil, if necessary. Add the onion and celery and cook until the onion is golden. In a large bowl mix the meat (including drippings), onion, and celery with the bread cubes. Add the almonds and seasonings. Add enough chicken broth to moisten.

Makes enough stuffing for a good-sized turkey, or 2 large chickens.

—JEFF RIZZO, musical director for
The Wizard of Oz National
Tour, 1998–1999

Gwen and Ray Bolger had one of the most successful marriages in Hollywood. The couple loved going out to eat, and it was over lunch at the old Montmartre Café on Hollywood Boulevard in 1929 that Ray proposed. For two years prior, the couple were separated geographically, but not emotionally. Finally, when Ray left New York during a break and returned to Los Angeles to be with his love, he decided it was time. Before they had finished lunch, he flatly said to Gwen: "I guess we'll just have to get married." The two were quite young (she was sixteen and he was twenty-two), but madly in love. Gwen followed Ray back to Port Chester, New York, for a civil ceremony, but the Justice of the Peace refused because the bride-to-be was legally underage. On July 9, 1929, the determined couple found a clergyman who performed the ceremony—resulting in a marriage that lasted fifty-seven years.

SEVENTH WONDER CHEESE DROP BISCUITS

2   cups all-purpose flour
1   tablespoon baking powder
1½   teaspoons baking soda
1½   teaspoons salt
5   to 6 tablespoons unsalted butter, cut into
       pieces and chilled
1½   cups finely shredded Cheddar cheese
1   cup heavy cream

In a large bowl combine the flour, baking powder, soda, and salt. With a pastry blender (or 2 knives) cut in the chilled butter pieces, tossing with the flour mixture to coat and separate the pieces. Blend the mixture until it resembles coarse cornmeal. Avoid letting the mixture become too soft and form a pastelike dough. Stir in the Cheddar cheese. Add the cream to the dough all at once. Mix just until moistened but not smooth. Use a teaspoon to drop biscuits onto an ungreased baking sheet about 1½ inches apart. Bake at 450° for about 12 minutes or until the biscuits are deep golden brown. Serve hot.

Serving suggestion: Split biscuits open with fork. Spread with honey whipped butter. Top with a generous spoonful of blueberry-currant jam.

MAKES ABOUT 12 BISCUITS.

—JACK HALEY JR., producer of television documentary, *The Wonderful Wizard of Oz: The Making of a Movie Classic,* hosted by Angela Lansbury

Wide-eyed Jack Haley Jr. is engrossed in the Oz tale, lovingly told by the Tin Man himself. Even at age five, young Haley had an unforgettable experience when he visited the Oz movie set, hand in hand with his father. "Munchkinland absolutely stunned me," Haley says. "I had never seen such startling colors or such strangely shaped dwellings where all these hundreds of curious people lived. Children today are at least somewhat prepared for their visit to Disneyland. I was definitely not ready for the visual impact of Oz." (Courtesy of Jack Haley Jr. Productions)

Tin Can Brown Bread

Note: *Collect 4 16-ounce tin cans—preferably ones that have been opened with the kind of can opener that leaves no sharp edges. Thoroughly wash and dry the cans. Set them aside to use as bread pans for baking.*

2   cups water
2   cups raisins
2   tablespoons butter
1   cup sugar
2   eggs, slightly beaten
1   teaspoon salt
2   teaspoons baking soda
1   teaspoon vanilla extract
2¾ cups all-purpose flour

In a small saucepan bring the water to a boil. Carefully drop in the raisins and simmer 15 minutes. Set aside to cool. In a large bowl cream together the butter and sugar. Stir in the eggs, salt, soda, and vanilla. Stir in the raisin mixture alternately with the flour. Oil the collected cans well and fill to half with batter. Bake at 350° for 1 hour.

MAKES 4 LOAVES.

—DENISE ORTH

Zucchini Bread

3   eggs, beaten
1   cup oil
2   cups sugar
2   teaspoons vanilla extract
2   cups grated zucchini
3   cups all-purpose flour
½   teaspoon baking powder
1   tablespoon baking soda
1   teaspoon salt
2   tablespoons ground cinnamon
½   cup chopped nuts

In a large bowl lightly beat the eggs. Add the oil and sugar. Stir in the vanilla and zucchini, blending well. In a medium bowl sift together the dry ingredients. Stir the dry ingredients into the egg mixture, blending thoroughly. Stir in the nuts.

Grease 2 loaf pans. Divide the batter between the prepared pans. Bake at 350° for 1 hour or until a tester inserted in the center comes out clean.

MAKES 2 LOAVES.

—VIRGIE AND LYLE CONVERSE, Dorothy Gage Memorial Garden, Bloomington, Illinois

VERY GOOD—BUT VERY MYSTERIOUS

EMERALD CITY MINT-PEA SOUP

1   teaspoon butter
1   shallot, minced
½   clove garlic, minced
1   cup chicken broth
     Pinch basil
     Pinch thyme
1   10½-ounce can condensed green pea
     soup
1½   cups half-and-half
     Salt and pepper to taste
3   tablespoons green crème de menthe (or
     to taste)

In a skillet heat the butter and sauté the shallot and garlic until soft and golden but not brown. Add the chicken broth, basil, and thyme. Bring to a boil and simmer for 2 minutes. Blend in the pea soup and half-and-half. Add the salt and pepper. Strain. Chill for at least 4 hours. Stir in the crème de menthe.

MAKES 4 SERVINGS.

EMERALD GREEN ONION PIE

1   9-inch pastry shell
1   egg yolk, beaten
¼   cup butter
3   cups chopped green onions including
     tops
2   cups thin cream, scalded
4   eggs, slightly beaten
     Salt and pepper to taste
     Basil to taste

Brush the pastry shell with beaten egg yolk. Bake at 450° for 5 minutes. Place an empty pie pan inside the pastry one, reduce the heat to 300°, and bake until slightly brown. Set aside.

In a skillet heat the butter and cook the onions until wilted. Place the cooked onions in the prepared pastry shell. In a medium bowl mix together the scalded cream, remaining eggs, salt, pepper, and basil. Carefully pour this mixture over the onions. Bake at 350° until set and the top browned.

MAKES 8 SERVINGS.

—BLANCHE COX

THE FAMILY CIRCUS® **By Bil Keane**

The WIZARD OF OZ

2-25
©1992 Bil Keane, Inc.
Dist. by Cowles Synd., Inc.

"Daddy, can we paint our front walk yellow?"

Dolly's Mud Pie

3 Tbl spoons dirt
1 mouthful water
Blend ~~ingridience~~ ~~ingreedents~~ the stuff together. Then squish around for two minutes, and serve to your little brother.

Both cartoons this page reprinted by permission of Bil Keane.

"HOLD ON TO YOUR BREATH" PASTA

This is one of our family favorites. It's tasty, it's fast, and we are definitely garlic lovers! If you have parsley in the garden, this is something you can cook up any time because you probably already have all the other ingredients on hand.

1	16-ounce package vermicelli (or spaghetti)
4	to 6 garlic cloves
8	ounces Parmesan cheese
½	cup olive oil
1	cup chopped fresh parsley
	Salt to taste

In a large pot of boiling salted water add a little oil to prevent pasta from sticking together and cook the vermicelli according to the package directions. While the pasta cooks, chop the garlic cloves and grate the Parmesan cheese. Set aside. When you think the pasta is done, throw a strand on the wall. If it sticks, it's done. If it doesn't, continue cooking. Drain the pasta and put in a large serving bowl. Add the olive oil, chopped garlic, half the parsley, and grated cheese. Toss and taste, adding more garlic, cheese, parsley, and salt to your own individual taste. Serve with a green salad and French bread.

After the meal, serve any remaining garlic as an Italian breath mint—and have the kids clean the wall.

MAKES 6 SERVINGS.

—BETTY ANN BRUNO, child Munchkin
in *Oz*, MGM

In the Kitchen with Daws Butler

Daws was very well acquainted with the kitchen, having first helped his mother and then me. Using the basic recipe on the Bisquick box for pancakes, he would add spices (like nutmeg or cinnamon) and nuts. He beat the egg white and then made pancakes in the shapes of our sons' initials: D, D, P, and C.

Early in our marriage we both worked. The first one home would start dinner. One day he was using a package of refrigerated biscuits and as he opened the container, it exploded and the biscuits landed on the kitchen ceiling. To this day I am leery of that type of packaging.

He continued the custom of starting dinner if I wasn't home. One evening he greeted me and a friend at the door with "I put the liver in a bowl of milk." At the surprised look on my friend's face, he added, "It makes the liver taste better."

—*Myrtis Butler*

"MARRIAGE CASSEROLE"

Master Chefs Gloria and Larry Mann

Into a dull void, place 2 people (dressed or undressed) at room temperature. Add equal portions of love and understanding. Fold in large portions of consideration and unselfishness. To the mixture, add extra-large doses of compromise. Ready to serve immediately. If done right serves 2 at least 75 years. Enjoy!

—LARRY MANN, voice of "Rusty the Tin Man"
in Rankin/Bass cartoon special
"Return to Oz" and in TV series
Tales of the Wizard of Oz

A 1962 comic book based on the TV series Tales of the Wizard of Oz, *produced by Rankin/Bass. Tales was a series of 130 five-minute cartoons, which aired in 1961.*

"Heavens to Murgatroyd!" Hardly a coward, Hanna-Barbera's flamboyant pink cartoon cat, Snagglepuss, delivers the Oz tale on this 1965 children's record album. Legendary cartoon actor Daws Butler (Yogi Bear, Huckleberry Hound et al.) provided the vocals. Admittedly, Butler's voice for Snagglepuss was essentially an impression of Bert Lahr.

MUNCHKIN TRIBAL MARINADE

Excellent on beef, chicken, or fish.

This is from the Hawaiian side of my family. It's a no-miss marinade: absolutely delicious, deceptively easy. It's best with fresh ginger, but you can use ground, if you can't get the fresh.

4   to 5 large garlic cloves, chopped
1   ½-inch piece fresh ginger (or ½ teaspoon powdered ginger)
1   tablespoon sugar
½   cup soy sauce
    Freshly ground pepper to taste

In a large bowl combine the garlic and ginger. Using the back of a spoon blend in the sugar. Add the soy sauce and pepper. If you're not going to use the marinade immediately, store in a closed jar in the refrigerator. Otherwise, in a shallow dish, just toss the meat or fish in the marinade so that all surfaces are coated, and mix it up every once in a while.

We prefer flank steak, sliced into diagonal strips, but this marinade is also wonderful on beef ribs and hamburgers. Beef should marinate for at least 2 hours—and you can leave it all day, if you're on a picnic, for instance. Chicken can marinate for less time (even half an hour seems to do it). Cut the chicken as if for frying. Fish is more absorbent and shouldn't marinate for more than half an hour or it will become too salty from the soy sauce.

Cooking: Best to barbecue, but you can also oven-broil or pan-fry. This is enough marinade for one flank steak, one chicken, or three or four fish fillets. If your beef is a little tough, add a shot of whiskey to the marinade as a tenderizer. Very good when accompanied by rice, a green vegetable, and a fruit salad.

—BETTY ANN BRUNO, child Munchkin
in *Oz,* MGM

Phyllis Diller prepares her famous "Garbage Soup" for the masses.

PHYLLIS DILLER'S GARBAGE SOUP

"Aha, so you won't take warning, eh?"

It's actually better to start your soup with 2 or 3 plates of boiling pieces of meat instead of— or along with—your soup bone.

First, you fill a big pot or caldron with water or hopefully with liquids you have saved from fixing frozen foods, preparing fresh vegetables, or liquids drained from canned vegetables. If you haven't saved enough of these, add water until the meat is covered. Bring to a boil, reduce the heat, and simmer for 3 or 4 hours. Remove the meat and let it cool so you can take all the lean meat and cut it into small pieces—less than bite-size—like dimes. Place the liquid in the refrigerator so the grease will congeal on top. Remove the grease.

Now add to the liquid: Chopped onion, carrots, and celery. These are basic. Other ingredients can be parsley, potato, green bell pepper.

Cook until these fresh ingredients are "done"— then add a large can of tomatoes (cut up) and 2 cans of S & W kidney beans. Add Lawry's Seasoned Salt, garlic salt, and onion salt.

Now take all the leftovers out of the refrigerator and chop them into dime-size pieces and add to soup. You can use spaghetti, peas, beans, pasta, corn, shrimp, any vegetable, leftover casserole, meat from restaurant doggie bags, leftover Mexican food, whatever. But DO chop it to dime size.

—PHYLLIS DILLER, W.W.W. in 1991 *Oz*
touring stage musical

SPAGHETTI SOUP

3   tablespoons oil
1½   pounds ground beef
1   large onion, chopped
1   teaspoon minced garlic
3   16-ounce cans kidney beans
1   16-ounce can chopped tomatoes
      Salt and pepper to taste
1   teaspoon sugar
1   16-ounce package spaghetti
      Parmesan cheese

In a large saucepan or Dutch oven heat the oil. Brown the ground beef, onion, and garlic. Add the kidney beans and tomatoes plus 2 cans of water. Bring to a boil. Add salt, pepper, and sugar. Boil over medium or low heat for 1 hour.

While the soup simmers, cook the spaghetti according to the package directions. Rinse, drain, and add to the soup. Add enough liquid to make it soupy. Cover and simmer. Serve with Parmesan cheese and fresh French bread.

MAKES 6 SERVINGS.

—MARCELLA KRANZLER, wife of Emil Kranzler,
Munchkin in *Oz*, MGM

TIN MAN'S CAN OF SPAM FRIED RICE

¼   cup diced bacon
1   12-ounce can Spam, diced
5   eggs, beaten
1   bunch green onions, chopped
5   to 6 cups cooked rice, cooled
      Soy sauce

In a large skillet or wok fry the bacon. Add the Spam before the bacon turns brown and crispy. Fry for 1 to 2 minutes. Add the eggs, stir into the mixture, and cook until the eggs are no longer runny. Add the green onions, mix well, and reduce the heat. Add the cooled rice and soy sauce to taste. Mix well before serving.

MAKES 4 TO 6 SERVINGS.

—NANCY K. ROBINSON, Dorothy's House,
Liberal, Kansas

Munchkin actor Emil Kranzler applying his signature and handprint in cement at the Yellow Brick Road Shop—a hub for the Chesterton, Indiana, annual Oz-Fest.

TOTO'S DELICIOUS DOGGIE BONES

4	cups whole wheat flour
½	cup cornmeal
½	cup rolled oats
2	tablespoons firmly packed brown sugar
1	egg, slightly beaten
2	tablespoons vegetable oil
	Juice from 1 small orange
1⅔	cups beef bouillon

In a large bowl combine the flour, cornmeal, oats, and brown sugar. Make a well in the center. In a small bowl combine the egg, oil, orange juice, and beef bouillon. Add the liquids to the flour mixture all at once, beating with an electric mixer.

Turn out onto a lightly floured surface and knead. Roll out dough to about ⅛-inch thickness and cut out with a dog-bone-shaped cookie cutter. Coat a baking sheet with non-stick spray. Place bones on the prepared sheet. Bake at 350° for 45 minutes. Turn the bones over halfway through the baking period.

MAKES ABOUT 3 DOZEN.

—JESSICA GROVÉ, Dorothy in *The Wizard of Oz* National Tour, 1998–1999

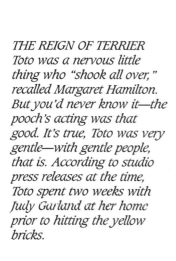

THE REIGN OF TERRIER Toto was a nervous little thing who "shook all over," recalled Margaret Hamilton. But you'd never know it—the pooch's acting was that good. It's true, Toto was very gentle—with gentle people, that is. According to studio press releases at the time, Toto spent two weeks with Judy Garland at her home prior to hitting the yellow bricks.

NEW HEART FOR BOB Celebrating a troubled Halloween in an eerie October 1987 episode of TV's Newhart *are Bob Newhart, Tom Poston, and Mary Frann. (Courtesy of Tom Poston)*

TOTO'S TREATS

2½   cups whole wheat flour
¼   cup wheat germ
¼   cup margarine, softened
1   clove garlic, crushed
1   egg, beaten
1   tablespoon molasses
¼   cup milk

In a large bowl combine the flour and wheat germ. Cut in the margarine. Stir in the garlic, egg, molasses, and milk. Add enough water so the mixture may be formed into a ball. Roll out on a floured surface. Cut into desired shapes. Bake on greased cookie sheets at 375° for 20 minutes. Cool before serving.

MAKES ABOUT 30 BISCUITS.

—KAILEY ARMSTRONG

VERY SIMPLE CHILI

Take your regular chili recipe. Instead of using rice in the chili, make a very strong garlic and butter sauce and pop one bag of microwave popcorn. Cover the popcorn with the sauce, then fold into the chili.

—TOM POSTON

Sweets from the Heart

Apricot Macaroons

"Who put the ape in apricot?"

½ cup dried apricots, cut into quarters
½ cup water
¾ cup plus 1 tablespoon sugar
4 egg whites
5 cups unsweetened shredded coconut

In a small saucepan combine the apricots, water, and 1 tablespoon sugar. Cook the apricots over medium heat until tender and about 1 tablespoon water remains. Cool slightly and transfer to a food processor fitted with a metal blade. Add the remaining ¾ cup of sugar, egg whites, and ½ cup of coconut. Process by first using on-off spurts, then allow the machine to run until the apricots are puréed.

Transfer to the large bowl of an electric mixer. Add the remaining 4½ cups of coconut. Beat on medium speed until the coconut is well blended. Stop the machine and check the texture. The mixture should hold together when pinched. Continue to mix, if necessary.

Prepare baking sheets by covering them with parchment paper or foil. Using your hands, shape the cookie mixture into pointed cone shapes. Arrange 1 inch apart on baking sheets. Bake at 350° for 15 to 20 minutes until the tops are well browned. Cool on a rack. Store in an airtight food container.

MAKES 24 TO 32 MACAROONS.

—ELIZABETH AND JERRY MAREN,
Munchkin in *Oz*, MGM

Munchkins Jerry Maren (left, as the Hamburglar) and Billy Curtis (center, as Mayor McCheese) later found profitable work in McDonald's fast-food commercials in the 1970s. (Courtesy of Jerry Maren)

Cocoanut Sweet

Cocoanut sweet
Honey-dew new
Jasmine an' cherry an' juniper berry
That's you

Cocoanut sweet
Buttercup true
Face that I see in the blue Caribbean,
That's you

Catch me the smile you smile
And I'll make this big world my tiny island
Shining with spice and sugar plum
Cage me the laugh you laugh
And I will make this tiny, shiny island
My little slice of kingdom come

The wind may blow
The hurricane whip up the sky
The vine go bare
The leaf go dry

But when you smile for me
Spring tumble out of the tree
The peach is ripe, the lime is green
The air is touched with tangerine

And cocoanut sweet
Honey-dew new
Ev'rything dear that wants to cheer
The nearness of you

How it all come true
Wherever we meet
The magic of cherry and berry
And cocoanut sweet

Lyrics to the song "Cocoanut Sweet" by E. Y. ("Yip") Harburg from the 1957 Broadway musical *Jamaica* (composer, Harold Arlen), reprinted by permission. The grammar may seem strange, but it was sung in the show by people with Caribbean dialects.

—The Harburg Foundation

E. Y. Harburg, called "Yip" by his friends, was one of the great lyricists and poets of our time. His son, Ernie, reminds us: "The word rainbow never appears in L. Frank Baum's book . . . it was Yip Harburg who put it in the film." (Courtesy of the Harburg Estate)

AUNTIE M&M'S COOKIES

1   cup margarine (good brand only, not diet margarine or butter)
¾   cup sugar
¾   cup firmly packed brown sugar
2   eggs, beaten
1   teaspoon vanilla extract
2½   cups sifted all-purpose flour
1   teaspoon baking soda
1   teaspoon salt
1   10-ounce package M&M's
1   cup chopped nuts

In a large bowl cream together the margarine and both sugars by hand. Add the eggs and vanilla extract. Stir to blend. In a medium bowl sift together the flour, baking soda, and salt. Add the dry ingredients into the creamed batter, mixing together until well blended. Stir in the M&M's and nuts. On nonstick baking sheets drop the batter by teaspoonfuls. Bake at 375° for 10 to 12 minutes until golden brown.

MAKES ABOUT 50 COOKIES.

—FRIEDA KARRAS

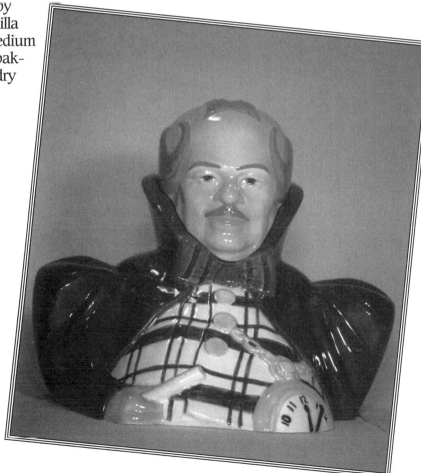

The Mayor of Munchkinland cookie jar, by Star Jars.

BAKED APPLES WITH HONEY AND ALMONDS

This was one of Hardy's favorites, reprinted from a 1930s actors' cookbook.

4   baking apples
1   teaspoon aromatic bitters
¼   cup honey
4   tablespoons chopped blanched almonds
2   tablespoons butter

Peel only the top half of the apples. Remove the cores without piercing the apples all the way through to prevent any of the apple juice and honey from running out of the apple as it cooks. In a small cup mix the aromatic bitters with the honey. Pour a tablespoon of honey mixture in each apple, spreading a little of the mixture over the tops of the apples to glaze them. Add a tablespoon of almonds to each apple. Dot with butter. Place in an 8 x 8 x 2-inch baking dish. Pour ½ cup of water around the apples to prevent them from burning on the bottom. Bake at 375° for 1 hour or until tender. Serve plain or top with whipped cream.

Note: A stuffing of dates and nut meats makes an appetizing variation for this dish.

—OLIVER HARDY, Tin Man in
The Wizard of Oz, 1925

A vintage lobby card for the 1925 Chadwick Pictures silent film version of The Wizard of Oz, *which starred Larry Semon as the Scarecrow, Oliver Hardy as the Tin Man, and Dorothy Dwan (Semon's wife) as Dorothy. Produced after L. Frank Baum's death, the film was co-written by his eldest son, Frank Jr.*

Another Fine Mess

Academy Award–winning director Leo McCarey appeared on Ralph Edwards's popular TV show, *This Is Your Life*, in 1954 to pay tribute to the comedy duo Stan Laurel and Oliver Hardy. McCarey has been credited for teaming the comedians in 1926, just a year after Hardy portrayed the Tin Man in a silent version of *The Wizard of Oz*. McCary recalled the legendary fusion:

". . . It seems that Babe (Oliver Hardy) was cooking a leg of lamb. For some reason, he left his arm in the oven too long, or something, and got it badly blistered. . . . We had to cut down his part in the next picture, so we decided to put Stan in the picture, too, to bolster up the comedy. When we saw the two of them on the screen together, we decided there was a real team, and from that time on, they really went places. All on account of Hardy having a little leg of lamb."

BECAUSE, BECAUSE PINEAPPLE UPSIDE DOWN CAKE

⅓   cup butter
½   cup firmly packed brown sugar
1   16-ounce can pineapple slices, drained and juice reserved
8   maraschino cherries
    Pecan halves
2   eggs
⅔   cup sugar
1   teaspoon vanilla extract
1   cup sifted all-purpose flour
⅓   teaspoon baking powder
¼   teaspoon salt

In a 10-inch baking dish, melt the butter. Sprinkle the brown sugar evenly over the butter. Arrange 8 pineapple slices with cherries and pecans in an attractive pattern on the butter-sugar coating. In a medium bowl beat the eggs until thick and lemon-colored, about 5 minutes. Gradually beat in the sugar. Beat in 6 tablespoons of reserved juice and vanilla. In a small bowl sift together the flour, baking powder, and salt. Combine with the egg mixture and mix well. Pour the batter carefully over the pineapple slices. Bake at 375° for 45 minutes or until a wooden toothpick inserted in the center comes out clean. Immediately turn upside down on a serving plate. Do not remove the pan for a few minutes. The brown sugar mixture will run down over the cake instead of clinging to pan. Serve warm with plain or whipped cream.

MAKES 8 SERVINGS.

—DONA MASSIN, assistant choreographer and Emerald City citizen in *Oz*, MGM

1939

Dona Massin, assistant choreographer on The Wizard of Oz, *taught the Munchkins their "skip" and Bert Lahr his steps. "Bert was horribly insecure," she reveals. "He had to have me as his audience all the time. When I taught him the skip I realized he didn't know his left foot from his right. Poor Bert . . . he was so clumsy, and I loved him for it."*

In Emerald City "we get up at twelve and start to work at one . . . take an hour for lunch and then at two we're done . . . jolly good fun!" Look for assistant choreographer Dona Massin, on the far left, holding clippers. (Courtesy of Dona Massin)

Nineteen-year-old Judy Garland out to dinner with her fiancé, David Rose, in Hollywood, June 11, 1941. The couple were married briefly, and they divorced amicably. (Beyond the Rainbow Archive)

BEEM'S BROWNIES

3	1-ounce squares unsweetened chocolate
6	1-ounce squares semisweet chocolate
9	tablespoons butter
3	eggs, beaten
1½	cups sugar
1½	cups all-purpose flour
¾	teaspoon salt
1½	cups walnuts
1½	cups mini marshmallows

In a double boiler over simmering water melt the unsweetened and semisweet chocolates and butter. Cool slightly. In a small bowl beat the eggs and work a small amount of the warm chocolate mixture into the eggs to warm them. Then add the warmed eggs into the remaining chocolate mixture. In a large bowl stir together the sugar, flour, and salt.

Gradually blend in the chocolate mixture, stirring until well combined. Measure out ¾ cup of the batter and reserve. In a 9-inch square pan place the remaining batter. Bake at 350° for 20 minutes.

In a medium bowl combine the reserved batter with the walnuts and marshmallows. When the brownies are removed from the oven, spread the topping over and return to the oven. Bake at 350° for an additional 7 to 10 minutes.

MAKES 8 TO 10 SERVINGS.

—ANITA AND BILL BEEM

*An original newspaper ad for the motion picture.
(Robert A. Baum Collection)*

BETTY TANNER'S WALDORF RED CAKE

½	cup shortening
2½	cups sugar, divided
2	eggs
2	teaspoons vanilla extract, divided
2	tablespoons cocoa
1	ounce red food coloring (plus several drops for frosting)
2½	cups sifted cake flour
1	teaspoon salt
1	cup buttermilk
1	teaspoon baking soda
1	teaspoon vinegar
1	cup milk
¼	cup all-purpose flour
1	cup butter
½	cup chopped pecans (optional)

In a large bowl cream together the shortening, 1½ cups of sugar, eggs, and 1 teaspoon of vanilla. In a cup make a paste of the cocoa and 1 ounce of food coloring. Add to the creamed mixture. In a small bowl stir together 2½ cups of cake flour and the salt. Alternately add the flour mixture and buttermilk to the creamed mixture. In a small bowl mix the soda and vinegar. Stir into the batter, blending well. Grease and flour two 9-inch round pans. Pour batter into the prepared pans. Bake at 350° for 30 to 35 minutes.

In a small saucepan cook the milk and ¼ cup of flour until thick, stirring constantly. Let cool. In a medium bowl cream the butter and remaining 1 cup sugar until smooth. Add the remaining 1 teaspoon of vanilla. Stir in the thickened milk and beat well. Add enough red food coloring to make the desired color of red. Add the pecans if desired. Frost the cooled cake with Yellow Brick Frosting (see page 224).

MAKES 8 SERVINGS.

—ANNE WHITE, sister of Betty Tanner,
Munchkin in *Oz,* MGM

CHOCOLATE ÉCLAIR TORTE

2	3-ounce packages instant French vanilla pudding mix
3	cups milk
1	9-ounce carton whipped topping
2	1-ounce squares Baker's unsweetened chocolate
3	tablespoons softened butter
2	tablespoons light Karo syrup
2	tablespoons milk
2	teaspoons vanilla extract
1½	cups confectioners' sugar
1	box graham crackers, divided

In a large mixing bowl beat both packages of pudding mix into 3 cups of milk. Fold in the whipped topping. Set aside.

In a small microwave-safe bowl melt the chocolate squares in the microwave. Remove from the microwave and stir in the softened butter. Stir in the Karo syrup, milk, and vanilla. Add the confectioners' sugar, beating until smooth.

Grease a 9 x 13-inch pan. Line the bottom of the prepared pan with graham cracker squares. Layer half of the pudding mixture over the crackers. Place another layer of crackers over the pudding. Layer in the remaining pudding, covering with a third layer of crackers. Layer the entire chocolate topping mixture over the last layer of crackers and refrigerate a minimum of 24 hours before serving.

Note: Can be prepared for a diabetic by substituting low-fat graham crackers, sugarless pudding mix, skim milk, and fat-free whipped topping, and omitting the chocolate topping.

MAKES 10 TO 16 SERVINGS.

—JANICE AND HERBERT LAHR, son of Bert Lahr

CINNAMON CHOCOLATE CAKE

1   cup water
1   cup margarine, divided
½   cup shortening
½   cup cocoa, divided
2   cups all-purpose flour
2   cups sugar
1   teaspoon ground cinnamon
1   teaspoon baking soda
½   cup buttermilk
2   eggs, beaten
2   teaspoons vanilla extract, divided
6   tablespoons milk
1   16-ounce package confectioners' sugar, sifted
1   cup chopped pecans (optional)

In a medium saucepan boil together the water, ½ cup of margarine, ½ cup of shortening, and ¼ cup of cocoa until melted. In a medium bowl combine the flour, sugar, and cinnamon. Add the chocolate mixture and beat well. In a measuring cup dissolve the baking soda in the buttermilk. Stir in the batter along with the eggs and 1 teaspoon of vanilla extract. Beat well. Grease and flour a 15½ x 10½ x 1-inch pan and fill with the batter. Bake at 400° for 15 minutes or until a toothpick inserted in the center comes out clean.

While the cake is baking, make the frosting. In a medium saucepan bring the milk and remaining ½ cup of margarine to a boil and remove from the heat. Stir in the remaining ¼ cup of cocoa, vanilla, confectioners' sugar, and pecans. Stir until smooth. Pour over the cake while it is still hot. The cake should be stored in, and served from, the pan.

MAKES 10 TO 12 SERVINGS.

—MYRNA AND CLARENCE SWENSEN,
Munchkin in *Oz*, MGM

Traffic halts as tiny folk trek to big job

TRAFFIC REALLY HALTS when this assemblage of pocketsize humans crosses Washington boulevard every morning to enter Metro-Goldwyn-Mayer studios. Recruited from all parts of the country by the studio, the 104 midgets play the gnomelike Munchkins in the musical spectacle "Wizard of Oz," from the story by L. Frank Baum. Police stop boulevard motorists when the group reports for work, and again when lunchtime comes around, to permit 104 miniature troupers to pass in safety.

Dorothy and Toto arrive in Munchkinville where the Good Witch appears and informs them they have been tricked into a return journey to Oz by the Wicked Witch. The Rankin/Bass color animated special "Return to Oz" was presented on NBC-TV's General Electric Fantasy Hour *in 1964 and 1965.*

CONWAY'S APPLE CRISP

5	to 8 Northern Spy apples, peeled and thinly sliced
1	cup sugar
1½	cups all-purpose flour, divided
1	teaspoon ground cinnamon
1	teaspoon vanilla extract
½	cup water
¾	cup firmly packed brown sugar
½	cup butter

In a round 8 x 3½-inch-deep casserole place the apples. In a small bowl mix together sugar, ½ cup flour, and cinnamon. Sprinkle over the apples. In a small cup add the vanilla to the water. Pour over the mixture. Prepare a pastry in a medium bowl by combining the 1 cup of flour and brown sugar. Cut in the butter using a fork or wooden spoon. Roll between sheets of waxed paper. Cut out circles and pat them down on top of the apples until they join together, forming a fairly smooth topping. Bake at 350° for 40 to 45 minutes or until the topping is brown and crispy.

Note: Northern Spy apples taste best. If you have to use a bland apple, try adding a bit of lemon juice.

MAKES 5 TO 8 SERVINGS.

—SUSAN CONWAY MITCHELL, voice of Dorothy in
Rankin/Bass "Return to Oz"

CORA'S COCONUT COOKIE BARS

A great treat with a cup of coffee!

½   cup butter, melted
1½   cups graham cracker crumbs
2   cups Angel Flake coconut
1   cup chopped nuts
1½   cups miniature marshmallows (optional)
1   14-ounce can sweetened condensed milk
2   1-ounce squares semisweet chocolate, melted

In a 13 x 9-inch pan place the butter. Sprinkle the graham cracker crumbs over the butter, pressing down with a fork. Sprinkle coconut on top of the crumbs. Add a layer of nuts followed by the marshmallows. Drizzle condensed milk evenly over the top. Bake at 350° for 25 to 30 minutes or until golden brown. Remove from the oven and drizzle with melted chocolate. Cool before cutting.

MAKES ABOUT 24 BARS.

—CORA, the Maxwell House Coffee Lady

WICKED NO MORE Margaret Hamilton became a popular spokeswoman in TV commercials as friendly "Cora," the Maxwell House coffee lady. A book of old-fashioned recipes featuring Cora on the cover was published by General Foods in 1977. Naturally, coffee recipes abound, with quotes such as this sprinkled throughout: "Cora says, 'Double the good taste of this dessert by serving it with lots of steaming coffee.'" (Beyond the Rainbow Archive)

CUSTARD RHUBARB PIE

1   heaping cup cubed rhubarb
1   unbaked 9-inch pastry shell
1   cup sugar
1   tablespoon butter
1   tablespoon all-purpose flour
¼   cup evaporated milk
2   eggs, beaten

Place the rhubarb in the pastry shell. In a small bowl cream together the sugar and butter. Add flour. Add the milk and eggs. Stir well and pour over the rhubarb. Bake at 425° for 20 to 25 minutes.

—VIRGIE AND LYLE CONVERSE, Dorothy Gage
Memorial Garden, Bloomington, Illinois

DOROTHY'S HUNK O' BROWNIES

½   cup butter
2   ounces Baker's unsweetened chocolate
2   eggs, beaten
½   cup all-purpose flour
1   cup sugar
½   teaspoon vanilla extract
1   cup chopped walnuts (optional)
1½ ounces Baker's unsweetened chocolate
2   tablespoons butter
1¼ cups confectioners' sugar
2   tablespoons milk (or as needed)

In a small saucepan melt ½ cup of butter and 2 ounces of chocolate over low heat. Remove from the heat and allow to cool slightly. In a medium bowl combine the eggs, flour, and sugar. Stir in the chocolate mixture and mix well. Stir in the vanilla and walnuts. Butter a shallow 8-inch square pan. Spread the batter in the prepared pan. Bake at 350° for 20 to 25 minutes.

In a small saucepan melt the remaining chocolate and butter together. Add the confectioners' sugar and enough milk to adequately stir the mixture. Spread lightly over the cooled pan of brownies.

MAKES 6 TO 8 SERVINGS.

—JOHN FRICKE, author of *Judy Garland: World's Greatest Entertainer*; coauthor of *Wizard of Oz Pictorial History* and *100 Years of Oz*

In 1962, after a six-year absence from television, Judy Garland returned to the small screen as star of "The Judy Garland Show," a tasty hour-long CBS special that aired Sunday, February 25, 1962. Appearing with her professionally for the first time were a couple of swells, Frank Sinatra and Dean Martin. The show was sponsored by Kitchens of Sara Lee.

EDNA BAUM'S ICE CREAMS
MACAROON ICE CREAM

1½   quarts milk
3   cups sugar
4   eggs, separated
½   teaspoon cornstarch
1   pint heavy cream
12   almond macaroons, dried and crumbled
1   small bottle maraschino cherries
1   teaspoon vanilla extract

In the top of a double boiler combine the milk, sugar, egg yolks, and cornstarch. Cook over simmering water until the mixture comes to a boil. Boil just 1 minute. Cool and fold in the beaten egg whites. Add the cream, macaroons, cherries including the juice, and vanilla. Pour into a freezing tray and freeze until firm, stirring well during the first hour of freezing.

MAKES 3 QUARTS.

NEW YORK ICE CREAM

1   pint milk
4   egg yolks, beaten
1½   cups sugar
1   quart heavy cream
1   teaspoon vanilla extract

In a double boiler over simmering water scald the milk. Gradually whisk a small amount of scalded milk into the egg yolks. Return the hot egg mixture to the scalded milk. Stir in the sugar and cook until the mixture comes to a boil. Boil just 1 minute. Cool and add the cream and vanilla. Pour into the freezing tray and freeze until firm, stirring well during the first hour of freezing.

MAKES 2 QUARTS.

ORANGE ICE CREAM

1   quart milk
6   egg yolks
3   cups sugar
2   cups orange juice
2   orange rinds, finely grated
1   pint cream, whipped

In a double boiler over simmering water scald the milk. Gradually whisk a small amount of scalded milk into the egg yolks. Return the hot egg mixture to the scalded milk. Stir in the sugar and cook until the mixture comes to a boil. Boil just 1 minute. Cool and add orange juice, grated rind, and the whipped cream. Pour into a freezing tray and freeze until firm, stirring well during the first hour of freezing.

—ROBERT BAUM, great-grandson
of L. Frank Baum

Maud Gage Baum holding her great-grandson, Robert, in 1942. (Robert A. Baum Collection)

EDNA BAUM'S LEMON MILK SHERBET

4   cups whole milk
3   cups sugar
4   egg yolks, beaten
1   teaspoon cornstarch
1   cup lemon juice

In the top of a double boiler combine the milk, sugar, egg yolks, and cornstarch. Cook until the mixture comes to a boil. Boil just 1 minute. Cool. Add the lemon juice. Pour into a freezing tray and freeze until firm, stirring well during the first hour of freezing.

MAKES 1 QUART.

Edna Baum (L. Frank Baum's daughter-in-law) reads an Oz book to her daughter, Florence, and son, Stanton, in 1934. (Robert A. Baum Collection)

—ROBERT BAUM, great-grandson
of L. Frank Baum

EDNA BAUM'S OATMEAL COOKIES

Can't have just one. Not nobody . . . not no how.

1   cup butter
1   cup firmly packed dark brown sugar
1¼   cups sugar
2   eggs
1½   cups all-purpose flour
1   teaspoon baking soda
1   teaspoon salt
1   teaspoon vanilla extract
4   cups quick-cooking oats
½   cup nuts (optional)

In a large bowl cream together the butter and sugars. Stir in the eggs, mixing thoroughly. In a medium bowl sift together the flour, soda, and salt. Add to the creamed mixture. Stir in the vanilla, oats, and nuts. Shape the dough into a roll, cover, and refrigerate overnight.

When ready to bake, grease cookie sheets. Slice the chilled dough in ½-inch slices and place on the prepared baking sheets. Bake at 325° for 12 minutes. Can be stored in a tin box when cool.

MAKES ABOUT 5 DOZEN COOKIES.

—ROBERT BAUM, great-grandson
of L. Frank Baum

EDNA BAUM'S SCOTCH SHORTBREAD

½   cup butter
½   cup sugar
2   cups all-purpose flour, sifted
½   teaspoon cornstarch
1   egg yolk (if needed for moisture)

In a medium bowl cream the butter and sugar until very smooth. Stir in the flour and cornstarch. Mix thoroughly with hands, adding egg yolk if the mixture is too dry. Chill. Line cookie sheets with waxed paper. Roll the dough to ⅓- to ½-inch thickness. Cut into fancy shapes, and pierce if desired. Place on prepared pans. Bake at 300° for 20 to 30 minutes. Cool completely before putting in a tin container.

Note: The tops do not brown during baking . . . nor does the shape of the cookies change.

By the way, there is no Scotch in this. It is an old-time delicacy from Scotland . . . crisp, thick, and buttery.

—ROBERT BAUM, great-grandson
of L. Frank Baum

In Oz, Dorothy and her pals dined on porridge, scrambled eggs, and white bread. Reprinted from Baum's original tale, The Wonderful Wizard of Oz *(1900). Artwork by W. W. Denslow.*

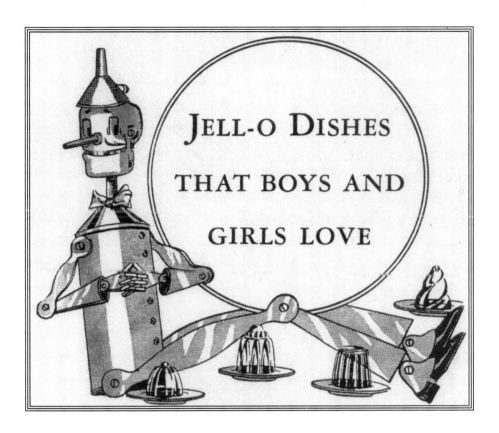

JELL-O DISHES
THAT BOYS AND
GIRLS LOVE

EMERALD CHIFFON MARBLE GELATIN

1   3-ounce package lime gelatin
¾   cup boiling water
1   cup cold water (see note)
1   cup whipped topping

In a medium bowl dissolve the gelatin in boiling water, stirring until well dissolved. Add the cold water. Remove ¾ cup of the mixture and set aside. Fold the whipped topping into the remaining gelatin. Alternately spoon plain gelatin and whipped topping mixture into 4 dessert glasses. Carefully zigzag a spatula or knife through the mixture to marble. Chill.

Note: For Munchkin Magic here's a little trick to shorten the required chilling time. Substitute 2 cups of ice cubes for the 1 cup of cold water when preparing the gelatin. Stir constantly until the gelatin starts to thicken, about 2 to 3 minutes. Remove any unmelted ice.

MAKES 4 SERVINGS.

—BILL COSBY, Wizard-Host of TV premiere, *Journey Back to Oz,* 1976

JELL-Oz

- The JELL-O company sponsored NBC's *Wizard of Oz* radio program in 1933 and 1934. Dorothy's popular radio adventures, based on all of the *Oz* books, were broadcast three times a week, across the United States. Listeners could send in box-fronts from JELL-O packages and receive a specially reprinted mini-*Oz* book with color images and recipes inside. The book urges Moms everywhere to treat the kids—why, treat the entire family!—to delicious JELL-O! Colorful and wobbly, it's great for any occasion.
- In the Emerald City scene, the spectral "horse of a different color," was actually two white palominos named Bill and Jake, "painted" with a gelatin product. According to studio press releases, during production, the steeds held up filming because they kept bobbing their heads, licking the brightly colored gelatin from their coats.

Magic Ice

1 package Lemon Jell-O
1 pint warm water
1 cup green Malaga grapes, halved and seeded

Dissolve Jell-O in warm water. Chill. When slightly thickened, fold in grapes. Chill until firm. Break with a spoon and pile lightly in sherbet glasses. The irregular mass looks like ice. Serves 6.

Emerald Fruit Cup

1 package Lime Jell-O
1 pint warm water
2 cups mixed fruit, diced (pears, peaches, cherries, canned pineapple, etc.)

Dissolve Jell-O in warm water. Turn into shallow pan. Chill until firm. Cut into small cubes. Combine with fruit. Pile into sherbet glasses, adding a small amount of fruit juice to each serving. Serves 8.

Junior Sailboats

1 package Orange or Lemon Jell-O
1 pint warm water
6 slices canned peaches

Dissolve Jell-O in warm water. Turn into sherbet glasses. Chill. Cut peaches in boat-shaped pieces. Cut small triangles of paper for sails. Insert a tooth pick through sail and into each peach slice, to hold sail erect. When Jell-O is thick enough to hold up peach boats, arrange one in center of each Jell-O lake. Chill until firm. Serves 6.

Cherry Whip

1 package Cherry Jell-O
1 pint warm water

Dissolve Jell-O in warm water. Chill until cold and syrupy. Place in bowl of cracked ice or ice water and whip with rotary egg beater until fluffy and thick like whipped cream. Pile lightly in sherbet glasses. Top each glass with cherry. Serve with custard sauce, if desired. Serves 8.

Raspberry Blocks with Pineapple

1 package Raspberry Jell-O
1 $\frac{1}{2}$ cups warm water
$\frac{1}{2}$ cup canned pineapple juice
1 cup canned pineapple, diced

Dissolve Jell-O in warm water. Add pineapple juice. Turn into loaf pan. Chill until firm. Cut in cubes. Pile lightly in sherbet glasses with pineapple. Serves 6.

EMERALD CITY GLIMMERING GELATIN DESSERT

2   3-ounce packages lime gelatin
¼   cup sugar
2   cups boiling water
1½   cups cold water
2   tablespoons green crème de menthe
     liqueur
1   envelope whipped topping mix
     Angel Flake coconut
1   1-ounce square semisweet chocolate
     (optional)

In a heat-resistant bowl dissolve the gelatin and sugar in boiling water. Add the cold water and liqueur. Pour 1 cup of the mixture into a 3-cup bowl and chill until slightly thickened. Pour the remaining mixture into a 9-inch square pan. Chill at least 3 hours or until firm. Meanwhile, prepare the whipped topping mix as directed on package. Blend into the slightly thickened gelatin in the 3-cup bowl. Chill about 3 hours until firm.

   In the center of a shallow serving bowl arrange a bed of coconut. Unmold the creamy gelatin. Cut the remaining gelatin in square pan into ½-inch cubes and arrange them around the mold. Garnish with chocolate curls if desired.

MAKES ABOUT 5 CUPS OR 8 TO 10 SERVINGS.

—LOIS JANUARY, Emerald City citizen in *Oz*, MGM

Toto's Trivia Tidbits

- How many times during *The Wizard of Oz* does the film cut to a close-up of Toto? (nine)
- Who portrayed the Winged Monkey that swooped down and kidnapped Toto during the haunted forest massacre scene? (According to Munchkin Hazel Derthick Resmondo, it was the late Walter Miller—a midget who also portrayed a Munchkin in the film.)
- Johnny Carson portrayed Toto in a hilarious comedy sketch on NBC's *The Tonight Show* in 1978.
- *Oz* author L. Frank Baum actually owned a dog he named Toto, while living at Ozcot—his spacious two-story home on Cherokee Avenue in Hollywood, California.
- How many times is the name Toto spoken in the MGM film? (forty-one)
- See Toto jump: Watch Toto closely, at the bottom of the screen during the Tin Man's solo dance number. Toto playfully follows the Tin Man, but when Jack Haley toots smoke from his funnel hat, nervous little Toto gets a sudden jolt.
- L. Frank Baum envisioned Toto not as a little gray dog, ". . . he was a little black dog, with long silky hair and small black eyes that twinkled merrily on either side of his funny, wee nose." (*The Wonderful Wizard of Oz*, 1900)
- Toto was owned by a German immigrant named Carl Spitz. The meticulous dog trainer began his Hollywood Dog Training School in 1927 and tutored several famous motion picture canine actors: "Cappy" (in the first *Moby Dick*), "Buck" (in *Call of the Wild*), "Prince Carl" (in *Wuthering Heights*), "Mr. Binkie" (in *The Light That Failed*), and "Musty" (in *Swiss Family Robinson*). Carl Spitz died in 1976.

GOOD AND WICKED BOURBON BALLS

2½ cups finely crushed vanilla wafers
2   tablespoons cocoa
1   cup confectioners' sugar
1   cup finely chopped walnuts
3   tablespoons corn syrup
¼   cup bourbon
    Confectioner's sugar

In a medium bowl combine the wafer crumbs, cocoa, sugar, and nuts. Add the corn syrup and bourbon. Mix well. In a shallow dish place a layer of confectioners' sugar. Form the crumb mixture into 1-inch balls and roll in sugar to coat. Store for a day or so in a covered container for the flavors to meld.

Note: To give the bourbon balls an extra good kick, soak some raisins in bourbon for a day. When making the balls, put a soaked raisin in the middle of each.

MAKES ABOUT 3½ DOZEN.

—MARY ELLEN ST. AUBIN, wife of Parnell St. Aubin, Munchkin in *Oz*, MGM

GOOSEBERRY PIE

1¾ cups sugar
¼   cup all-purpose flour
½   teaspoon ground cinnamon
2   teaspoons cognac
1½ teaspoons lemon juice
4   cups fresh gooseberries
1   to 2 tablespoons butter
    Pastry for 2-crust 9-inch pie

In a small bowl combine the sugar, flour, and cinnamon. Add cognac and lemon juice and stir to mix. In a medium bowl place the berries and sprinkle with the sugar mixture.

Stir gently until well blended. Let stand for 15 minutes.

Line a 9-inch pie pan with pie dough. Pour the fruit into the pie shell. Dot with the desired amount of butter. Cover the pie with a well-pricked top or with a lattice. Bake at 450° for 10 minutes. Reduce the heat to 350° and bake 35 to 40 minutes or until golden brown.

MAKES 6 TO 8 SERVINGS.

—ADRIANA CASELOTTI, voice of Walt Disney's *Snow White*, who also sings a line in MGM's *Oz*

Whistle while you cook . . . Young Adriana Caselotti, the voice of Walt Disney's Snow White, *also lent a lilt to Oz during the Tin Man's solo ("Wherefore art thou, Romeo?"). Here, in 1939, appearing on the Prudence Penny radio program (the Martha Stewart of the day), Caselotti serves delicious treats. Notice the tiny Disney dwarf figures on the platter. (Ray Savage Collection)*

Grandma Baum's Ginger Drop Cakes

My seventeen years of research with Matilda Jewell Gage, niece of Oz creator L. Frank Baum, were nearly completed; we had been through her entire house summer after summer locating historical documents. When I raved about her sugar cookies over lunch one day, she brought out her battered, ancient family cookbook to get me the "receipt" (as they referred to recipes in her generation) and I realized that I might have missed one important source of history. "Do you have any family recipes in there, Matilda?" I asked hopefully. This gem emerged.

1	egg
1	cup sour cream
½	cup firmly packed brown sugar
1	cup molasses
1	tablespoon melted butter
2	cups all-purpose flour
1	teaspoon ground cinnamon
1	teaspoon ground ginger
1	teaspoon baking soda

In a small bowl beat the egg lightly. Add the sour cream, sugar, molasses, and butter. In a medium bowl combine the flour, cinnamon, ginger, and soda. Pour in the egg mixture and stir just until the dry ingredients are moistened. Line muffin pans with paper cups. Fill the cups two-thirds full with batter. Bake at 400° for 15 minutes.

These may be steamed later and served as a pudding with butterscotch sauce.

MAKES 1 DOZEN.

—CYNTHIA STANTON BAUM,
mother of L. Frank Baum
(Contributed by Dr. Sally Roesch Wagner)

GREAT AND POWERFUL RUM CAKE

1   cup chopped pecans
1   18½-ounce package yellow cake mix
1   3¾-ounce package instant vanilla
     pudding mix
4   eggs
½   cup cold water
½   cup oil
1   cup Bacardi dark rum, divided
½   cup butter
¼   cup water
½   cup sugar

Grease and flour a 10-inch tube pan. Sprinkle pecans over the bottom of the pan. In a large bowl mix together the cake and pudding mixes, eggs, ½ cup of cold water, oil, and ½ cup of rum. Pour the batter gently over the pecans in the bottom of the pan. Bake at 325° for 40 to 50 minutes. Set the cake aside to cool.

In a small saucepan melt the butter. Stir in ¼ cup of water and the sugar. Boil for 5 minutes, stirring constantly. Remove from the heat. Stir in the remaining rum. Invert the cake onto a serving plate. Prick the top of the cake with a toothpick. Dribble glaze on the top and sides. Allow the cake to absorb the glaze. Repeat until the glaze is used up.

Note: A bundt pan may be substituted for tube pan, if desired.

— JEAN SHEETS

Frank Morgan helps serve up some grub to the men at a Palm Springs, California, U.S. Air Corps canteen, circa 1942.

GREATEST IN OZ GOOEY BUTTER CAKE

1   18½-ounce package yellow cake mix
4   eggs
½   cup butter, melted and cooled
1   8-ounce package cream cheese, softened
1   16-ounce package confectioners' sugar

Grease and flour a 13 x 9-inch pan. In a medium bowl combine the cake mix with 2 eggs and the melted butter. Spread in the prepared pan.

In a medium bowl combine the cream cheese, remaining eggs, and sugar. Pour over the top of the cake batter. Bake at 350° for 30 to 40 minutes.

MAKES 8 TO 12 SERVINGS.

—BETTY VON HOFFMANN

HAUNTED FOREST COOKIES

"Seize them!"

¼   cup shortening
¼   cup butter, softened (or margarine)
⅔   cup sugar
1   egg
1   teaspoon vanilla extract
1¼   cups all-purpose flour
⅓   cup cocoa
¼   teaspoon salt
¼   cup chopped almonds (or walnuts)
¼   cup sugar
⅓   cup cherry preserves

In a medium bowl cream the shortening, butter, ⅔ cup of sugar, egg, and vanilla. Stir in the flour, cocoa, salt, and nuts until well blended. Wrap and chill the dough 1 hour (or up to 2 days).

Lightly grease baking sheets. In a shallow dish place the remaining sugar. Shape the chilled cookie dough into 1-inch balls. Roll the balls in sugar. Place 1 inch apart on the prepared baking sheets. With your thumb, make an imprint in the center of each cookie. Bake at 350° for 10 to 12 minutes. Remove from the baking sheets and cool. Fill the center of each cookie with ½ teaspoon of preserves.

Note: Store cooled, unfilled cookies in airtight containers in the freezer for up to 3 months. Before serving, fill the centers with preserves.

MAKES 28 TO 30 COOKIES.

—JAN VANDERWALL

HOLY COW CAKE

1   18½-ounce package German chocolate cake mix
1   14-ounce can sweetened condensed milk
1   jar caramel ice cream topping
1   12-ounce carton whipped topping
3   toffee candy bars, crushed

Prepare the cake batter according to the package directions and pour into a 9 x 13-inch pan. Bake according to the package directions. When done, remove from oven. While the cake is still hot poke holes with a large fork. Pour condensed milk over the cake. Then spread with caramel topping. Refrigerate overnight. Before serving top with whipped topping and sprinkle with crushed toffee bars.

MAKES 8 TO 12 SERVINGS.

—FRED MEYER, former secretary,
International Wizard of Oz Club

"I'M MELTING, MELTING" WORLD-FAMOUS LEMON BARS

1½	cups all-purpose flour
½	cup confectioners' sugar
½	teaspoon lemon zest
¾	cup butter
6	eggs
3	cups sugar
½	cup all-purpose flour
¾	cup lemon juice
1	tablespoon lemon extract

In a small bowl combine 1½ cups of flour, the confectioners' sugar, and lemon zest. Cut in the butter and press into a 9 x 13-inch glass baking pan. Bake at 325° for 25 minutes.

While the crust bakes prepare the filling. In a medium bowl lightly beat the eggs. Stir in the sugar, remaining flour, juice, and extract. When the crust is removed from the oven, spread the filling over the hot crust. Bake at 300° for 40 minutes. Cool and sprinkle with confectioners' sugar. Chill overnight and cut into bars.

MAKES 12 SERVINGS.

—JOANNE WORLEY, W.W.W. in *The Wizard of Oz* National Tour, 1999

"It's No Place for Dorothy Around a Pigsty"

Magazine journalist Dudley Early visited the set of *Oz* researching behind-the-scenes activities. In his 1939 feature article, Early reported the heroics of one of the film's crew in *The Family Circle* magazine.

When Judy Garland was doing her farm scenes, she had to walk a fence and fall into a pigpen. The first time she did it she landed among the baby pigs and the mamma pig charged her. Al Shenberg, the assistant director, rescued Judy. But Toto the dog got mad at the pig for chasing Judy and jumped into the pen, charging the pig, which promptly decided to meet him halfway. Toto realized his mistake too late, momentum carrying him right up to the point of danger. Mamma pig might have done serious damage to a valuable dog had not Shenberg gone to the rescue again. For his acts of valor the entire company the next day solemnly presented Shenberg with a jar of pickled pigs' feet and a medal made from the rind off a ham, suspended from a dime-store chain. They insisted that Shenberg wear the medal all day, but relented when it began to melt under the hot lights . . . and stink.

You can bet your bippy JoAnne Worley made a splendid Wicked Witch in Radio City Entertainment's The Wizard of Oz on tour in 1999.

Ray Bolger, Jack Haley, and Margaret Hamilton reunited in 1970 for a rare photo session and series of interviews advertising NBC's telecast of The Wizard of Oz, Sunday evening, March 15, 1970. The costars lamented that Judy Garland, who had died recently, was not with them to share the warm memories. Said Hamilton in an interview: "Judy Garland was an absolute darling, a warm human being and very professional; she was one of the happiest people on the set, too. Judy was excited about her part in the picture . . . she realized it was going to be a wonderful thing in her career . . . everybody on the set loved her."

IMPOSSEROUS CUSTARD PIE

4   eggs
2   cups milk less 2 tablespoons
1   teaspoon vanilla extract
6   tablespoons butter, softened
½   cup all-purpose flour
½   teaspoon salt
1   cup sugar
1   cup coconut

Grease and flour a deep 9-inch pie pan. In a blender pulse the entire conglomeration 5 or 6 times for 10 seconds each time on the mix setting. Pour into the prepared pie pan. Bake at 350° for 50 minutes or until the top is golden. Forms its own crust!

MAKES 6 TO 8 SERVINGS.

—BRAD WELAGE

IMPRESSIVE BERRIES AFLAME!

"How about a little fire, Scarecrow?"

1   quart strawberries
3   tablespoons sugar
1½   quarts vanilla ice cream
1   28-ounce can pitted Bing cherries
¾   cup currant jelly
½   cup brandy

About 2 hours before serving, wash and hull the strawberries. Place in a bowl, sprinkle them with sugar, and refrigerate. Make ice cream balls. Wrap and freeze them for later use.

At serving time, drain the strawberries and cherries. In a chafing dish over direct heat melt the currant jelly, stirring gently. Add the drained fruits. Heat slowly, stirring constantly, until simmering. Pour the brandy into the center of the fruits. Do not stir. Let the brandy heat undisturbed. When it is warmed, carefully light with a match. Spoon the flaming fruit sauce over the individual servings of ice cream balls.

Note: Sugar cubes soaked in lemon extract may be substituted for the brandy. Arrange soaked cubes on fruit and light. Remove cubes before serving fruit.

MAKES 8 SERVINGS.

—EUGENIA ARGER

Swift & Company began producing a line of OZ peanut butter in the 1940s and continued sporadically until the 1970s. The peanut butter was packaged in collectible tin containers and decorative glass tumblers. (Bill Beem Collection)

IRRESISTIBLE PEANUT BUTTER COOKIE

¾   cup creamy peanut butter
½   cup shortening
1¼   cups firmly packed light brown sugar
3   tablespoons milk
1   tablespoon vanilla extract
1   egg
1¾   cups all-purpose flour
¾   teaspoon salt
¾   teaspoon baking soda

In a large bowl combine the peanut butter, shortening, sugar, milk, and vanilla. Beat at medium speed of an electric mixer until well blended. Add the egg and beat just until blended. In a medium bowl combine the flour, salt, and soda. Add to the creamed mixture at low speed. Mix just until blended. On an ungreased baking sheet drop the batter by heaping teaspoonfuls 2 inches apart. Flatten slightly in a crisscross pattern with the tines of a fork. Bake at 375° for 7 to 8 minutes or until set and just beginning to brown. Cool 2 minutes on a baking sheet before removing to wire racks.

MAKES 3 DOZEN COOKIES.

—ELLA RUTH WILLINGHAM

Wonderful recipes with Swift's **OZ** peanut butter

MARTHA LOGAN · HOME ECONOMIST · SWIFT & COMPANY

tin woodman's sundae

Spoon OZ Peanut Butter Sauce or OZ Peanut Butter Fudge Sauce over vanilla ice cream. Top with a red heart cut from a maraschino cherry.

OZ peanut butter sauce

Yield: ¾ cup

¼ cup Swift's OZ Peanut Butter
1 cup sugar
½ cup water
⅔ cup light corn syrup
½ teaspoon salt

Combine sugar, water, corn syrup, and salt in a saucepan. Bring to a boil and boil rapidly for 1 minute. Remove from heat. Cool without stirring until syrup has reached room temperature. Add peanut butter and blend until smooth. The sauce may be kept in a covered jar in the refrigerator.

peanut butter fudge sauce

Yield: 3 cups

1 cup Swift's OZ Peanut Butter
2 squares (1 ounce each) unsweetened chocolate
½ cup water
1½ cups corn syrup
⅛ teaspoon salt
1 teaspoon vanilla

Combine chocolate and water in a saucepan. Place over low heat 2 minutes, or until chocolate is melted and the mixture is thick. Remove from heat; add syrup and salt. Simmer 10 minutes; stir occasionally. Add vanilla. Put peanut butter into mixing bowl and stir to cream. Add chocolate mixture slowly to the peanut butter and blend well. Serve warm or cold over ice cream.

Casey Colgan portrays the Scarecrow in The Wizard of Oz *National Tour, a stage version produced by Radio City Entertainment (1999).*

ISOSCELES TRIANGLES

Smart choice!

1	cup butter (or margarine)
1	cup confectioners' sugar
1	egg
1	tablespoon water
2	cups all-purpose flour
1	teaspoon cream of tartar
1	teaspoon baking soda
½	cup sugar

In a medium bowl cream together the butter and confectioners' sugar. Add the egg and water. Beat well. In a separate bowl sift together the flour, cream of tartar, and soda. Add to the creamed mixture. Beat well. On a floured surface roll the dough ⅛ inch thick. In a shallow dish place the sugar. Using a knife dipped in butter, cut the dough into triangles. Dip the triangles in the sugar. Arrange on ungreased cookie sheets. Bake at 350° for 9 to 10 minutes.

MAKES ABOUT 3 DOZEN COOKIES.

—CASEY COLGAN, Scarecrow in *The Wizard of Oz* National Tour, 1999

JACK PUMPKINHEAD'S COBBLER

1   18½-ounce package yellow cake mix,
     divided
¾   cup cold margarine, divided
4   eggs, divided
1   29-ounce can pumpkin
¾   cup evaporated milk
¾   cup firmly packed brown sugar
2   teaspoons ground cinnamon
1   teaspoon vanilla extract
½   cup sugar
1   cup chopped pecans (optional)
     Ice cream or whipped topping (optional)

Measure out 1 cup of cake mix and reserve
for use later. In a medium mixing bowl place
the remainder of the cake mix and cut in ½
cup of margarine. Add 1 egg. In an ungreased
9 x 13-inch pan spread this mixture.

In a medium bowl combine the canned
pumpkin, 3 eggs, evaporated milk, brown
sugar, cinnamon, and vanilla. Pour into the
pan over the first layer.

In a small bowl combine the reserved 1
cup of cake mix and sugar. Cut in ¼ cup of
margarine until course and crumbly.
Sprinkle over the top of the pumpkin layer,
then add chopped pecans if desired. Bake at
350° for 45 to 50 minutes and serve with
vanilla ice cream or whipped topping.

—BRIAN HENSON, performed Jack Pumpkinhead
in Disney's *Return to Oz*

One of the corporate tie-ins with Disney's Return to Oz
motion picture in 1985. A natural. (Jay Scarfone/
William Stillman Wizard of Oz Collection)

KANSAS PRAIRIE COOKIES

1	cup butter
1	cup shortening
4	eggs
2	tablespoons vanilla extract
2	cups sugar
1	16-ounce package brown sugar
4	cups all-purpose flour
2	tablespoons baking soda
2	tablespoons baking powder
2	cups oatmeal
1	cup grated coconut
1	12-ounce package chocolate chips
2	cups chopped pecans
2	cups crispy rice cereal

In a very large bowl cream together the butter, shortening, eggs, and vanilla. Add the sugars. In a medium bowl stir together the flour, soda, and baking powder. Gradually stir the dry ingredients into the egg mixture. Add the oatmeal, coconut, chips, nuts, and rice cereal. Using a cookie dropper (like a small ice cream scoop), put no more than 12 cookies on each ungreased cookie sheet. These cookies spread, so don't crowd them. Bake at 350° for 12 to 15 minutes.

—AMY CASSIMATIS

Fourteen Munchkin actors reunited in 1990 in Grand Rapids, Minnesota, the birthplace of Judy Garland. Fifty years after Oz, this was one of the largest reunions of Munchkins. (Photo by Elaine Willingham)

Several of the Singer Midgets pose inside a normal-size refrigerator. Many of the little people who worked as Munchkins in The Wizard of Oz *were quite tiny, standing just above three feet tall.*

LEMON ICE BOX PIE

1	small carton (2 eggs) egg substitute
1	14-ounce can fat-free sweetened condensed milk
½	cup lemon juice (juice of 3 lemons)
1	graham cracker pie crust
1	8-ounce carton fat-free whipped topping

In a small bowl whisk together the egg substitute and condensed milk. Stir in the lemon juice until mixture is smooth. Pour into the graham cracker crust. Spread whipped topping over the top. Chill overnight.

—VICKIE OWNBY

Lemon Meringue Pie

1½   cups sugar
⅓   cup plus 1 tablespoon cornstarch
1½   cups water
3   egg yolks, slightly beaten
3   tablespoons butter (or margarine)
2   teaspoons grated lemon peel
½   cup lemon juice
1   9-inch baked pie shell
3   egg whites
¼   teaspoon cream of tartar
6   tablespoons sugar
½   teaspoon vanilla extract

In a 1½-quart saucepan mix the 1½ cups sugar and cornstarch. Stir in the water gradually. Cook over medium heat, stirring constantly, until the mixture thickens and boils. Boil and stir for 1 minute. Remove from the heat and stir at least half of the hot mixture gradually into the egg yolks. Blend back into the hot mixture in the saucepan. Boil and stir for 1 minute. Remove from the heat and stir in the butter, lemon peel, and lemon juice. Pour into the pie shell.

In a medium bowl beat the egg whites and cream of tartar until foamy. Beat in 6 tablespoons of sugar, one tablespoon at a time. Continue beating until stiff and glossy; do not underbeat. Beat in the vanilla. Spread the meringue onto the hot pie filling, carefully sealing it to the edge of the crust to prevent shrinking or weeping. Bake at 400° about 10 minutes, until a delicate brown. Cool away from any draft.

Makes 6 to 8 servings.

—MILTON BERLE, voice of the Cowardly Lion
in *Journey Back to Oz*

JOURNEY BACK TO OZ *Interestingly enough, this ninety-minute animated feature starred Judy Garland's daughter, Liza Minnelli, as the voice of Dorothy, and Margaret Hamilton as the voice of kindly Aunt Em. Once again, Dorothy is swept up in a Kansas cyclone and whisked off to Oz where the Scarecrow (voice of Mickey Rooney) is now king. This time, Dorothy's nemesis is Mombi, an evil witch, voiced by Ethel Merman. A host of stars lent their voices as well, including Danny Thomas as the Tin Man, Milton Berle as the Cowardly Lion, Paul Lynde as Jack Pumpkinhead, Risë Stevens as Glinda, and Herschel Bernadi as Woodenhead. The feature, produced by Filmation (Norm Prescott and Lou Scheimer), had an interesting journey of its own. Though it was made in 1964, the film was not released theatrically until 1974. In December 1976, an elongated version ran on ABC-TV with live film of Bill Cosby as the Wizard-Host, who watched the adventure from a hot-air balloon and attempted to assist the characters (in cutaways much like on Cosby's* Fat Albert *cartoon show). Music and lyrics were created by Sammy Cahn and James Van Heusen. A soundtrack album of the special was released and eventually the animated portion was released on home video by MGM/UA.*

THE PRICE OF COURAGE
The original prop Medal of
Courage presented to the
Cowardly Lion in the MGM
film The Wizard of Oz *was*
auctioned in 1997 by
Sotheby's, Beverly Hills. It
sold for $29,000 to a fan
who reportedly blurted,
"Shucks folks, I'm speech-
less!"

LION'S WALNUT TREASURE BARS

"Wrap 'em up in cellophant."

½	cup shortening
1	cup firmly packed brown sugar
1	egg
¼	cup milk
¼	cup sherry wine
1⅔	cups sifted all-purpose flour
1	tablespoon instant coffee powder
¾	teaspoon salt
½	teaspoon baking powder
½	teaspoon baking soda
½	teaspoon ground cinnamon
1	cup coarsely chopped walnuts
1	cup semisweet chocolate morsels
2¼	cups confectioners' sugar, sifted
4½	teaspoons butter, softened
2	tablespoons sherry wine
1	tablespoon milk
1	teaspoon instant coffee powder

In a medium bowl cream together the shortening, brown sugar, and egg. Add ¼ cup of milk and ¼ cup of sherry (batter may look curdled at this point, but will smooth out when flour is added). Resift the flour with 1 tablespoon of coffee powder, salt, baking powder, soda, and cinnamon. Add to the creamed mixture and blend to a smooth batter. Stir in the walnuts and chocolate morsels.

Grease a 10 x 15-inch jelly roll pan. Spread the batter in the prepared pan. Bake at 375° for about 20 minutes or until the top springs back when touched lightly. Cool in the pan.

In a small bowl prepare the frosting by combining the confectioners' sugar with the remaining butter, sherry, milk, and coffee powder. Beat until smooth. Spread the cooled baked layer with frosting. Decorate the top with additional walnuts and chocolate morsels if desired. Cut into bars and wrap.

—BLANCHE COX

LOLLIPOPS, OH BOY!

Direct from the Guild

1   cup water
2   cups sugar
¾   cup light corn syrup
1   tablespoon butter
     Food coloring (vegetable dye, color of
     your choice)
¼   teaspoon oil of peppermint (or cinna-
     mon; or 1 teaspoon oil of orange, lime,
     or wintergreen; or ⅛ teaspoon oil of
     anise)
1   teaspoon powdered citric acid (optional)

In a large heavy pan bring the water to a boil. Remove from the heat. Add the sugar, corn syrup, and butter. Stir until dissolved. Return to the heat. When boiling, cover for about 3 minutes so the steam can wash down any crystals on the sides of the pan. Uncover and cook at high heat, without stirring, to the hard-crack stage at 300°. Prepare a slab or molds by brushing them well with butter or oil. Have stiffened lollipop cords on the oiled slab ready to receive the patties. Remove candy mixture from the heat and cool to 160°.

Add a few drops of vegetable coloring. Choose a color suitable to the flavor you have decided to use. Add the flavoring of your choice, also adding citric acid if using a fruit flavor.

If you have no molds, form into balls by pouring a small amount of the candy onto an oiled slab. Keep the rest in the pan over very low heat. Cut the candy on the slab into squares with scissors and roll quickly into balls. Insert the lollipop cords. Continue to pour the candy onto the slab as needed, but do not scrape the pan. Remove the lollipops from the slab just as soon as they are firm so as not to crack them. Wrap individually so as not to become sticky.

Note: Do not use an alcohol-based flavor like vanilla extract because it will evaporate in the intense heat. Be sure to use a flavor based instead on essential oils.

—ELIZABETH AND JERRY MAREN,
Lollipop Munchkin in *Oz,* MGM

Munchkins Margaret Pellegrini, Jerry Maren, and Ruth Duccini were involved in media promotion in Hollywood with the Yellow Brick Road Museum Tour bus, which trekked across the country exhibiting rare Oz artifacts in 1997. The tour, sponsored by Greyhound, Turner Entertainment, MGM/UA Home Video and Planet Hollywood, commemorated Turner's final video release of the motion picture this century. (Photo by Steve Cox)

SWEETS FOR THE SWEET   Gift in hand, the Lollipop Guild presents Dorothy with a treat. Although for years urban legend had it that the three little tough guys were children, they in fact, were three midgets: Jackie Gerlich, Gerard Marenghi (a.k.a. Jerry Maren), and Harry Earles (a.k.a. Harry Doll). (Courtesy of Jerry Maren)

LULLABYE LEAGUE'S FAMOUS PINK FROSTING

½   cup margarine
4   cups confectioners' sugar, sifted
1   teaspoon vanilla extract
4   to 5 drops red food coloring
    Heavy cream (optional)

In a medium bowl beat the margarine until soft and cream-colored. Beat in the sugar gradually, blending until creamy and smooth. Beat in the vanilla extract and red food color-ing until the frosting is the desired shade of pink. If the frosting needs thinning, add heavy cream a teaspoonful at a time.

MAKES FROSTING FOR ONE 2- TO 3-LAYER CAKE.

—NITA KREBS, Lullabye League Munchkin
in *Oz*, MGM

MAGIC COOKIE BARS

Wally was working on the movie Earthquake *and got a new production secretary. She became a very good and popular script supervisor. She was a wonderful cook with a wealth of recipes and was always bringing food to the office. My first contact with her was when I called the office and told her, "You've got to go!" I then elaborated that Wally was gaining weight and it was her fault. However, the best part is that Wally started using her recipes. We served them at our big—mostly motion pix people—parties and they became famous among the many who knew Wally as a Gourmet.*

½	cup butter
1½	cups graham cracker crumbs
1	cup chopped walnuts (or nuts of your choice)
1	6-ounce package chocolate chips
1	3½-ounce can Angel Flake coconut
1	14-ounce can sweetened condensed milk

In a small pan melt the butter and pour into a 13 x 9 x 2-inch pan. Sprinkle graham cracker crumbs as first layer. Then layer over with nuts, then chocolate chips, then coconut. Pour over layers the condensed milk. Bake at 350° for 25 minutes or until golden brown. Allow to cool before cutting into bars.

MAKES ABOUT 2 DOZEN.

—SUE DWIGGINS WORSLEY, wife of Wallace Worsley, script supervisor for *Oz*, MGM

Script supervisor Wallace Worsley works with the cast on the set of The Wizard of Oz. *(Courtesy of Sue Dwiggins Worsley)*

SHE WAS HUNGRY! Margaret Hamilton must've been famished, digging right in, at this party for Victor Fleming on the set of The Wizard of Oz, February 1939. (Mickey Carroll Collection)

MAHLE CAKES

1   cup plus 6 tablespoons butter
1   16-ounce box brown sugar
4   eggs, slightly beaten
2   teaspoons vanilla extract
2   cups all-purpose flour
2   teaspoons baking powder
1½   cups chopped pecans (or walnuts)
     Confectioners' sugar

In a medium saucepan melt the butter. Add the brown sugar and mix well. Cool slightly. Stir in the eggs and vanilla extract and mix well. Add the flour, baking powder, and pecans, blending well. Grease and flour a 9 x 13-inch pan. Pour batter into prepared pan. Bake at 350° for 30 to 35 minutes. Cool for 30 minutes, then sprinkle with confectioners' sugar. Cut into squares.

MAKES 12 SQUARES.

—JEAN AND ART CARNEY

MARGARET HAMILTON'S BERRY DELIGHT

6   egg yolks
1   cup sugar
1   cup sherry
1   cup cream
2   pints strawberries
2   teaspoons confectioners' sugar
½   cup Cointreau liqueur

In the top of a double boiler beat the egg yolks until fluffy. Add the sugar and beat until lemon-colored. Add the sherry. Cook over simmering water until thickened. Cool and add the cream. Set aside to cool. Then refrigerate until ready to serve.

Clean the strawberries and place in a small bowl. Sprinkle with confectioners' sugar and Cointreau. Let stand for 1 hour. Serve the strawberries with the sauce.

—HAMILTON MESERVE, son of
Margaret Hamilton

MUNCHKIN KARL'S BUTTERMILK POUND CAKE

1   cup butter
3   cups sugar
4   eggs
1   teaspoon vanilla extract
1   teaspoon lemon extract
¼   teaspoon baking soda
1   cup buttermilk
3   cups all-purpose flour

In a medium bowl cream the butter and sugar. Add one egg at a time, beating well after each addition. Add the extracts. Add the soda to the buttermilk in a measuring cup and stir until dissolved. Add the flour alternating with the buttermilk to creamed mixture.

Grease and flour a tube pan. Pour the batter into the prepared pan. Bake at 325° for 1 hour and 15 minutes.

MAKES 12 SERVINGS.

—KARL SLOVER, Munchkin in *Oz*, MGM

MUNCHKIN MARGARET'S FLOWERPOT CUPCAKES

1   18½-ounce package yellow cake mix
½   cup margarine
4   cups confectioners' sugar
1   teaspoon vanilla extract
4   drops green food coloring
4   drops yellow food coloring
        Candies for decorating

Prepare the cupcakes according to package directions. Bake in muffin pans using paper liners. Set aside to cool.

In a medium bowl beat the margarine until soft and cream-colored. Then add the sugar gradually. Blend until creamy and smooth. Beat in the vanilla. Divide the frosting in half. Add green coloring to one portion and yellow to the other. When completely cool frost the cupcakes. Decorate with flowered mint patties or gumdrop fruit slices shaped like flowers. Use a long gumdrop on a toothpick for a stem and insert in the top.

MAKES ABOUT 12 CUPCAKES.

—MARGARET PELLEGRINI,
Munchkin in *Oz*, MGM

Munchkin Margaret Pellegrini tries out a fresh "Munchkin" donut hole at Dunkin' Donuts during an in-store promotion in 1989.

MUNCHKIN MARGARET'S MILLION-DOLLAR PIES

1   8-ounce can peaches
1   8-ounce can mandarin oranges
1   8-ounce can crushed pineapple
1   15-ounce can sweetened condensed milk
¼   cup lemon juice
1   12-ounce container whipped topping
2   graham cracker crumb pie crusts

Drain the canned fruits, reserving the juice for later use in punch, etc. In a large bowl combine the drained fruits, milk, and lemon juice. Fold in the whipped topping. Spread half the mixture into each of the graham cracker crusts. Chill in the refrigerator until serving time.

MAKES 2 PIES, 6 TO 8 SERVINGS EACH.

—MARGARET PELLEGRINI,
Munchkin in Oz, MGM

MUNCHKIN ROCKY ROAD S'MORES BARS

½   cup butter (or margarine)
½   cup firmly packed brown sugar
1   cup all-purpose flour
½   cup graham cracker crumbs
2   cups miniature marshmallows
1   6-ounce package semisweet chocolate morsels
½   cup chopped walnuts

In a medium bowl cream the butter and brown sugar until fluffy. In a separate bowl combine the flour and cracker crumbs. Add to the creamed mixture, mixing well. Press onto the bottom of a greased 9-inch square pan. Sprinkle over with marshmallows, chocolate morsels and walnuts. Bake at 375° for 15 to 20 minutes or until golden brown. Cool before cutting into bars.

MAKES 2 DOZEN.

—TINY DOLL, Munchkin in Oz, MGM

A handful of Munchkins (no pun intended) gather for a photograph with producer Mervyn LeRoy and director Victor Fleming. Lollipop Guild Munchkin Harry Earles (a.k.a. Harry Doll), in striped stockings, was a celebrity in his own right at the time. Earles had costarred with Lon Chaney in a silent and talky version of The Unholy Three (1925, 1930) and costarred with his midget sister in another MGM feature, a horror flick called Freaks (1932).

MUNCHKIN STRAWBERRY SHORTCAKE

Get it?

1	quart strawberries, hulled and cut into halves
2	tablespoons orange liqueur (or orange juice)
½	cup sugar, divided
3	cups sifted all-purpose flour
4	teaspoons baking powder
½	teaspoon salt
¾	cup unsalted butter
1	cup light cream (or milk)
	Whipped cream

In a small bowl mix the berries with liqueur and ¼ cup of sugar. Cover and chill for several hours. In a medium bowl sift the flour with baking powder, salt, and the remaining ¼ cup of sugar. Using a pastry blender or 2 knives cut in the butter until crumbs are the size of small peas. Add the light cream all at once. Stir just enough to moisten the dry particles. Turn the dough out onto a lightly floured board and knead just a few times to shape into a smooth ball. With a rolling pin or with fingers, shape the dough into an oblong about 6 x 9 inches. With a sharp knife, cut the oblong into six 3-inch squares. Place on a lightly greased cookie sheet and bake at 425° for 15 to 20 minutes or until browned. Split the shortcakes in half while hot. Spoon the berries over the bottom half. Top with the second half. Add more berries and top with whipped cream. Serve immediately.

MAKES 6 SERVINGS.

—ELIZABETH AND JERRY MAREN,
Lollipop Munchkin in *Oz*, MGM

Jerry Maren was a hardworking "Little Oscar" on the West Coast, appearing on TV shows, at supermarket openings, and at charity events. These folks are but a few of the famous personalities who sampled fine Oscar Mayer meats along with Jerry in promotions. (In the collage look for: Frank Sinatra, Bob Hope, Eddie Bracken, Charley Weaver, Stan Freberg, and Hoot Gibson.)

Nikko—ringleader of the Wicked Witch's winged monkeys—was portrayed in the MGM film by diminutive actor Pat Walshe.

NIKKO'S WINGED MONKEY PIE

You'll "Fly! Fly!"

25   chocolate wafers
5   tablespoons melted butter
25   large marshmallows
⅔   cup milk
3   ounces crème de menthe
1½   ounces white Crème de Cacao
½   pint heavy cream
1   square unsweetened chocolate

Crush the chocolate cookies. In a small bowl combine the crumbs and melted butter. Press the mixture into a 9-inch pie dish. Freeze to set. In the top of a double boiler melt the marshmallows and milk over simmering water. Cool. Add the crème de menthe and Crème de Cacao.

In a medium chilled bowl and using chilled beaters whip the cream until very stiff and fold into the marshmallow mixture. Pour into the frozen pie shell. Top with shaved unsweetened chocolate. Freeze until a few minutes before serving.

MAKES 6 TO 8 SERVINGS.

—MARTY KLEBBA, Nikko in *The Wizard of Oz*
National Tour, 1998–1999

PEANUT BRITTLE

This is one of my dad's very favorites, and he asked that I submit it. I usually make this every year, for his birthday and Father's Day gifts.

1½   cups sugar
½   cup Karo syrup
¾   cup water
      Pinch salt
2   cups raw Spanish peanuts
2   tablespoons butter
1   tablespoon baking soda
1   teaspoon vanilla extract

In a medium saucepan cook the sugar, Karo syrup, water, and salt to 230° on a candy thermometer. Add the peanuts and butter and cook to 300°, stirring constantly. Remove from the fire and add the baking soda and vanilla. Beat briskly 4 to 5 strokes, pour quickly into a buttered cookie sheet, and let cool. Break into pieces.

MAKES ABOUT 1½ POUNDS.

—JO-ANN KEITH, daughter of Charlie Schram, makeup artist for *Oz,* MGM

PEANUT BUTTER FUDGE PIE

1   graham cracker pie crust
1   8-ounce carton whipped topping
⅓   cup fudge sauce
½   cup peanut butter
1   cup cold milk
1   4-ounce package vanilla instant
    pudding mix

In the bottom of graham cracker crust spread 1 cup of whipped topping. Freeze for 1 hour or more. Carefully spread the fudge sauce over the whipped topping. In a medium bowl place the peanut butter and gradually stir in the milk until smooth. Add the pudding mix and beat with a wire whisk for 1 to 2 minutes. Fold in the remaining whipped topping. Carefully spoon this mixture over the sauce. Freeze.

MAKES 6 TO 8 SERVINGS.

—THELMA HAMILTON

PEPARKAKAR (GINGER SNAPS)

Charlie and I have been married 62 years. How well I remember when he took me to MGM to see the Wizard of Oz *set. It was such a treat!*

1   cup butter or margarine
1¼   cups sugar
1   egg
2   tablespoons molasses
2½   cups all-purpose flour
1   teaspoon baking soda
1   teaspoon baking powder
2   teaspoons cinnamon
2   teaspoons ground ginger
2   teaspoons ground cloves
2   teaspoons ground allspice
1   teaspoon ground cardamom

In a large bowl cream the butter or margarine. Add the sugar, then egg, and then molasses. Sift in the dry ingredients. Mix well. Roll out and cut with fancy cookie cutters. Place on a greased cookie sheet.

Bake at 350° for 20 minutes.

This dough can be prepared ahead of time, wrapped in foil, and placed in the refrigerator until ready to bake.

MAKES ABOUT 3 DOZEN.

—ANN-MARIE AND CHARLIE SCHRAM,
Bert Lahr's makeup artist

PINEAPPLE NUT BARS

½ cup butter
¼ cup sugar
1 cup all-purpose flour
2 eggs
½ teaspoon vanilla extract
1 13 ounce can crushed pineapple, drained
⅓ cup all-purpose flour
1 cup firmly packed brown sugar
¼ teaspoon baking powder
¼ teaspoon salt
½ cup chopped nuts

Grease a 9 x 13-inch baking pan. In a small bowl cream the butter and sugar together. Add the flour and mix well. Press into the bottom of the prepared pan. Bake at 350° for 25 minutes.

In a medium bowl beat the eggs lightly. Stir in the vanilla and pineapple. In a separate bowl stir together the flour, brown sugar, baking powder, salt, and nuts. Add to the pineapple mixture and stir to blend well. Spread over the baked crust and bake at 350° for 30 minutes. Allow to cool. Cut into square bars.

MAKES 6 TO 8 SERVINGS.

—BILL STILLMAN, coauthor of *Wizard of Oz Pictorial History, The Wizard of Oz Collector's Treasury, The Wizardry of Oz*

Tavern on the (Emerald) Green

A child of Hollywood, Warner LeRoy (son of MGM *Oz* producer Mervyn LeRoy) spent his formative years roaming the back lots of Warner Brothers—the studio his maternal grandfather founded in 1923. In 1938 when his father was overseeing the production of *The Wizard of Oz*, three-year-old Warner was brought to the Munchkinland set and introduced to Dorothy, Glinda, and some of the tiny actors. Nearly the same height as the Munchkins then, LeRoy recalls little of the experience today, but remains an admirer of his father's most famous motion picture production.

Warner LeRoy, a Stanford University graduate, moved east in the 1950s and became one of the founders of the off-Broadway movement, directing several productions. He acquired a taste for the restaurant business, and in 1966 he opened his first establishment, Maxwell's Plum, in New York City. The public saw a former flat coffee shop become a culinary venture that would revolutionize the restaurant industry. Maxwell's Plum became an overnight sensation, a maget for the singles scene, with elegant—even flamboyant—interiors and no dress code. Its success was due, in part, to its unique arrangement as the first restaurant to have a formal dining room, a bar, and a casual sidewalk café under one roof.

In 1974, LeRoy assumed the lease on New York's famous Tavern on the Green and spent $10 million transforming the aged establishment into a dazzling culinary four-star fantasy that has become one of the highest-grossing restaurants in the United States. It is *the* dining experience in the Big Apple. Additionally, LeRoy opened a Maxwell's Plum in San Francisco, the Potomac in Washington, D.C., and planned a spectacular New York reopening in 1999 for his newest acquisition, the Russian Tea Room.

PINK LULLABYE PIE

3 egg yolks, slightly beaten
1 cup water
¼ cup sugar
1 3-ounce package red gelatin (any flavor)
½ cup cold water
1 tablespoon lemon juice
1 tablespoon grenadine syrup (optional)
1 envelope whipped topping mix
3 egg whites
   Dash salt
4 tablespoons sugar
1 baked 9-inch pie shell, cooled
1 square semisweet chocolate (optional, for chocolate curl garnish)

In the top of a double boiler combine the egg yolks and 1 cup of water. Add ¼ cup of sugar and mix well. Cook and stir over boiling water until the mixture coats a spoon, stirring constantly. Remove from the heat. Add the gelatin and stir until dissolved. Add ½ cup of cold water, lemon juice, and grenadine. Chill until thickened.

Prepare the whipped topping mix according to the package directions. In a medium bowl beat the egg whites and salt until foamy throughout. Add 4 tablespoons of sugar, one at a time, beating thoroughly after each addition. Continue beating until the mixture will form soft, rounded peaks. Fold into the gelatin mixture. Fold in 1 cup of the prepared whipped topping. Chill again, if necessary, until the mixture will mound. Spoon into the pie shell. Chill about 4 hours or until firm. Garnish with the remaining whipped topping and chocolate curls, if desired.

MAKES 6 TO 8 SERVINGS.

—NITA KREBS, Munchkin in *Oz*, MGM

POPCORN MOUNTAIN CRACKLE

1 bag microwave popcorn
1¾ cups sugar
½ cup light molasses
¾ cup light corn syrup
2 tablespoons butter (or margarine)

In a microwave pop the corn according to the package directions. Pour into a large bowl. Set aside.

In a large saucepan mix the sugar, molasses, corn syrup, and butter. Boil until the syrup registers 285° on a candy thermometer or until it forms a hard ball in cold water. While the syrup boils grease a cookie sheet. Set aside. When the syrup is ready stir it into the popcorn. With the back of a buttered wooden spoon, spread the mixture on the prepared cookie sheet, shaping into a 14-inch square. Cool; then break into pieces. Store in an airtight container.

MAKES ABOUT 3 DOZEN PIECES, DEPENDING ON SIZE.

—JOSEPH M. WHITE, Munchkin
in *Under the Rainbow*

POPPY FIELD CAKE

3   eggs
1   cup plus 2 tablespoons oil
1½   teaspoons almond flavor
1½   teaspoons butter flavor
1½   teaspoons vanilla extract
2¼   cups sugar
1½   cups milk
3   cups all-purpose flour
1½   teaspoons baking powder
4½   teaspoons poppy seeds
¼   cup orange juice
¾   cup sugar
½   teaspoon vanilla extract
½   teaspoon melted butter

In a large bowl combine the eggs, oil, almond, and butter flavors, 1½ teaspoons of vanilla, 2½ cups sugar, and milk. Stir to blend. In a medium bowl stir together the flour, baking powder, and poppy seeds. Add to the egg mixture. Beat with a mixer for 2 minutes. Grease and flour a tube pan. Pour the batter into the prepared pan. Bake at 350° for 1 hour.

While the cake is baking prepare the glaze. In a small bowl combine the orange juice, remaining sugar, vanilla, and melted butter. When the cake comes from the oven pour the glaze over the top.

Note: Cake will crack on top.

MAKES 12 SERVINGS.

—TINA CASSIMATIS

POPPY FIELD SNOWDRIFTS

". . . something with poison in it."

1   cup cold strong coffee
2½   tablespoons brandy
2   envelopes unflavored gelatin
¼   cup sugar
¼   cup half-and-half
2   cups crushed ice

In a blender place the coffee, brandy, and gelatin. Cover and blend for 40 seconds. Add the sugar and blend 10 seconds. Add half-and-half and crushed ice. Cover and blend for 1 minute, then let stand in the blender for another minute. Pour into 6 individual parfait glasses. The mixture will firm up without refrigeration, but if you are in a hurry, refrigerate briefly.

MAKES 6 SERVINGS.

—STEVE COX

PUMPKIN ICE CREAM PIE

1½ cups fine graham cracker crumbs
(18 crackers)
¼ cup sugar
½ cup melted butter (or margarine)
1 cup canned pumpkin (or mashed cooked
pumpkin)
½ cup firmly packed brown sugar
½ teaspoon salt
½ teaspoon ground cinnamon
½ teaspoon ground ginger
¼ teaspoon grated nutmeg
1 quart vanilla ice cream (or butter pecan,
walnut, pecan praline)
Chopped walnuts for garnish (or
pecans)

In a small bowl combine the graham cracker
crumbs, sugar, and melted butter. Mix well
and press firmly into a buttered 9-inch pie
plate. Chill for about 45 minutes.

In a medium bowl combine the pumpkin, brown sugar, salt, and spices. Stir the
ice cream to soften. Fold into the pumpkin
mixture. Spoon into the crust. Freeze until
firm. Garnish with walnuts.

MAKES 6 TO 8 SERVINGS.

—BLANCHE COX

RAINBOW DESSERT

1½ cups white rice
1 16-ounce can fruit cocktail, undrained
1 16-ounce can pineapple chunks
¼ cup butter

In a large saucepan cook the rice according to
the package directions. While the rice is cooking butter a 13 x 9-inch ovenproof glass dish.
When the rice is done spread it into the prepared dish. In a small bowl mix the fruit cocktail and pineapple chunks. Pour over the rice.
Dot the top with butter. Bake at 350° for
about 1 hour. Serve hot or chilled. May also
be eaten as a main course.

After preparation, this colorful-looking
dish very much resembles the rainbow of
which Dorothy sings, not to mention the
bright hues that greet our heroine in the
Land of Oz.

MAKES 5 OR 6 HELPINGS.

—DOUG MCCLELLAND, author of *Down the
Yellow Brick Road: The Making of
The Wizard of Oz,* the first book
published on the film

RAINBOW SHERBET ROLL

3	eggs
1	cup sugar
⅓	cup water
1	teaspoon vanilla extract
¾	cup all-purpose flour
1	teaspoon baking powder
¼	teaspoon salt
	Confectioners' sugar
	Raspberry, orange, and lime sherbet

Line a 15½ x 10½ x 1-inch jelly roll pan with aluminum foil (or waxed paper) and grease generously. In a small mixer bowl beat the eggs on high speed until very thick and lemon-colored, about 5 minutes. Pour the eggs into a large mixer bowl. Beat in the sugar gradually. Beat in the water and vanilla on low speed. Add the flour, baking powder, and salt gradually, beating just until the batter is smooth. Pour into the prepared pan. Bake at 375° for 12 to 15 minutes, until a wooden pick inserted in center comes out clean.

Immediately loosen the cake from the edges of the pan. Invert on a towel sprinkled generously with confectioners' sugar. Carefully remove the foil. Trim off the stiff edges if necessary. While hot, carefully roll the cake and towel from the narrow end. Cool on a wire rack for at least 30 minutes. Unroll the cake and remove the towel. Spread raspberry sherbet on ⅓ of the cake, orange sherbet on next ⅓, and lime sherbet on the remaining cake. Roll up. Place seam side down on an 18 x 12-inch piece of aluminum foil. Wrap securely in foil and freeze. Remove from the freezer 15 minutes before serving.

Makes 12 servings.

—TINA CASSIMATIS

ROBERTA'S COFFEE CAKE

½	cup shortening
¾	cup sugar
1	teaspoon vanilla extract
3	eggs
2	cups sifted all-purpose flour
1	teaspoon baking powder
1	teaspoon baking soda
1	8-ounce carton sour cream
6	tablespoons butter (or softened margarine)
1	cup firmly packed brown sugar
2	teaspoons ground cinnamon
1	cup chopped nuts

Grease and line the bottom of a 10-inch tube pan with waxed paper. In a large bowl cream the shortening, sugar, and vanilla thoroughly. Add the eggs one at a time, beating well after each one. In a separate bowl sift the flour, baking powder, and soda together. Add to the creamed mixture, alternating with the sour cream, blending after each addition. Spread half of the batter in the prepared tube pan. In a bowl cream the butter, brown sugar, and cinnamon together. Add the nuts and mix well. Dot the batter in the pan evenly with half of the nut mixture, being careful to avoid having this mixture touch the edges of the pan. Cover with the remaining batter. Dot with the remaining nut mixture. Bake at 350° for 50 minutes. Cool the cake 30 minutes and then remove from pan.

Note: Putting the nut mixture away from the edges of the cake will cause the cake to have a better appearance and it will slice nicely.

—ROBERTA BAUMAN

RON'S SWINGIN' CHEESECAKE

(Great for sugar-free or carbohydrate-restricted diet)

4   8-ounce packages cream cheese, softened
1¾ cups Equal Spoonful (or Splenda)
½   cup cocoa
4   large eggs
2   tablespoons heavy cream
1   teaspoon vanilla extract

Butter a 9-inch springform pan. Using an electric mixer beat the cream cheese on medium speed until smooth. Slowly beat in the sweetener, then the cocoa. Add the eggs one at a time and beat well after each addition. Add the cream and vanilla extract, scrape down the bowl, and stir to combine. Pour into the prepared pan and smooth the top. Bake at 350° for 10 minutes. Turn the heat down to 275° and bake for 1 hour. Turn off the oven. Run a knife around the edge of the pan and return the pan to the oven to cool slowly. Will firm up in the center as it cools. After the cheesecake cools, cover it with plastic wrap and refrigerate overnight, or up to 3 days. When ready to serve, run a knife around the edge of the pan again and remove the sides of the springform pan.

Protein approx. 8.5g; fat 28g; carbohydrates 4.5g.

MAKES 12 SERVINGS.

—RON GIBBS, assistant director, *The Wizard of Oz* National Tour, 1998–1999

SNICKERDOODLES

1   11-ounce package butterscotch morsels
¼   cup peanut butter

1⅓ cups canned chow mein noodles
1   cup skinless salted peanuts

In the top of a double boiler over simmering water melt the butterscotch morsels and peanut butter, stirring while melting. When melted, remove from the heat and stir in the noodles and peanuts. Spread waxed paper on 2 baking sheets. With the mixture still in the double boiler to keep it workable, drop by spoonfuls on prepared pans. Allow to cool. Takes about 1 hour to harden.

Optional: Can use a combination of chocolate and butterscotch morsels.

Note: My mom, Jean, prefers the thinner rice noodles to the chow mein variety.

MAKES 3 TO 4 DOZEN.

—DAVID ELLZEY, Scarecrow in TV movie *The Dreamer of Oz*

David Ellzey portrayed the Scarecrow in the 1990 TV movie The Dreamer of Oz.

syrup in a thin stream into the egg whites, beating constantly until the mixture loses its shine and thickens. Stir in the vanilla and nuts. Immediately drop by teaspoonfuls on waxed paper.

MAKES 25 PIECES.

TIN MAN FUNNEL CAKES

1⅓ cups all-purpose flour
6 tablespoons sugar
1 teaspoon salt
½ teaspoon baking soda
¾ teaspoon baking powder
1 egg, beaten
⅔ cup milk
Oil for frying
Confectioners' sugar

In a large bowl sift together the flour, sugar, salt, baking soda, and baking powder. In a separate bowl mix together the egg and milk. Add the liquid mixture to the dry ingredients and beat until smooth. If the batter is too thick, add more milk. In a skillet heat 1 inch of oil. Placing a finger over the bottom of a funnel pour in some batter. Over the hot oil release the batter in a spiral motion. Fry until golden brown, turning once. Remove from the pan and drain on a paper plate. Sprinkle with confectioners' sugar. Serve hot.

—MARY MACHENS

Jack Haley and his wife, Florence, attending an awards dinner in 1960.

SURRENDER DIVINITY

3 cups sugar
½ cup light corn syrup
⅔ cup water
¼ teaspoon salt
2 egg whites
¼ teaspoon vanilla extract
1 cup chopped nuts

Spread a 12-inch strip of waxed paper on the counter surface. In a 3-quart bowl microwave the sugar, syrup, and water for 10 minutes on high. In a bowl add salt to the egg whites and beat on high speed until stiff. Slowly pour the

TIN MAN'S RUSTY COFFEE CAKE

Goes together in a hurry—and disappears fast!

½	cup shortening
1½	cups sugar
2	eggs
2	teaspoons vanilla extract
1	cup milk
2	cups sifted all-purpose flour
1	tablespoon baking powder
½	teaspoon salt
6	tablespoons confectioners' sugar
2	teaspoons ground cinnamon
2	tablespoons butter, softened (or margarine)

In a large bowl place the shortening and gradually add the sugar, creaming until fluffy. Add the eggs, beating well. Add vanilla and milk. In a medium bowl sift together the flour, baking powder, and salt. Add the dry ingredients to the creamed mixture. Beat until smooth. Grease a 9 x 13-inch pan. Pour the batter into the prepared pan. Bake at 375° for 20 to 25 minutes. While the cake is baking, in a small bowl combine the confectioners' sugar and cinnamon. Set aside. When the cake tests done, remove from the oven and spread the top with butter. Sift the sugar mixture over the butter. Serve warm.

MAKES 8 SERVINGS.

—BLANCHE COX

AT HOME IN OZ When the star wasn't filmed below the waist, she preferred to wear comfy house slippers rather than ruby slipper pumps. (Beyond the Rainbow Archive)

THE TIN MAN'S EMPTY CAN COBBLER

No oil can necessary.

1   21-ounce can fruit pie filling of your choice
1   8-ounce can crushed pineapple (including the juice)
1   18½-ounce boxed cake mix (flavor of your choice)
1   cup margarine, sliced into patties
½   cup chopped nuts (optional)

In an 11 x 17-inch ungreased cake pan layer the pie filling, pineapple, and dry cake mix. Scatter margarine patties on top and sprinkle with nuts if desired. Bake at 350° for 30 to 40 minutes or until golden brown.

MAKES 6 TO 8 SERVINGS.

—DONNA BEDWELL

THE WICKED WITCH'S GO-TO-SLEEP MINTS

". . . attractive to the eye and soothing to the smell"

2   egg whites (room temperature)
½   teaspoon cream of tartar
¾   cup sugar
    Pinch salt
3   drops green food coloring
1   6-ounce package semisweet mint flavored chocolate chips

Preheat the oven to 375°. In a medium bowl beat the egg whites and cream of tartar while gradually adding sugar, salt, and coloring. When stiff peaks are formed, stir in the chocolate chips. Drop by teaspoonfuls onto ungreased cookie sheets. Turn the oven off and put the mints into the oven to set overnight. Mints will be ready the next morning.

Note: If regular chocolate chips are used, use ¾ teaspoon of peppermint extract mixed into batter.

MAKES 50 MINT DROPS.

—PHIL POTEMPA

TOTO-LY DELICIOUS APPLE CAKE

4   cups peeled, cored, and chopped apples
1¼   cups sugar
2   eggs, beaten
½   cup oil
1   teaspoon vanilla extract
2   cups all-purpose flour
½   teaspoon salt
2   teaspoons baking soda
2   teaspoons ground cinnamon
1   cup chopped walnuts
1   cup sugar
½   cup butter
½   cup milk
¼   cup rum (or brandy)

Grease and flour a 9 x 13-inch pan. In a medium bowl combine the apples and 1¼ cups of sugar and let stand for 30 minutes.

In a large bowl beat together the eggs, oil, and vanilla. In a small bowl stir together the flour, salt, soda, and cinnamon and sift. Stir the flour mixture into the batter alternately with the apples and nuts. Pour the batter into the prepared pan. Bake at 350° for 45 minutes to 1 hour, until a toothpick inserted in the center comes out clean.

While the cake is baking, prepare the topping. In a small saucepan boil together 1 cup of sugar, the butter, and milk for 10 minutes. Stir in the rum and pour the hot topping over the hot cake. Allow to soak at least 1 hour before serving.

MAKES 8 SERVINGS.

—HANGO DENNISON

TRUMPETER APPLE CRUMBLE

2   pounds apples, peeled, cored, and thinly
     sliced
3   tablespoons lemon juice
1   cup firmly packed brown sugar
1¼   cups all-purpose flour
½   cup butter
½   teaspoon ground cinnamon
1   teaspoon grated lemon rind
     Vanilla ice cream (optional)

In a large bowl drizzle the apple slices with lemon juice. In a small bowl combine ½ cup of brown sugar and ¼ cup of flour. Toss the apples with the sugar mixture. Place in a 2½-quart ovenproof baking dish. In a small bowl thoroughly mix the butter, remaining 1 cup of flour, and cinnamon. Add the lemon rind and remaining ½ cup of sugar. Sprinkle over the apples. Bake at 350° for 30 minutes or until the top is golden brown. Serve warm. Delicious topped with vanilla ice cream!

—KARL SLOVER, Munchkin in *Oz*, MGM

FROM RAGS TO WITCHES   Yappy little "Toto," a female cairn terrier originally known as "Terry," was owned and trained by Carl Spitz. Toto's film career actually stretched back prior to Oz. According to Carl Spitz's personal scrapbooks, Toto was a year old when he adopted her in 1933. One of her earliest appearances on film is with Shirley Temple in the heartwarming film Bright Eyes (1934), in which Toto plays "Rags," the companion of Shirley's godfather, Luke, who ends up giving the dog to Shirley. That same year, Toto appeared in a Paramount release, Ready for Love. In 1935, Toto shined in the United Artists picture The Dark Angel, and the following year, appeared with Spencer Tracy in the drama Fury. Besides Oz, a handful of films followed: The Buccaneer (1938); Barefoot Boy (1938); Bad Little Angel (1939); Calling Philo Vance (1939); and Twin Beds (1942). Producer/writer Willard Carroll put it best: "Toto's intrepid spirit lives on in several films. Toto will always be remembered as the catalyst for all the action in The Wizard of Oz. For without Toto, Dorothy and we would never have gone to Oz."

UNCLE HENRY'S BREAD PUDDING WITH WHISKEY SAUCE

½   loaf French bread, torn into small pieces (about 4 cups)
2   cups whole milk
½   cup chopped pitted dates or raisins (see Note)
3   eggs, slightly beaten
1   cup sugar
¼   cup butter or margarine, melted
1   tablespoon vanilla extract
2   teaspoons ground cinnamon

Whiskey Sauce:
¼   cup butter or margarine, melted
½   cup sugar
1   egg yolk
2   tablespoons water
2   tablespoons bourbon

In a large bowl combine the bread, milk, and dates. Let stand 15 minutes or until the bread is softened, stirring often. In a separate bowl beat together the eggs, sugar, melted butter, vanilla, and cinnamon. Stir into the bread mixture until blended. Turn into a greased 8-inch square baking dish. Bake at 350° for 40 to 50 minutes or until a knife inserted in the center comes out clean. Meanwhile, prepare the Whiskey Sauce.

In a small saucepan melt the butter or margarine. Stir in the sugar, egg yolk, and water. Cook and stir over medium-low heat until the sugar dissolves. Stir in 2 tablespoons of bourbon.

MAKES ⅔ CUP OF SAUCE.

Serve the pudding warm with Whiskey Sauce. Garnish with apple chunks and sweet woodruff or mint leaves (optional).

Note: You can substitute fresh or canned peaches.

MAKES 9 SERVINGS.

—DEL ARMSTRONG, makeup artist for *Oz,* MGM

The beautiful Gene Tierney as Elly May and Charley Grapewin as Jeeter Lester in the film version of Tobacco Road *(1941). Grapewin, who died in 1956, was an accomplished actor and author of several books before he portrayed sympathetic Uncle Henry in* The Wizard of Oz. *It's not widely known, however, that Grapewin appeared in one of the original stage presentations of Oz after the musical comedy premiered at Chicago's Grand Opera House in 1902, hit Broadway in 1903, and toured the country. (Of course, L. Frank Baum's original stage version did not resemble any subsequent motion pictures, nor include the phenomenal music written specifically for MGM's 1939 classic version.)*

VERY SWEETLY CREAM OF COCONUT CAKE

1   18½-ounce box yellow cake mix
1   15½-ounce can cream of coconut
1   10-ounce container frozen whipped
    topping (Cool Whip)
½   cup shredded coconut (optional)

Prepare the cake according to the package directions and bake. Let cool. Poke holes all over the top of the cake and pour cream of coconut over it, letting it soak into the cake. Frost with Cool Whip. Sprinkle with shredded coconut, if desired. Keep refrigerated.

MAKES 8 SERVINGS.

—MYRNA AND CLARENCE SWENSEN,
Munchkin in *Oz*, MGM

VICTOR WETTER'S FRUIT COBBLER

1   cup margarine, room temperature
1   cup sugar
3   cups all-purpose flour
2   21-ounce cans pie filling of your choice
    Ground cinnamon

In a medium bowl cream together the margarine and sugar. Stir in the flour and mix well. In an ungreased 9 x 13-inch pan spread ½ inch of batter. Spread the pie filling over the batter. Add the remaining batter on top. Sprinkle with cinnamon. Bake at 300° for 1 hour.

MAKES 8 TO 12 SERVINGS.

—EDNA WETTER, wife of Victor Wetter,
Munchkin soldier in *Oz*, MGM

WALLY'S CARROT CAKE

1½   cups salad oil
2   cups sugar
3   eggs
2   teaspoons vanilla extract
2   cups all-purpose flour
2   teaspoons baking soda
1   teaspoon baking powder
2   teaspoons ground cinnamon
2   teaspoons salt
1   16-ounce can crushed unsweetened
      pineapple, undrained
1½   cups flaked coconut
2   cups shredded carrots
1   cup chopped nuts
1   3-ounce package cream cheese, softened
3   tablespoons butter, softened (or
      margarine)
2   cups sifted confectioners' sugar
1   teaspoon vanilla extract

Grease a 9 x 13-inch pan. In a large bowl mix
the oil, sugar, eggs, and vanilla. In a separate
bowl stir together the flour, soda, baking
powder, cinnamon, and salt. Combine with
the egg mixture and stir to blend well. Fold
into the batter the pineapple, coconut, carrots,
and nuts. The batter will be runny. Pour into
the prepared pan. Bake at 325° for about 1
hour and 30 minutes or until a toothpick
inserted in the center comes out clean. Allow
the cake to cool completely before frosting.

    In a small bowl beat the cream cheese
and butter at medium speed with an electric
mixer until fluffy. Gradually add the confectioners' sugar, beating the mixture well. Stir
in the vanilla. Spread over the cake when it
has cooled.

MAKES 8 TO 12 SERVINGS.

—SUE DWIGGINS WORSLEY, wife of Wallace
Worsley, script clerk for *Oz*, MGM

WICKED WITCH'S MINT SQUARES

They'll melt in your mouth.

3   1-ounce squares unsweetened chocolate
¾   cup margarine
1½   cups sugar
¾   cup all-purpose flour, sifted
3   eggs
¾   teaspoon vanilla extract
½   cup plus 2½ tablespoons butter
1   16-ounce package confectioners' sugar
2   teaspoons peppermint extract
3   drops green food coloring
2   1-ounce squares semisweet chocolate
2½   tablespoons shortening

Grease and flour a 16 x 11-inch jelly roll pan.
In a small saucepan melt the unsweetened
chocolate and ¾ cup of margarine. Stir well,
remove from the heat, and add the sugar,
flour, eggs, and vanilla. Spread on the prepared pan. Bake at 375° for 12 to 15 minutes.
Let cool.

    In a small bowl cream together the but-
ter, confectioners' sugar, peppermint extract,
and food coloring until light and fluffy.
Spread on the cooled chocolate layer. Place in
the refrigerator for 30 minutes.

    In a small saucepan over low heat melt
the semisweet chocolate and shortening,
stirring until smooth. Drizzle over the mint
layer. Cool and cut into squares.

MAKES 60 BARS.

WINKIE CHOCOLATE PEANUT BUTTER PIE

"Oreo-eeyoo-o! Oreo-eeyoo-o!"

22   Oreo cookies, finely crushed
¼   cup butter, melted (or margarine)

½   cup creamy peanut butter
1   cup sliced bananas (2 medium)
2   4-ounce packages instant chocolate
    pudding mix
3   cups milk
    Whipped topping
    Unsweetened chocolate curls for garnish

In a small bowl combine the cookie crumbs and butter. Press the mixture firmly into the bottom and sides of a 9-inch pie plate. Refrigerate for 30 minutes.

Spread the peanut butter over the bottom of the prepared crust. Arrange the bananas over the peanut butter and set aside. In a medium bowl beat with a mixer at low speed for 1 minute the pudding mix and milk. Pour the pudding over the bananas. Refrigerate at least 2 hours before serving. Top with whipped topping and shaved unsweetened chocolate.

—MURRAY WOOD, Munchkin in *Oz,* MGM

YELLOW BRICK CAKE

1   cup butter, softened
3   cups sugar
6   eggs
3   cups all-purpose flour
½   teaspoon salt
¼   teaspoon baking soda
1   cup sour cream
1   teaspoon vanilla extract
½   teaspoon almond extract
½   teaspoon ground mace

Grease an 8-cup bundt pan. In the large bowl of an electric mixer cream the butter and sugar on low speed. Add the eggs one at a time, beating well after each addition. Into a separate bowl sift the flour, salt, and baking soda. Beat into the sugar mixture alternately with the sour cream. Mix in the extracts and mace. Pour into the prepared pan. Bake at 350°, checking with a cake tester after 50 minutes. Do not bake more than 1 hour or the cake will be dry. Dust with confectioners' sugar when cooled.

MAKES 12 SERVINGS.

—IRENE LANE

(*Ray Savage collection*)

This is the re-release ad—
This is the first time The WIZARD made money at the box office—
Good luck!
Ray Bolger
The SCARECROW

YELLOW BRICK FROSTING

12 ounces cream cheese
6   tablespoons butter
1   16-ounce package confectioners' sugar
2   teaspoons vanilla extract
    Yellow food coloring
¼   cup chopped walnuts (optional)
    Gold dust candy sprinkles

In a medium bowl cream together the cream cheese, butter, sugar, and vanilla. Gradually add the coloring, a drop at a time, until the desired color is reached. Keep the frosting cold or it will melt. Frost the cake and sprinkle with edible gold dust sprinkles.

Note: Good served on Betty Tanner's Waldorf Red Cake (see p. 172).

—JAMIE ROCCO, musical staging, *The Wizard of Oz* National Tour, 1998–1999

YELLOW BRICK ROAD CAKE

Just follow the directions . . .

1   18½-ounce box lemon cake mix
2   3-ounce packages lemon gelatin
1   cup boiling water
    Ice cubes
    Zest of one lemon
½   cup Domino Lemon Confectioners' Sugar

Mickey Rooney commiserates with Ray Bolger outside the Oz soundstage at MGM.

Prepare the cake mix according to the package directions. Bake in a 9 x 12-inch pan.

While the cake cools prepare the gelatin. In a heat-resistant quart measuring pitcher dissolve both packages of gelatin in the boiling water, stirring until completely dissolved. Then add enough ice cubes to make a total of 2 cups of liquid. Stir until all the ice is dissolved and the mixture starts to thicken.

Pierce the cooled cake with a large fork at ½-inch intervals. Carefully pour the gelatin over cake. Refrigerate for 3 hours. Dip the cake pan in warm water for 10 seconds, then unmold onto a serving plate. Sprinkle with lemon zest and top with yellow lemon confectioners' sugar. Refrigerate at least 1 hour or until ready to serve.

To serve, cut into brick shapes by cutting 6 slices across the width of cake. In the first row, make a single cut in the middle of the row. In next row, cut into thirds. Repeat the pattern of these 2 rows on remainder of cake so as to form brick pattern.

Note: Can remove the cake bricks and place on a sandwich board to resemble The Yellow Brick Road. Decorate with the Oz PVC figures.

MAKES 10 TO 12 SERVINGS.

—JAN AND MICKEY ROONEY, Wizard in *The Wizard of Oz* National Tour, 1998–1999

Mickey Rooney and Eartha Kitt are featured in the 1998 cast recording of the touring production of The Wizard of Oz. The CD features Jessica Grové as Dorothy, Lara Teeter as the Scarecrow, Dirk Lumbard as the Tin Man, and Ken Page as the Cowardly Lion.

Jessica Grové (starring as Dorothy in the 1999 touring stage production of Oz) with costar Mickey Rooney and his wife, Jan Chamberlin Rooney. (Photo by Katie Grové)

Here's to the next one hundred years of Oz!

Recipe Index

——⟨⟨⟨⟩⟩⟩——

Oz Index

About the Authors

—⟨∞⟩—

ELAINE WILLINGHAM owns and operates Beyond the Rainbow, the premier mail-order business specializing in Judy Garland/*Wizard of Oz* collectibles, which was founded in 1985. A lifelong admirer of Garland, *Oz,* and musical theater, Willingham edited and published *Beyond the Rainbow Collector's Exchange,* a journal for MGM *Oz* aficionados, for seven years. Within the past decade, Willingham has orchestrated several triumphant *Oz* conventions and events in St. Louis; Las Vegas; Culver City, California; and Bloomington, Illinois. From her offices in St. Louis, she maintains an immensely popular *Wizard of Oz* Web site at www.beyondtherainbow2oz.com. Willingham is business manager for Stages St. Louis, one of the most popular musical theater companies in the Midwest; she lives with her husband, Jimmi, and two cats, Sammy and Sake.

STEVE COX is the author of a dozen books on film and television, including the hugely successful *The Munchkins Remember* (revised as: *The Munchkins of Oz*), as well as *The Abbott & Costello Story, The Beverly Hillbillies, Here's Johnny!, The Munsters, Here on Gilligan's Isle* (with Russell Johnson), *The Hooterville Handbook: A Viewer's Guide to Green Acres, Dreaming of Jeannie: TV's Prime-Time in a Bottle,* and *The Addams Chronicles.* Cox worked closely with Buddy Ebsen on the actor's autobiography, *The Other Side of Oz.* An occasional contributor to the *Los Angeles Times* and *TV Guide,* he lives in Southern California.

LYMAN FRANK BAUM & MAUD GAGE BAUM

+ FRANK JOSLYN BAUM

1ST WIFE:
HELEN LOUISE SNOW

THEIR CHILDREN:
* JOSLYN STANTON BAUM & ELIZABETH POLLACK

THEIR CHILDREN:
** ROGER BAUM & CHARLENE
** LYNN BAUM AND LARRY WOLF
** FRANK ALDEN BAUM &
1ST WIFE, HALLIE J. LINCOLN
2ND WIFE, LOUISE BALME

2ND WIFE:
ROSINE AGNES BRUBECK

STEPCHILDREN:
* THOMAS EDWARD BRUBECK
* PATRICIA ANN BRUBECK
* DONALD PHILLIP BRUBECK

3RD WIFE:
MARGARET ELIZABETH LIGON

+ ROBERT STANTON BAUM

WIFE:
EDNA DUCKER

SON:
* ROBERT ALLISON BAUM & PHYLLIS ANN MILLSAP

THEIR SON:
** ROBERT ALLISON BAUM JR. & CLAIRE YORKER

THEIR CHILDREN:
* CHRISTINE GAIL BAUM
* CAROLYN ELIZABETH BAUM

SON:
** STANTON GAGE BAUM & GWEN ELLEN LUTZ

THEIR CHILDREN:
** JANET ELLEN BAUM & STANLEY WARE
** MARGARET BAUM & RANDY SMELTZER

DAUGHTER:
* FLORENCE BAUM & GEORGE E. HURST

THEIR CHILDREN:
** SUSAN MARNEY HURST & KURT SKARIN
** KIMBERLY HURST & KARL JOHNSON
** GIGI HURST & SKIP WALLACE
** PATRICIA LEE HURST & PETER AHRENS
** ROBERT SCOTT HURST

+ HARRY NEAL BAUM

1ST WIFE:
MARY NILES

THEIR CHILDREN:
* WILLIAM NILES BAUM
* HENRY BARRON NILES II (FORMERLY HARRY NEAL BAUM JR.) & GRACE ANDREWS

THEIR CHILDREN:
** HARRY BARRON NILES III
** JENNIFER NILES
* JUDITH GAGE BAUM & EDMOND RONEKEY

2ND WIFE:
HELEN BATES

3RD WIFE:
BRENDA BAUM TURNER
* STEPCHILD ANN HOWELL
* SON RICHARD HOLIER BAUM & ROSEMARY

THEIR CHILDREN:
** GREGORY N. & KAREN BAUM
** RICHARD L. & BARBARA BAUM
** WILLIAM E. & KAREN BAUM
* JAMES J. BAUM

+ KENNETH GAGE BAUM

WIFE:
DOROTHY DUCE BAUM

DAUGHTER:
* OZMA BAUM & KENNETH AUSTIN MANTELE

THEIR CHILDREN:
** DOROTHY MANTELE MORENA
** CRAIG FREDRIC MANTELE & MIMI MANTELE
* JANET HILDA BAUM & JOHN W. DONALDSON JR.

THEIR CHILDREN:
** BONNIE MCFARLAND
** MCFARLAND DONALDSON
** JOHN WILCOX DONALDSON III